That's All I'm Sayin'

MICHAEL BRANDON

DEDICATION

To my wife Glynis
And my son Alex.

Author's Note

To the lonely kids who feel life has cut them out. Fitting in is hard, feeling left out, is even harder.

I have an image in my memory, of standing behind a screen door, waiting for friends to pick me up.

My father, (I fondly refer to as the Gutter Confucius) said, what doesn't kill you, makes you stronger. That might be true but it's not the full truth. There is only you, one unique you, and nobody else can be **you**. I believe it's our part of destiny, to make that YOU, all the **YOU**, you are capable of being.

I regret certain attitudes and actions in the past, only because I don't agree with them today. That's the way it was, or maybe better said, that's the way I was. So here is the truth, as I remember it.

Arthur Miller says, in *A View from The Bridge*, "The flat air in my office suddenly washes in with the green scent of the sea and dust in the air is blown away and the thought comes…"

Foreword

I have known Michael for many years, funnily enough, not from his Hollywood days or the famous *Dempsey and Makepeace* series. Instead, I have been fortunate to call him a close and beloved friend after his wife, Glynis, introduced us at a dinner party. I remember laughing so much that I was in tears; he is the most entertaining, genuine, and brilliant storyteller.

Michael also has a unique empathy and deep understanding of life. His ability to make me laugh has never faded over the years - he has an incredible gift for lifting my spirits.

He was somewhat taken aback when I told him I had written a leading role for him - as a psychopath. The character had to be amusing, trustworthy, and give no indication of his terrifying darkness. Michael was astonishing. His acting talent and ability to portray such a complex character were truly impressive; he is a class act of the highest level.

Truthfully, his depth of understanding and genuine kindness to others make me deeply thankful to know him. It has been a special honour to read his memoir shortly before publication. Learning about his past life and career was not only fascinating but, unsurprisingly, had me laughing again. His memoir is entertaining, heartfelt, and truly compelling.

Michael really is a star.

Lynda La Plante

Contents

Prologue

October 1984. The stretch Merc limo pulled up outside Peel Cottage, 80 Peel Street, Kensington, London, England. My driver, Bill Darvil, was pointing to one of those historic blue plaques next to the door. Sir William Russell Flint, a famous artist, lived and died here. As I understood it, the current owner, Brian Clark, was an artist as well – stained glass and totemic art, whatever. The estate agent, presenting the house, also told me Brian's grandfather was the last hangman of London. That's kind of unique. Imagine that, Grandpa, tell me a story!

I was in the UK for six months of filming. It was the first season of a police action-drama co-produced by England and the US called *Dempsey and Makepeace*. I played Dempsey, a brash, irreverent New York detective, to my irresistible co-star Glynis Barber's genteel Lady Harriet Makepeace (more about her later).

This was the only house the rental agent had to show me since my panicked call this morning. I barely looked at the interior of the house; I just tested all the radiators. This house had heat, praise the Lord. I had to get out of my friend Michael Proudlock's house.

Proudlock was a middle-aged Etonian (Eton College grad and owner of the Foxtrot Oscar, a famous Chelsea restaurant) and I nearly froze to death the night I spent in his Holland Park house. He'd insisted I stay at his home while I looked for a house during filming. Everyone had gone to bed, and I was freezing and couldn't find a thermostat. A thin layer of ice was forming in the toilet. I put on everything in my suitcase and tried the meditations from Shirley MacLaine's book claiming monks could dry sheets using their body heat if they slept naked. Didn't work, a cold night on the tundra!

In the morning, after he finished his forty-five-minute bath with the Financial Times, Proudlock found me in his kitchen hugging an oven called an AGA. I made rings in the air with my breath to demonstrate how cold his house was, and he said, "In England, Brandon, we don't turn on the heat till November." In America, we turn it on when we are cold. They obviously didn't teach plumbing on the Eton curriculum.

The estate agent gave me a tour of Peel Cottage, the only house available on her books, and I noticed a man peeling vegetables in the kitchen. I asked her if he was the owner, and she laughed and said, "No, he's your chef and houseman."

Being from Brooklyn, I just stared at her and asked, "Does he live here with me?"

"No, he comes every morning and stays if you need him. He's a Le Cordon Bleu chef."

I never ate a cordon bleu. It could be an eel thing; they eat them here. "No, take him with you."

She crossed her arms. "Can't – it's an inherent condition of the landlord's; Pablo stays."

I had her call the owner, currently in Italy. Brian said, "Michael, give Pablo one week, if he hasn't changed your life for the better, I'll fly him to Italy." I was so desperate not to return to the Etonian ice age that I agreed on one condition, I must move in today! That sorted, I turned up the heat and went to retrieve my luggage.

At the Proudlocks' igloo, lunch was being served. English Sunday lunch is a tradition in the UK – when people eat, drink, and laugh while sitting for hours. I could no longer feel my ass, besides everything at lunch wasn't quite dead enough for my boring American tastebuds. Sorry to say, I am a well-done boy. Michael Proudlock, an incredibly charming man, and Lena, his beautiful wife, were very welcoming, wonderful, and warm. It was the country, not the hospitality that was cold. By the time I bid my friends farewell, it was dark outside and only mid-afternoon. What is that?

I was starving by the time I returned to Peel Cottage. Pablo was waiting to lead me to the dining room, a room I didn't remember even seeing that morning because I was so focused on radiators. The long, highly polished enamel table with metal inlays was a product of the current owner's totemic art, surrounded by eight high-backed chairs.

Here was the remarkable thing. I looked up as I was about to snap my napkin and drop it on my lap and observed the half-naked body of a woman coming through the ceiling! She was holding a chandelier like a torch, lighting the dining room! Pablo was suddenly standing next to me, holding a bottle of wine hovering over an empty glass. I nodded and he poured. Our first communication.

I looked in front of me and there was a plate with something on it. "What is that?"

Pablo had a soft Colombian accent. "Avocado, with smoked haddock, covered with caviar."

I had never eaten any of those things. I asked him if he did a BLT. He had a curious look, so I demonstrated bacon (flat, straight fingers), lettuce (wiggly, crunchy fingers), tomato (fingers forming a circle), in a sandwich (two flat hands).

Pablo pensively nodded. "For lunch?"

I nodded in agreement, but Pablo didn't leave. Surprisingly, he straightened my napkin and stood waiting, his eyes on my plate. It was a Colombian standoff. I slowly picked up a fork and bravely took a bite of the starter, as they call it in this country. A starter indeed!

My virginal palate assailed with pleasures never known to me. An entirely new experience of taste, a new style of living, and all because I was looking for hot radiators. This was like discovering classical music. There was a concert going on in my mouth. I groaned with pleasure, and Pablo's face exploded into a warm smile of satisfaction.

I sat back, looked up at this woman coming through the ceiling, sipping my glass of Pouilly-Fuissé. A driver, a chef, a houseman, and a huge house named Peel Cottage complete with hot radiators.

Pablo left me to enjoy my meal and then walked past the dining room with my luggage, which he unpacked, ironed, and hung in the closet.

How about that? Not to mention, starring in what would be the most popular TV series in the country.

It seemed that I had it all. It did not come easy, I can tell you that...

CHAPTER 1

The Truth, As I Remember It

1945. I came from an American ghetto called Brownsville, Brooklyn. Before me, it fostered Meyer Lansky, Bugsy Siegel (Murder Incorporated), and The Three Stooges, and after me, Mike Tyson. Fondly referred to as the murder capital of New York, Brownsville is now chic.

My father was in the US Army during the Second World War. He made Master Sergeant, serving in Motor Divisions. He oversaw three hundred Spanish-speaking soldiers, despite not speaking Spanish himself. Miriam, my mom, and I lived with her parents, Hymie and Sonya Tumen. My grandparents had fled the Russian pogroms in the late 1800s to England. They lived in London for years, setting up three tailoring factories before sailing to America around 1910. They arrived at Ellis Island, New York.

My father (Master Sergeant Sol not Saul Feldman) came home after the war and went to work at a gas station across from Ebbets Field, home of the Brooklyn Dodgers. Sol worked seven days a week to pay for an apartment with heat in one room. He told me I was probably conceived in a tow truck because he worked so much. We lived on Lenox Road, which was around the corner from a huge hospital called Bellevue that my mother whispered was a nut house filled with crazy people. We all lived in the front bedroom on the second floor of the walk-up Brownstone because that's where the heat was (it's now worth millions). My toy gas station was kept in the back bedroom, which we called the cold room. My mother would put on my hat and coat and send me in to play.

I remember rock fights in the empty lot across from Bellevue Hospital and not being good at it. You don't duck in a rock fight - I got my first concussion. I remember getting caught playing 'show me yours and I'll show you mine' with the girl next door. She didn't have anything to show; I had only slightly more. Maybe that's why our mothers were so angry? We were five years old.

I remember school fire drills. They marched us outside, but for the air raid drills, the ones for atomic bomb attacks, we sat on the hallway floor with our hands on our heads. Putting hands on heads to protect us from atomic bombs and my forefathers coming over on the Mayflower were the two biggest lies I was taught in school.

When I was five, my father, opened his own garage in Brooklyn with two of his old army buddies. It was called Sol, Harry, and Shimmy's. The garage, a serious repair station, was successful, and later that year, we moved from Brooklyn to Kew Gardens in Queens. The neighborhood was full of two-story terraced housing developments surrounding a big, trampled square like an ancient Roman fort. In our school, we didn't have regular classes. There were too many kids (it was the baby boom), so they split the day into triple sessions. You went from 9 to 11, or 11 to 1, or 1 to 3. You only had two books: How to Read and How to Write. You had to leave them for the next class. That's why no one can read my sideways handwriting to this day!

There was a construction site behind Kew Gardens that was a virtual Disneyland before they ever thought of Disneyland or anything virtual. It was made up of enormous piles of sand and gravel on a dirt lot. A city boy's dream. We played King of the Mountain.

I discovered movies. I was eight years old. A box of Dots (American wine gums) and a double feature with cartoons. I loved the movies! Westerns and science fiction, all kinds of movies. I would stay till my mother came yelling and made me leave. I wish she had come to pick me up the day I watched War of the Worlds twice and then had to make that long walk home alone, looking out for snaky aliens.

I saw my first Schwinn bike in the store window and made a million wishes for it. My father took me to a cheap place to get a bike, and I didn't like any of them. He was angry with me, but I begged him to take me to the Schwinn store where the guy looked at me and said I needed a 24-inch bike, and he didn't have one.

My father was literally dragging me out the door when I yelled, "What about that one?" I was pointing to the blue beauty in the window.

He said, "It's a 26-inch," and then, "Wait a minute, it is a 24, kid."

The bike was blue with white wall tires and a battery horn in the crossbar. I was the happiest kid in the world. Maybe the guy said that so I could get it anyway. What's two inches? I crashed into another kid on the un-grassy green and was bandaged for days. The bike was fine. I would clothespin playing cards in the spokes for motorcycle sounds.

My mother used to make me malteds, U-bet chocolate syrup, and milk. Mom hid a raw egg in the drink, saying it was good for me, but I despised them. I refused to drink any more until she promised me there was no egg in it. There was a malted waiting on the table at breakfast. I stared at it and then looked at her, and she swore there was no egg in it. I took the tiniest sip to see if there was any egg, and there wasn't. (She didn't stir it to trick me.) When I drank it, a raw yolk slid down my throat, making me gag and throw up.

This was the first time I realized that Mothers lie! I never ate an egg again. Just the sound of whisking eggs makes me nauseous. Whup, whup, whup. I'm nauseous writing this.

In the hot N.Y. summers, my family would drive up to the Jewish Alps, upstate in Monticello, New York. Families rented cabins for two weeks or even months if you were rich. (If you had money, you went to Grossinger's Catskill Resort or the Concord Hotel.) Usually, it was the same families from your neighborhood. Screen doors slamming all day and night. Men smoking and playing cards. Women smoking, cooking, and yelling at their children. My father used to go to work and drive back up on weekends. A neighbor took me to the swimming hole where I would catch tiny salamanders. When we were going back to the cabin, I tied my towel around my waist, but the neighbor lady pulled off my bathing suit from underneath.

She wasn't even my mother, and she stripped me.

She smiled, "You can't walk back wearing a wet bathing suit." It's haunted me all my life. I guess I was at the age where I was becoming aware of my body otherwise, why would I remember that?

She was my mother's friend, Phyllis, and the same lady that picked me up at school when I fell on the cement playground and hit my head for my second concussion. I waited on a hardwood bench in the office, vomiting for hours because they didn't have school nurses then. They couldn't reach my mother, and finally, Phyllis took me home. I held tightly onto my pants that day; you can be sure of that! I had to have a foam pillow for my concussed head, and I still use one out of habit. Ah, the foam pillows, that's when it began. I'll get to that.

On April 20, 1953, my ninth birthday, we moved to Valley Stream, Long Island. My mother's nasal New York pronunciation was "Lawn Guyland." It was just across the Brooklyn/ Queens County line with a ten-cent toll on the highway just behind the trees at the back of our house. My father got off at the exit before and drove an extra ten minutes, so he didn't have to pay a dime. He used to say if I had a nickel for every moron paying the ten-cent toll in a day I'd be a rich man, when I was a kid, I worked for five cents an HOUR pushing a vegetable cart. If I had a nickel for every time I heard my dad tell the vegetable cart story, I have owned the vegetable cart!

My family was moving up in the world. Although Valley Stream was more like sideways, being the first town past

Queens, so you could say that you lived on Long Island. It was a nice house, with a backyard and a driveway leading to a garage at the side. There were fruit trees, crabapple and plum, and a lawn that went all the way to the curb with no sidewalk. I hated our lawn because my father made me mow it. To me, it was like living on a farm. I was a cement-city kid. I needed a sidewalk.

I shared a room with my four-year-younger brother, Elliot, who was born a couple of weeks after we moved in. My sister Debra was born five years later. I hated hearing my parents argue through the wall, and I felt big enough to move upstairs to one of the two empty bedrooms. It was so scary up there, but I liked having my own bedroom even if the wallpaper was slanted rows of roses that turned into walking spiders when you stared at them. I would shut the light and run for the covers before the monsters got me. I could hear the traffic whooshing by on the highway. Years later, when I first heard waves at the beach, it reminded me of the highway behind my house.

The Long Island schools were progressive, which meant I came from a stupid city school. I was the missing link to the Neanderthal because I only joined the class in late April. I was the new dumb kid. I had to write my name on the blackboard, and no one could read it. My sideways-up writing was hilarious to the class. Assholes. The teacher put a big pile of books on my desk.

"You want me to pass these out?"

Mrs. Earl smiled and said, "No, they're yours."

I looked at this huge stack. "I have to carry these every day?"

More hilarity from the class.

"No, you can keep them in your locker."

"What's a locker?"

I overcame feeling like the class chimp by love-dreaming all day. Trudy Rose sat in front of me. I could smell her hair, and she was pretty. I was in love. But there was also Hope Cooperman. She sat across from me and had the whitest teeth I had ever seen. When she smiled, the sun came out. If there's an afterlife, I want to come back as a tooth in Hope Cooperman's mouth. At night I couldn't sleep, I was so in love. I couldn't decide which one I was going to marry. Trudy or Hope? It didn't really matter because neither one would speak to me.

Thank God for my foam pillow. That pillow could kiss. One side was Trudy, and the other was Hope. I kissed that pillow to sleep. The thing about a foam pillow, it almost kisses back. No, really, there's that little bit of give and pushback. That pillow was the best date I had in twelve years of school and the second-longest relationship of my life.

I had to put my feelings out there. I wrote a love letter to Trudy Rose and signed it Your Secret Admirer. I snuck it into her desk. I watched her read it, but she obviously recognized my sideways-up handwriting immediately.

She stood up and turned around, pointing straight at me, and said out loud for the teacher and class to hear, "That boy wrote me a secret admirer letter."

There are certain moments in your life when you want to just shrink up inside your own testicle sac. That's all that was left of me sitting on my chair. It's this kind of shit that can do a kid in for life. It was not the reaction I'd hoped for. Hope … there was still Hope.

It was 1959; I was fifteen, and it was my junior prom. I walked up to Hope Cooperman. You had no idea how long that walk across the gym floor took. I asked her to dance. My mom had taught me the box step.

She looked at me and said, "Dance with you?" and her girlfriends all burst out laughing. I could see those beautiful teeth laughing all the way back across the gym. Hope was kind; I think it was her friends.

That's why I had my 45s. I collected records. I had hundreds of them and used to come home from school and go up to my room and lip-sync into the mirror on the back of the closet door. There I could release all my emotions of love and desire, rejection, and pain. My 45s were my life. In the morning, I put on the Teddy Bears' "*To Know Him Is to Love Him*" to fortify myself for the school day. I believed if they just took the time to get to know me, they might like me, but nobody gave a shit.

The only person who gave me any attention was Malcolm Flemighetti, my personal Nazi. He would knock down my books, kick my papers down the hall, punch my arms black and blue, and take the canned Moosabec sardine sandwich that my mother made me daily on white bread with butter and mush it under his shoe. That I didn't mind so much – they were disgusting – but still, my mother made them. Flemighetti held me solely responsible for the death of Jesus.

I was denying my faith, trying to fit in with the Italian/Irish guys. The drunk principal called us 'animals' over the school intercom after a mutilated squirrel was found hanging from the flagpole at the school entrance. I hated gym, or anywhere I was vulnerable to getting picked on. If you hang out with the tough guys, you get left alone pretty much unless they were bored. I was a funny chameleon, so I blended into the pack. Blending was my new religion.

I came home to my 45s. I put on Paul Anka's "*Lonely Boy*," the theme to my life, and lip-synced into the mirror. I could let my feelings out, but the funny thing is, remembering back, I never sang out loud.

I got my first job working in the State Park refreshment stand on weekends. The park was just down the road from our house, and I could walk to work. I grilled burgers and sold charcoal and potato chips over the counter. One day I looked over the counter and my aunt and uncle were staring at me – my father's brother and sister. Uncle Jack had a deli in Brooklyn, and Aunt Leah had the biggest arms I had ever seen. They were bigger than my legs. "What are you doing here?" they asked. "I work here," I told them, "We live up the block." They insisted on going home with me. I went to knock on the door; it must have been a Sunday because my dad was staring through the screen door at me. Finally, he opened the door, and his brother and sister entered, chattering away. He put his hand on my chest and stopped me from going by. He looked at me, "Why did you bring them here?" "They're your brother and sister," I replied. He said, "Don't ever do this again." I didn't understand it. My father wasn't big on family. Mostly his family. He seemed more comfortable with Mom's relatives. Maybe that's who I am with my brother and sister. Elliot and Debra are both younger than me, and I love them both, but there's a kind of gap. More than the Atlantic Ocean. I'll ask them about it someday.

One day, my mother came into my room. My mother always had this expression like God smeared a little piece of shit right under her nose. She had this thick, nasal Brooklyn voice that I'm sure caused my lifelong tinnitus.

"Look at this room… It's a pigpen… It's disgusting!" She started knocking all my stuff around. Then she grabbed the 45 from the record player.

"Ma… don't touch the 45. Don't touch the record, Ma."

But she did.

I tried to grab it back, and we both had two fingers in Paul Anka… in the big hole… and it was twisting this way and that… and I didn't want it to break, so I whipped my fingers out and she flew backward… out the door… down the stairs… right on the beat… "I – just – a – lone – ly"… BOOM… and she was lying there like she's broken or dead, but the record was okay, thank God, and very slowly she got up.

"Ma… You okay?"

"Wait till your father gets home!"

Like an asshole, I waited. I should've just left – got the fuck outta here – but I'd got nowhere to go. Where was I gonna go?

I went to the basement… to the 'red toolbox', the Holy Grail. God built the world with that toolbox. Hands off to everybody but my father. I got a hook lock, a slide bolt, and a padlock, got back upstairs, and hooked all this up. Like Fort Knox. Under other circumstances, my father might've been proud of me.

Then my father's headlights crossed my ceiling as he pulled into the driveway, and I heard through my newly reinforced door my mother's adenoidal squeal: "Michael pushed me down the stairs!"

I didn't; I just pulled my fingers out of Paul Anka's hole.

"Where is he?"

"In. His. Room!"

BOOM... BOOM... BOOM... My father was climbing the same stairs my mother had just bounced down. My father was a very big man.

Fe Fi Fo Fum... I smell the blood of my idiot son. "Open this door!"

I could see the doorknob twisting back and forth.

"If I open this door, you're going to kill me."

"If you don't open this door, I'm going to kill you!"

"No!"

"You got three seconds to open this door. One..."

"We who are about to die salute you!"

"Two..."

I loved mythology, but the gods had abandoned me.

"Three!"

He hit that door. The locks... the door... the molding... all of it came flying like a piece of cardboard. The plaster dust was floating around him like the smoke of hell. He stood there on top of the shattered door... leaning over me... picked me up by the shirt into the air.

"You ever... EVER... lay a finger on my wife again, I'll bust your skull open... Understand me?" And he dropped me.

17

My wife? That's my mother! I got the picture. First his wife... then me. He just handed me my umbilical cord.

When summer came, it was like he owned me. I was his indentured servant. He woke me up at 5 o'clock, dragged me down to his garage in Brooklyn where I had to pump gas, check the oil and tire pressure, and burn my hands on boiling radiator caps.

They once sent me to summer camp when I was twelve, but it sucked. I had to share a bug-infested cabin with six other boys. One short-sheeted me, so when I tried to put my feet straight, the sheet tore. I waited till four a.m. and then whacked him with a tennis racquet and jumped back into bed pretending to be asleep. The counselors told him it was a nightmare, and we should all go back to sleep. After I ran away three times, my parents had to take me home.

Dad did pay me something for working at the station, and I got tips from his customers, if he was watching, but his hope was that I would take over the business someday. Never going to happen. On the drive into Brooklyn, we would stop at the Kobe Diner for breakfast. Cops, cabbies, and working men sat inside this chrome train car eating. I would sit on the red leather revolving stool flipping the counter jukebox, looking at songs as I ate pancakes. Dad said, "Don't be an asshole like your friends. Learn a trade. I have a trade, and I can work anywhere in the world."

"Pop, you never left Brooklyn."

Pop had no formal education, but he went to Gutter College. He had street smarts, which he tried to endow upon me like Confucius. My father grew up in the gutters of New

York, pushing a vegetable cart for a nickel (five cents) a day. The Gutter Confucius spewed the wisdom of the streets. After lunch, in the grease-covered office, Dad stood up.

(Dad) "Follow me… Keep your eyes open and your mouth shut!"

He handed me a little shovel… pointed to a fresh pile of dog crap.

"Scoop it up!"

I scooped it up. He held open his empty brown paper lunch bag.

"Put it in the bag."

I dropped it in the bag. Then he folded the bag at the top, very neatly… Took his time… when he was satisfied,

"Presentation is important."

Then he walked over to one of his New York cabbie customers (the sign of a good mechanic is that the cops and cabbies came to his garage).

"Hey, Kenny… You want this?"

(Kenny) "What's in it?"

"Gimme ten, you'll find out!"

(Kenny) "I'll give you five!"

"Never mind. Morty, you want this?"

(Kenny) "Alright, alright! I'll take it. I'll take it!"

"Gimme the ten."

He took the ten… He handed Kenny the bag… He walked me away.

"Now, let that be a lesson to you."

"What exactly is the lesson here, Pop?"

"You can sell shit to anybody!"

I had to get outta there. These weren't my parents. I keep waiting for the mother ship to come and rescue me. Take me back to my own people.

Why did I have this life? Taking all this rejection? Getting beat up every day by Flemighetti? Two thousand years of retroactive persecution? Who needs this shit?

It was the first week back at school after the summer holidays, and Flemighetti put a live bloodsucker worm down the back of my shirt, which made me scream like a girl and dance like a puppet fool to get it out. Everyone was laughing while I watched Flemighetti mush my mother's sardine sandwich under his shoe. Something snapped; I'd had enough, my first bloodlust arrived.

I yelled, "That's it! I've had enough of you, Flemighetti, you want to fight, let's fight. C'mon!" I held up my puny fists. The hallway was crammed with kids making a circle around us. Flemighetti's six-foot-six frame hovered close to me. "Not now, kike, after school when nobody can stop us."

The bloodlust melted. I now had to wait for eight classes to get the shit kicked out of me in front of the entire school. English was the last class of the day. Forty-five minutes till my execution. I entered the classroom like a dead man walking. Flemighetti's eyes were drooling death at me from across the room. Mr. Lummit, our English teacher, wasn't there. He had quit the day before after Flemighetti held him out of the third-story window by his heels. Lummit started crying when Flemighetti let go of one of his ankles, making him swear on his family not to tell anyone before he would pull him back inside.

Our new substitute teacher was leaning on the front of his desk waiting for everyone to come in, sit down, and shut up, which made us noisier. But just the way he was leaning, doing nothing, made it uncomfortable, and very quickly it did, in fact, get quiet. Then he pointed to his name on the board: Mr. Stagg.

He looked over the class. "So, this is the bad class. They call you the animals in the office." (We laughed proudly.) "So, who is the toughest person in this class?"

Nobody said a word, but the glances at the seat in the last row said it all.

Mr. Stagg checked the seating chart and called out, "Malcolm Flemighetti. Malcolm, are you the toughest guy in the class?"

No response.

"I'd like to meet the toughest guy in the class." Stagg held out his hand. "What do you say, Malcolm?"

Flemighetti hated to be called Malcolm. He hadn't even bothered to look away from the window where he watched traffic in front of the school.

Stagg stood up. "C'mon, Malcolm, I'll meet you halfway."

Flemighetti turned his piggy eyes on Stagg. He rose, all six-foot-six of him, almost a foot taller than Stagg.

Stagg began walking up the aisle toward Flemighetti, who started toward Stagg, bouncing the knuckles of his ham-sized fists on each of the desks as he lumbered forward. Maybe after he kills Stagg, he'll forget about me.

Still extending his hand, Stagg said, "Nice to meet you, Malcolm."

Flemighetti grabbed Stagg's hand, and the next thing, Flemighetti was flying. He came down on his back, and Stagg had his shoe pressed into Flemighetti's neck, still holding his arm locked straight. Flemighetti couldn't move.

Stagg leaned over him and said, "Now, Mr. Flemighetti, I'm the toughest guy in this class!"

He didn't let go until Malcolm acknowledged his statement with a blink and a nod. Then Stagg helped him up. Stagg rules! Today, of course, Mr. Stagg would get arrested for child abuse.

I thought I had a stay of execution, but it only made Flemighetti enraged. As I exited Central High, he was looming across the street. It's not school property there; I couldn't run. Half the student body had turned up to see what he would do to me. They weren't disappointed either. Flem pushed me around and smacked me to get me to put my hands up. He hit me a couple of times, and I swung back once, and that was when my head bounced back and forth between his huge fists. I didn't know what to do; I stood there taking this pounding until my hands dropped by my sides. He hit me a couple more times, and I think I just sat down. He made more derogatory racist remarks and hunkered off, taking the crowd with him.

I felt something touching my face, and I flinched. It was a tissue in the hand of Roberta Villager. She was a beautiful girl and out of my league, but there she was, being so gentle and kind. She helped me up and walked with me until we came to our different paths. She asked if I was okay; I nodded. She walked away but not forever.

CHAPTER 2

Fuckin Wonder

1961. At sixteen, I got my junior driver's license. I took a driver's ed course so I could get my license early. This meant I could drive during the day and at night with anyone who had a full license. My father taught me to drive in the cemetery; he said, "You can't kill anyone here."

Now that I had a license, I could drive myself to a dermatologist, who would burn my face with dry ice. It made my whole face peel and relieved me of the awful acne I had at the time. I would go to his office on Christmas Holiday, Easter break, and before summer ended and school started again so no one would see the awful peeling scabs of skin. It didn't work – the pimples came back – and I still couldn't get dates.

I got a job after school. I heard about it from an older guy, Mitch, who lived on my street. He was always working on his car.

He said, "Hey, kid, you want a cool job after school?" He handed me a card. "Call and ask for Danny and tell him you got a driver's license."

I went to work for these guys, Danny and Gary Domino. They were the owners and had a couple of associates, Bert and Tiny. I referred to them as the Goons. They called me The Fuckin Wonder. The only name I can give my job title is 'diverter'. Things that were supposed to go one place went another. It was like a pharmaceutical wholesale business and these guys were 'jobbers'. The name on the front door was the same name as on the back door but spelled backwards. Where they get the stuff, never mind; where it goes, don't ask. What came in one door went out the other.

Okay, to briefly explain what a diverter does, you need to understand that every product has a code. Everything, everything, is coded in one way or another. It could be an ink stamp on the bottom of a can or a number on a label or an impression pressed into the bottom of a tube. My job was to remove all the codes so the merchandise couldn't be traced back to us. Obviously, there was a lot of money made because it eliminated all the middlemen – from manufacturer direct to consumer.

The day I met Bert; he walked into Danny's office. He was wearing a black shirt with a white tie and said with a strangled whisper, "Where's ya boss?"

I thought he was kidding around. I replied in a mobster-like manner, "He's downstairs polishing his pistol."

He pulled a chrome 38 out of his jacket and put it cocked to my face saying, "Duz it look like dis?"

Holy shit! I apologized profusely to say the least.

Bert controlled the Philadelphia districts of the business. Months later, I came up with decoding information that saved

Bert's business, and after, he sent me a bottle of Dom every Christmas.

On certain days of the week, Danny gave me a brand-new Cadillac to drive and deliver envelopes. Once I opened an envelope and it was filled with cash. I carefully sealed it back up.

When I got back to the warehouse, Danny yelled, "Hey, Fuckin' Wonder, c'mere. You do not open envelopes. Do you understand that?"

I said, "I didn't take nothin'."

Danny smirked. "I know you didn't take nothin'. That's why I am speaking with you!"

I got the message.

My father brought home a car for me. He bought and sold cars every day at his garage. It was a three-year-old, 1958 white Buick Special. A V-8 engine and more chrome than the Kobe Diner. It was a huge beauty with chrome torpedoes sticking out of the grill. The white elephant. It cost me three hundred dollars – my entire savings from the Goons. I was admiring it from my seat next to the window in eighth-period English, the seat in front of Flemighetti, from which he would snap my ears, when the bell rang. Flemighetti made his snide broadcast: "Was that the bell? Where did the time go?"

I was trying to escape class, but Stagg said, "Mike, you stay after."

I barked, "I didn't do nothin'," and Stagg said, "For that, you can stay after the whole week."

Flemighetti and the other 'animals' went OOOH like I was badass. Most of them took to carving an A on their arms with a beer bottle opener since the principal called us animals over the loudspeaker system. I lived in fear that Flemighetti would take it upon himself to tattoo me personally.

Stagg waited till everyone was gone. Then he said, "Michael, you're not like those assholes; you've got a brain. Don't worry, I won't tell anyone. I read what work you've done, and I can see you like literature. I am going to keep you after every day to do the work, and they can think it's because I got it in for you."

Because of Mr. Stagg, I not only graduated from high school, but I also won a Regents Scholarship at New York University. Thank you, Mr. Stagg!

If an inspired teacher believes in you, they can change your life.

At the 1962 graduation ceremony, I was 17 and the principal reluctantly handed me my diploma. Leaning in too close – I could smell his breath – he said, "I never thought I would be giving one of these to you."

I wanted to hold up my middle finger and say, "I never thought I would be giving you one of these," but I saw my father was sitting out there. I could hear the Gutter Confucius in my head: Son, just because you got spokes up your ass, don't think you're a big wheel.

My good friend Gary - who I always called GAAA, was getting married. His brother and I took the subway to Brooklyn for the wedding, only to find Gary's bride crying in the street. A crowd had gathered, agitated and upset. Someone had stolen the gold candelabras from the church—candelabras that had been blessed by the Pope. The entire Italian community was outraged.

Word quickly spread, and calls were made. It was soon made clear to certain neighborhoods that if the candelabras weren't returned within the hour, there would be no business on the streets that night.

Not long after, a call came in, and a bag was discreetly left behind. The wedding went ahead, and the couple was blessed before the now-returned candelabras. Some might call it a miracle.

I was working full-time for the Goons and had also started working in a bagel bakery at crazy hours in the morning. My dad's friend, a bagel baker, offered me work as his Kettleman—the apprenticeship to becoming a full bagel baker, fulfilling my dad's dream of me having a trade. So, I boiled bagels in a huge kettle, set them out on slim boards, and loaded them into the oven. Usually, it was a four-hour shift that paid very well, and taking home a dozen hot bagels right from the oven was a tasty bonus. But one morning, while driving home from the bakery, my steering wheel turned into a huge bagel in my mind, and I took it as a sign. I quit. My dad was angry, but I told him I'd rather be a lawyer and would go to law school.

Still working for the Goons during the day, I started attending law school on my scholarship in the evenings, but it was so boring. This was not the law I watched on TV. The law professor pointed at me, "You, define cybernation." I didn't have a clue. "A nation of Cybers, where the people have blue skin." Then this guy next to me jumped up, "Cybernation is the second step in automation where machines work machines." I jumped up, banging my desk, "Objection, I object to this badgering of the witness, your honor." I felt like a real lawyer. It was my last class.

Maybe it was auspicious because, as I got to my car, there was a pain in my back that was excruciating. I could hardly get into my car. I lifted my legs in and drove home two-footed. I climbed out like a hundred-year-old man and shuffled into the house. Everyone was asleep, so I pulled myself up the stairs to my room. I got into bed, but after a few hours, the pain was so terrible I needed help. I couldn't get up. My legs wouldn't move. I banged on the floor with my shoe till I heard my dad at the bottom of the stairs.

"What the hell is with all the noise?"

"Pop, I can't move my legs."

He yelled at me. "Why not?"

"I don't know why not. I just can't move them."

As he came into my room, my mother was behind him, her facial expression looked like God had smeared a smellier piece of shit under her nose.

Mom was ogling me. "Yeah, the doctor said this would happen."

"What are you talking about, Ma?"

"When you were born, you had a tail. Some people do. It's called an extended coccyx or something. The doctor said when you were seventeen or eighteen, you might need an operation."

"Why didn't you tell me?"

"I didn't want to worry you."

I had this operation, and I've never experienced more pain than this, ever. The surgery itself took five hours, and I was awake with my butt in the air and people coming around saying, "Hi, how's it going?" They took a chunk out of my lower back. My father said afterward, "Hey, you won't believe this, I saw your ass in a jar. It was the size of a small pineapple."

They weren't sure if I would walk properly again. Football was never on the cards anyway. If I could have climbed out of the window and dropped to my death, I would have, but the window only opened four inches at the top. The pain never stopped. They wouldn't give me anything - not enough, anyway.

The nurse said, "I can't give you any more medicine, but if you look across the hospital from your window at midnight, I'll make you feel better."

It was a square of twelve windows in the nurses' dorm, and she had gotten a bunch of nurses to do a striptease for me. I love nurses.

I didn't know karma from a hole in my ass. But looking back, I now see that the operation may have saved my ass. It caused me to fail the physical induction at the draft board. Forty-two of the forty-five guys on that army bus to the induction center on Whitehall Street were shipped directly to boot camp and then Vietnam. I might have taken a bullet in the ass now, for life later. It wasn't my choice! This was fate. It took months balancing on the doorknobs between the bathroom and the closet opposite it, teaching myself to walk. I had embarrassingly awful procedures and humiliating examinations, even by my mother changing bandages.

I was walking slowly with a cane, going to an examination, and I met this girl and asked her out. I think she was attracted to the limp. She was a model, and her photo was on the cover of the paperback How to Marry a Harvard Man.

Rita Cepf. I took her to The Black Rose, a bar in Queens, with a live jazz band, but there was a musicians' strike because of this thing called 'disco,' and no musicians were playing. A DJ played records while I poured out my life to a total stranger. I didn't want to go back to law school, and I didn't want to go back to the Goons. I was deeply lost!

Rita was laughing so hard, I stopped talking and looked at her. "What's so funny?"

She broke up twice trying to tell me, and finally said, "You're funny. You should be an actor or a comedian."

It was like that guy who hits the metal gong at the beginning of those old Rank films: BWONGGGGG. But the Hammer hit me right on the forehead with a flash, and my whole being resonated like a giant gong.

Yes, that's it. I didn't know what I wanted until this moment. Was that life possible for a guy like me?

"How do you become an actor?" I asked.

"You go to a school."

"What school?"

"There are lots: the Actors Studio or The American Academy of Dramatic Arts."

Thank you, Rita Cepf, I'll never forget you. Sorry I never called again but thank you.

Two days later, on one of my 'envelope drops' in the Goon Caddie, I cruised by the American Academy of Dramatic Arts on Madison Ave. I walked in and looked around and saw a door with a sign: Admissions – Bryn Morgan. He looked up, quite surprised when I barged into his office.

"I'd like to join up."

"It's not the Army, I'm sorry, and you are?"

"My name's Michael Feldman."

"Do you have an appointment, Mr. Feldman?"

"How much?"

"The first semester is $300, but you must audition for acceptance."

"Audition? Lemme get this straight. You're asking me to act before you've taught me how? Does that make sense? Tell you what, I'll give you six hundred and we skip the audition part. Get right into it."

"You trying to bribe me?"

"I'm just trying to eeeease the path here ... Know what I mean?" (See, that's what the Goons taught me.)

"Sorry, but that's not going to happen. You need to audition, and if you're accepted, then tuition is discussed. Don't worry, it's okay that you haven't acted before; we just need to get a gauge of you. Fill out the application forms, Mr. Feldman, and book an appointment for an audition. Look, here's an application form and a book of scenes. Learn a scene. We hold auditions every Wednesday afternoon from 3 p.m."

I slumped back to the Caddie. That was a short career ... not how I thought it would go. I flipped through the book of scenes. I didn't recognize anything. But why would I? I'd never seen a play!

It was Wednesday. I didn't want to wait a whole 'nother week, so I thought Hamlet! That's acting, right? There was a bookstore across the street, so I bought Hamlet and flipped through till I found the speech. You know, The Speech. I learned it in an hour; well, the gist of it.

It was three o'clock, so I went back in, and there were all these people in costumes. They looked like pilgrims. Costumes? I didn't think of that, but it was too late.

I walked up to the desk. "Hi, I'm here for my audition!"

"What's your name?"

Name? I gotta come up with a proper acting name. My favorite actor was Brando ... Brando ... nnnn. "Michael Brandon!"

"Your name's not on the list."

"Really? I just came all the way in from Long Island on a train to do this. I gave up a day's work. Look, I'm here. This is gonna be my life! Please, please, could you look again?"

She stared at me; I guess she had heard it all before. Then a pilgrim came out from a door behind the desk. The secretary gave me a smile and whispered, "Just go right in." She winked and nodded at the door.

"Really? Thank you. Thank you so much." I thought, I just did my first acting!

What's the difference between acting and being a convincing liar?

So, I went in, and there was this long table with about eight to ten people—like a panel. All Class A theater people, all very educated-looking, and sitting at the end of the table was the admissions guy, Bryn Morgan, whom I had met an hour ago, and he was just glaring at me.

Then this dignified-looking gray lady in the middle - gray hair, gray skin, huge gray glasses, could hardly lift her head from the weight of the gray pearls around her neck - asked, "What's your name?"

"Michael … uh … Brandon."

"I can't seem to find your details, Mr. Brandon."

"I don't have any spare details with me."

Bryn Morgan, the admissions guy, knew "there were no details." He also knew I didn't have an appointment, and my name was not Brandon.

"Okay … what are you going to do for us, Mr. Brandon?"

"Do for you?"

"What scene?"

"Oh, Hamlet!"

The admissions guy leaned way back in his chair with his hands behind his head. "This I've got to see."

"All right, when you're ready."

I knew the words! And I … I was off...

"TO BE or NOT TO BE … THAT'S A FUCKIN' QUESTION!"

I hadn't got a clue what I was saying. I might as well have been speaking Farsi or Dothraki … I got to the only line I thought I had a sense of - "this bare bodkin" (naked body, right?). Inspired, I tore open my shirt and vest, and the buttons went flying … bouncing off the gray lady's enormous glasses; bing, bing, bing, and the admissions guy started laughing in this inhaling, high screechy way like this was the funniest thing he'd ever seen (shriek! shriek!). Then, he fell to his knees, and he couldn't stop (shriek! shriek!). Like he couldn't get air. I thought he might be dying, but I carried on.

I didn't know what I was doing ... but they all thought it hysterical. What they didn't know was, I was doing it straight!

The letter arrived.

I was in! Accepted into The American Academy of Dramatic Arts!

I'm gonna be an actor!

CHAPTER 3

Gisele

New York City, 1965. I started at the Academy of Dramatic Arts feeling as any kid would at a new school—nervous and out of place. But these were very different people from any I had ever met before. Not only did they look different, but they were also strangely friendly and genuinely fascinated to be there. I wasn't an outcast here, maybe because everybody here was an outcast. One day you're lonely and unhappy and life stinks; then something like this happens, and it all changes. Fate, luck, or Rita Cepf?

The first AADA semester began. Day One. My acting class with Max Fischer. We sat in the academy's small theatre. I say that now. Before this, the only thing near a theatre for me was an auditorium at school. Theatres are scary. The new students filled the first three rows. Max stood silently watching us like a hungry Tyrannosaurus. He wore a black turtleneck under his tattered sport jacket. His shoulders seemed to be covered in dust, which I later recognized as the dandruff that snowed down from his storm of wild white hair. When he spoke, it was with a Russian accent. I thought he might be Stanislavski himself, who wrote An Actor Prepares, an acting bible. He yelled at us like we were idiots. Maybe he was projecting. He looked at me, "You," he said, "do you read newspapers?" I said, "No." "NO? Why not?" I swallowed; "They are bullshit." He looked at me so intensely, I thought he was going to bite me. "An honest answer. You must watch. See everything. Look at people. Study life. It's the best book you can read on acting." Max was a wonderful teacher. In one lesson, he taught me I didn't know anything about acting.

I found a roommate in Walker Daniels. Walker was older, a struggling actor/singer/philosopher who had a one-bedroom apartment on the Lower East Side, and he was one of the most passionate humans I had ever met. Passion was at the heart of every conversation and argument that would sometimes go on all night in our smoky apartment with fellow Academy students Stacey Keach, Cleavon Little, and Danny DeVito, voicing out on the Vietnam War, segregation, acting; Stanislavski acting, Marlon Brando and method acting, all to the background music of Bob Dylan. We covered the windows with foil so as not to be interrupted by the light of day.

During the first semester, I was assigned my first role in a play, and because of my "hysterical" audition of Hamlet, I was given the role of Benedick in Much Ado About Nothing. Can you believe it? Shakespeare! This was a huge problem for two reasons: One, I couldn't understand a word of it, and two, my parents would be coming, and my father would see me wearing tights. When I told my parents I was quitting my job to be an actor, I overheard my father say to my mother, "Next he'll want to borrow your clothes."

When the day came, I was freaking out, to put it mildly. The costume person was yelling, "Where's your dance belt?" My what? He pointed at my crotch and said, "It goes under your tights. You're showing through on stage."

Then someone was frantically calling my name. "Benedick, you're on!"

So, I grabbed a pile of scarves off the wardrobe table and shoved them down the front of my tights. That should cover me! I walked out with this enormous bulge in my tights, and the actress playing Beatrice took one look, screamed, and ran offstage.

Meanwhile, my father, at lights up, was lights out. He slept through the entire play, and my mother didn't understand a word of it. Afterwards, I got a lecture from Frances Fuller, the gray-haired lady from my audition, also the head of the Academy. My justification was Benedick had a hard-on for Beatrice. Ms. Fuller's response: "Do you have anything to fall back on?"

It was a student requirement to attend other student plays. I went along because up till this point, I had never seen a play. It was Gigi, a musical (you mean, they're acting and then they start singing a song?). I had no interest in a musical, but then I saw Gisele. The most beautiful woman I had ever seen in my life. Gisele Kalli was a delicate, half-French/half-Greek elfin vision. She had that blue-black hair I had only seen in DC comics, cut short like Audrey Hepburn. Sophisticated, demure, elegant, and so out of my reach, I could have been born without arms.

She stepped on stage, and I was smitten. Her eyes were a color blue I didn't have a word for. They were lit from within, like pinholes in the sky. They sparkled every time I looked at them for the next two years at the Academy.

Once or twice, she smiled and in her soft French accent said, *"Hello, Michele."*

I was unable to speak back to her. She was silk; I was a dishrag. Why would a woman who looked like her ever want to talk to a guy like me?

Two years later, it was graduation day at the Academy, the class of 1967. A ceremony and diplomas.

"Now, you are an actor," laughed Walker Daniels as he put his arm over my shoulder.

I had a diploma, but I didn't feel ready to go out there. I was overwhelmed by the different techniques and various methods of acting. I couldn't stop staring at Gisele across the hall.

Walker said, "Talk to her, man."

I said, "No, what's the point? What can I say to her?"

Walker had listened to my secret longings for two years. "If you don't, then I will!"

"If you walk near her, I'll leave here and never speak to you again."

Walker pleaded. "This is it, man. The end of the line. She's gone tomorrow. Take a chance."

I couldn't do it. She was a dream beyond my imagination.

Luck stepped in, and I was invited to join a workshop at the Actors Studio. They did scene work and plays and performed for Lee Strasberg. This was an exciting time, and many famous actors came to and from these workshops. This was the kind of work I needed to get deeper into my work.

Michael Simone, the workshop's intense director, with his bizarrely half-frozen scarred face showing through a wiry black beard that made him very dramatic looking, was calling out names of who would be scene partners.

He called my name and then called, "Gisele Kalli."

My head whirled around and there she was, three rows behind me. She waved when I looked at her. Michael Simone randomly picked us to do a scene together. He told us the play and the specific scene to do and to bring it in next week.

After class, Gisele came to me and said it would be easier for her if I came to her apartment to work. She was on call as a translator at the UN where she spoke five languages fluently, but my favorite was her English with the French accent. She lived on the Upper East Side on 72nd Street. The doorman made me feel unworthy when I arrived the next day. He checked me out and then let me up to the 19th floor.

Her apartment was elegant, with a piano and a curtain of blue and clear glass beads leading into the kitchen. I was studying a sculpture when she asked me if I would like prosciutto and melón. I mumbled something as I didn't know what the hell she had said. Then she put a plate of cantaloupe and ham in front of me (phew!). We talked easily, laughed, and learned our scene. A good first day after two years.

We got together a couple more times, and each time we talked a lot, laughed a lot, and worked hard on the scene. Then we did the scene in the workshop.

Very near the beginning, Simone stopped us. He stood up, waving his hands, and yelled out, "Stop!" He turned to me and said, "Do you like this girl?"

"What?!" I said.

"Do you like Gisele? Do you find this woman attractive?"

I felt like I was under an X-ray machine, and everybody could see right through to my exposed heart. I stuttered, "Yeah, sure."

"Really?" he said. "You like her?"

I said, "Yes, I like her!"

"Do you just like her or do you want to fuck her?"

I was stuck. I couldn't speak. I wanted to say, "Yes, I want to fuck her," but it was too raw. I couldn't express my real feelings. I felt totally exposed in front of her and the class.

Thankfully, Simone spoke. "Well, the guy in this scene wants to fuck her. But I don't get that from you. I want to stop this scene for now. I want to see it next week. I want to see a guy who wants this woman and a woman who wants it."

It was one of the most embarrassing moments in my life. I felt humiliated. But Gisele and I laughed a great deal about it while we carried on working and getting to know each other much better, and it was working for us in the scene. Then one night, she confided to me that she was engaged to one of the teachers at the Academy. I was devastated.

Gisele said, "Yes, it's been a while. Sorry I didn't tell you." Then she said, "Could you do me a favor, *Michele*?" She always called me *Michele*.

I said, "Of course," and she said there was an English theater company playing at the Martin Beck Theatre, the RSC, and they were doing a limited engagement of *Marat/Sade*, and would I take her? She explained that her fiancé was also a theater critic, and going to the theater was his work, and he did it better alone. It was the last performance, and she asked if I would please accompany her. "Please Michele, take me?"

Those eyes, that mouth, I would take her anywhere. I said "Absolutely," but then realized I had no money. "I have to stop by my apartment to get my wallet." (Then I could hit Walker up for a loan.)

Gisele said, "There is no time; please don't worry. I have plenty of money. I model and translate," and she stuck a hundred-dollar bill into my shirt pocket. "We better go!"

Marat/Sade was mind-blowing. This was another world to me. RSC stood for Royal Shakespeare Company. Such production and acting as I had never imagined. My first real theater *experience*. Gisele and I went on and on about all we'd seen and felt in the play and forgot where we were. We did a walk-and-talk across the city and were on Third Avenue somehow. We were so buzzed that we only stopped talking when we heard the jazz saxophone. It was August 11, a hot, humid New York summer night. The saxophone's raw growls were coming from inside Yellow Fingers, a restaurant during the day but at night it turned into a jazz club downstairs. It's why you love New York City.

Gisele stood in the doorway, listening. "I love the jazz. You like the jazz, *Michele*?"

I was drinking her every second. With the soft lights of Third Avenue as a backdrop and a sexy jazz score, Gisele was the only thing in focus.

"I love jazz."

After a furtive glance of agreement, we climbed down the dark stairwell to a smoldering hot jazz band. The sax was hotter than the room, and Gisele took my hand, and we were just dancing close. I might have imagined I was in France at the end of the war, but I didn't need to dream. The girl of my dreams was hugging me close, her head buried on my chest. It was a perfect moment. I held her close to me as we swayed to the steamy jazz, and I could feel her body through her clothes. I could feel her thin silk dress and where her stockings began underneath. I saw a droplet of sweat running down her neck, and I secretly caught it with my lips.

Then Gisele said, "*Michele*, the music is stopped."

I didn't notice; I didn't care. I was a little embarrassed but oh-so-in-the-moment happy. Gisele's face looked the same. We made our way up the stairs to the world above. I took her home as slowly as I could. We held hands and walked the twenty-three blocks to her apartment. I never wanted to get there. I gave an occasional glance at the way her head tilted and her delicate neck.

At her apartment door, she turned to me. "*Michele*, I had such a wonderful evening, thank you so much." And she gave me a kiss and said, "Goodnight, *Michele*."

But she didn't close the door, and we looked at each other until it was just about too long, and she began to close the door, but I held it open, and she said, "What are you doing?"

"Not tonight. I can't leave, not tonight."

Gisele smiled. "What are you talking about?"

"Gisele, I can't leave you."

The next moment happened by itself. I pushed open the door and, lifting her like a silk scarf, carried her to the bedroom and tore off her dress. She couldn't believe it, and truthfully neither could I.

I pulled her into a kiss, and she grabbed my face firmly in her hands, saying, "*Michele*, I don't want you! I don't want you!"

I stopped, frozen in the hottest moment of my life. I looked at her and she was ravishing, but I wasn't a rapist. I looked into her eyes and said, "You don't want me?"

She looked back at me, her face softened, and she said in that soft French whisper, "Maybe just a little."

I ravished her; we ravished each other. It was, for me, the first time it counted. Nothing had ever come close to this. Without a doubt, the two years of waiting and wanting her were worth it. No thinking – just passion. The wonder in her eyes as well as the desire in both our eyes. I couldn't stop looking into those eyes. We steamed up the windows in summer. Then we felt the morning light.

I floated down Third Avenue like Gene Kelly in *Singin' in The Rain*. I was dream happy. The bakery trucks were bringing, and the garbage trucks were taking. A delivery man sensed my happiness and tossed me an orange. The city at dawn.

I called the next day and the next, but there was no answer. I knew she had to have felt what I felt. She had to! I was getting more upset with each unanswered ring. I began to doubt what I felt. I told Walker what happened. He was happy for me. Gisele and I had to work on our scene, and that was my motivation for going uptown to her apartment a few days later.

Maybe her phone was broken. The doorman wouldn't let me in. I waited till he was helping a woman from a cab with groceries, and then I slipped by and took the stairs just as Giselle and I had done the other night. It was far less romantic now. What a climb.

I got to her door and rang. Rang again. Nothing. It was the right apartment, right floor. I checked several times. On impulse, I tried the door, and it opened. I stood back, shocked. This apartment was empty. I stared at it from the door. I thought it must be the wrong apartment till I saw the floor protectors for the piano legs. The round cushioned casters were still where the piano had been. Then I saw the Greek beads on the kitchen window, the marks where the sofa had been. This was her apartment, but it was empty. She was gone.

She wasn't at the Actors Studio workshop. I kept staring at the door till Simone said, "Maybe I should move the stage to the back of the room". I was getting desperate, so I went to the Academy and stalked the halls waiting to find Mr Husband-to-be, my old teacher and Gisele's fiancé. I was nervous about this. What if she told him about us? *US*?

He walked right by me. He turned. "Oh Michael, right?"

"Yeah, I was wondering, um … Gisele and I are working on a scene … We're in a workshop together at the Studio."

"I know." He nodded.

"I haven't been able to reach her, and I was wondering if you knew…"

He had the saddest expression on his face. "I don't know where she is. I haven't heard from her in days, and I don't know how to reach her. Sorry."

I felt for him, but I said, "Thanks," and skulked away. I never saw him after that.

Summer 1988 – twenty-two years later – Ramatuelle, South of France, near St Tropez.

I had finished the 80s classic hit TV series *Dempsey and Makepeace*, and my co-star Glynis Barber and I were now a couple. A very romantic tale to come, but not at this moment, as we'd recently split up. So, instead of being here on holiday together with our English friends, Frank and Michelle, our hosts allowed us to split the two weeks and take one week each. Glynis had finished her week in the South of France, and now it was my turn.

After a glorious lunch at *Cinquante-Cinq*, the French pronunciation of the infamous St. Tropez Club 55, we returned to the villa for a relaxing afternoon around the pool. Drinks and massages, as one does. A long way for this boy, eh?

We were reclining around the pool, Frank was on the phone, moving the world, and I was reading a TV script.

Michelle explained in a sulking tone, "Michael, I am really upset. I left my book at the restaurant. I was so looking forward to reading a hot love story this afternoon by the pool. Please could you tell me one?"

I had watched these period English films where guests are meant to entertain their hosts – that's why their guests or their daughters sing, and the men play piano or recite romantic prose – but so far in my life I had never experienced it personally. Michelle put on her best *oh please?* expression and I was the guest, so I reached deep back and told her the story of Gisele. Only now I was a bit worldlier, and I could embellish my memories with new understandings and descriptions. The color of Gisele's eyes, not on my chart back then, were now the color of the water in Tiberius's cave on the Island of Capri, where the Roman emperor would have his divine bath in glowing blue waters unknown anywhere else in the world. Gisele's eyes were lit with that same shimmering sparkle.

However, the ending was sadly the same; she was gone, and I never saw her again.

A good guest, I took my leave to shower before dinner. But the memories haunted me. We build rust around our hearts to forget, but I didn't forget because I never knew what happened to Gisele.

London – my house in Hampstead – two weeks later.

A call from Michelle in Ramatuelle, South of France.

She was very excited; so much so, I could hardly understand what she was saying. "French? You said French, the girl in your story was French?"

"Yes, actually half French and half Greek."

Michelle screamed, "She's Greek." I thought perhaps too much Rosé at Club 55. Then she said, "My friend Bonnie just came to stay a week after you left. She came from Greece, where she was staying with a Greek friend of hers named Gisele. I started to speak, but she shut me down. Wait for this, this girl Gisele told her the same story you told me!"

That's impossible, but Michelle continued, saying, "The thing is, Gisele told Bonnie that the guy was American, and Bonnie thought it can't be you, then said that you play an American cop in that TV series but you're English! But when Bonnie told me, I said, 'No, Michael is American, he's not English.' You're not English, right?"

I told her gently that I wasn't. I was (am), in fact (sorry!) American.

Another scream followed. Michelle was beyond herself with excitement, and I could hear Bonnie screaming along with her in the background. "He's American, he's American! You're right, it's him!" You'd have thought they'd just found out they were twin sisters separated at birth.

"Michael, do you want the phone number of Gisele? She spends most of the year in Cannes where she lives. In the summers, she visits family in Greece."

I wrote the number down.

Two weeks later, I had a meeting with a director and a producer who wanted me to do four movies back-to-back in the South of France working with Robert Mitchum and David Carradine. Glynis and I went to France to find a house in Antibes, on the Med, around the corner from the Hotel Du Cap in Cap d'Antibes.

Glynis had returned to London. I was a couple of weeks into the filming, and one night I was alone in the Roc d'azur, the name of the house I rented with the gate that opened to the Med. I was holding the piece of paper with Gisele's number. If it *was* Gisele … I was so torn about this. I felt guilty because I loved Glynis, whom I was in a most tempestuous relationship with, but commitment had been elusive up to now. Not that Gisele meant anything contrary to or in betrayal of our relationship. This had nothing to do with Glynis; this was a twenty-two-year-old mystery, and I needed to know the answer!

I called the number, and a woman answered the phone. "*Allo?*"

A silence and then I said, "Gisele?"

She gasped. "Oh my God. I can't believe I am speaking with you after so long." Gisele told me of a bistro on the road to Cannes. "We could meet."

An hour later I was sitting at a table with an umbrella, staring at the candleflame dancing through my wine glass. It was twenty-two years since she disappeared after that amazing night. Now I was sitting here, and I knew in my head she was still the image of twenty-two years ago.

What if an old woman walked in with a cane? What if she walked in and she looked the same – she hadn't aged at all? And sat down looking at my puzzled face and told me she is my daughter? That Gisele had run away and had my daughter who looked exactly like her!

The fantasies ended when the real Gisele walked into the café. I stood up and we looked at each other and it felt just like we were breathing in at the same time. Gisele, still beautiful in the way French women don't age. Not like an old Greek woman in black drapes skinning fish. She was still pixie-like and delicate and elegant.

The waiter came.

Giselle nodded to my glass. "*Le meme.*"

Until the wine came, nothing was said.

"You look the same."

"So do you."

A little small talk. She was happily married, had two children, and gave up show business shortly after the Academy. She was never really committed to a career but had watched *Mission Casse-Cou*, the French name for *Dempsey and Makepeace*, which it turns out was a bigger hit in France than it was in the UK where it was made. She was happy for my success. I told her about Glynis and how I even felt guilty being here. We sipped our wine.

Finally, I said, "Why? Why did you leave? The most amazing night of my life, the theater, the jazz, the dancing, the lovemaking … you! It couldn't have been more perfect. Then you were gone. Why?"

Gisele's eyes, those eyes, filled with tears. Big, twinkling tears. "Because, *Michele*, what was I to do? I was engaged to be married, but I had never felt like that before, I had never loved like that before. How could I marry this man who had never made me feel like I felt this night? I could not. I ran away."

"But what about you and me?"

"You and me? What did I know about you? You were funny, nice, so sweet, good-looking, you were young, and you made me feel like no other man. But to you, I was just a girl, one night."

"Just a girl? One night? Gisele, I was in love with you from the moment I saw you in *Gigi*. I was in love with you every day for two years at the Academy. I waited two years for that one night. I wanted to take you in my arms every time we passed in the hall. I could not have been more excited when I saw you at the Actors Studio and, when we became friends, I fell deeper in love with you."

The large tears finally made their way down from her eyes as she looked at me. "*Michele*, how was I to know this? You never told me!"

"Gisele, I never thought you could love me."

As I drove her home along Boulevard de la Croisette. I'm sure we were both thinking of alternative life possibilities. We could see that in each other's eyes when we hugged goodbye. We were grateful and without regrets. We were both good with our lives.

If you love someone, it's good to tell them before it's too late.

CHAPTER 4

Academy Years 1965–1967
Brooklyn to Broadway

New York City. During the first year at the American Academy of Dramatic Arts, I became friends with a girl in my scene class named Geedee Hayden. Turned out she was Grace Kelly's niece and grew up in the Kelly mansion in Philadelphia. We were buddies, two young aspiring actors in the Big Apple. Our friendship was about laughs, and learning, not coupling. Geedee was a unique girl, who loved to be home alone, pour herself a scotch, light a cigarette, put on fishnet tights, top hat and tap shoes, and do all the Fred Astaire/Ginger Rogers routines. She knew them by heart.

Geedee was a great actress. I saw her perform *Royal Gambit* at the Academy with Stacey Keach and I was in awe of her work. Geedee knew early on that she caved in at the audition process. Many great actors just didn't want to live with that kind of pressure. After we graduated from the Academy, Geedee went to work for the talent manager Bill Treusch and took care of his biggest clients like Christopher Walken.

The return to the Academy for the second year was by invitation only. I can't say I wasn't happy to get the invitation letter. After my collision with Frances Fuller, I thought they would drop me. It was a week before the start of semester when I had horrible tonsillitis. The doctor said they must come out and if I did it right away, I would be fine in a week. Moments later, I was strapped in a chair and the doctor told me to open my mouth and he had shears in his hand. I said, "Whoa! I am still awake"! The doctor casually said, "Oh, we don't put you out, or sedate because you could swallow your tongue. Don't worry, it will be over in a minute". While he was talking a nurse shoved a device that forced my tongue down and my mouth wide open. I was yanking my arms, but I was strapped firmly. I was freaking out and making Frankenstein noises. He reached into my mouth and cut off one tonsil and then sheared the other and took out the two bloody lumps with a little basket. The nurse said, "Doctor he's having heart palpitations". That's all I remember till I woke up in a room. My throat felt like somebody had put out a torch in my mouth. The doctor came in and all I could do was garble angry Frankenstein noises at the monster. But he understood me. The Doctor said, "If I told you the truth, would you have done it?" Incredible! Maybe, I found the missing Nazi, Josef Mengele?

During the second year at the Academy, Geedee fell in love with another acting student named Andy Rubin and the three of us became storybook pals. Andy worked as a page at NBC while attending auditions, along with another page, David Geffen, who became Geffen Studios. Andy and Geedee were my best mates, and we were often kicking our legs in the air, laughing. It was the best of times.

When I moved out to LA in 1969, they followed a year later. A few great years after that, Geedee and Andy sadly split up. She left LA and I lost touch with her, till very recently. Andy was aways there for me, helping me with scenes for auditions and working on the parts we played. We were bullshit detectors for one another. As well as shoulders to cry on for the parts we didn't get or the girls that got away. The best part was our inexhaustible humor. In my personal glossary Andy was found under soulmate.

Andy had a very decent career; he co-starred with Walter Matthau in *Casey's Shadow*, a co-starring role in Police Academy and a TV series with Peter Boyle, and he guested with Michael Douglas in *The Streets of San Francisco*.

Andy had a long live-in relationship with Debra Winger, who was the little sister of Wonder Woman, Lynda Carter, when he started dating her. Debra was vibrant, funny, and confrontational. Her career accelerated with *TGIF*, An *Officer and a Gentleman*, *Urban Cowboy* and *Terms of Endearment*. Debra became a big movie star. The three of us all lived out at the ranch houses and later in my house in Brentwood. Andy and I stayed best friends for fifty years until he passed away in 2016. My buddy, Andy remembered everything I did better than me and I could sure use him now, writing this book. I miss him.

Meanwhile, back in New York City, 1967, over two years of intense study had gone by. Now I was an actor. I felt like one of those baby turtles in a wildlife documentary. You climb out of the sand, take a quick look around and run for the sea before you get eaten by predators. I believe there is a slightly higher survival rate for turtles than actors.

I was twenty-one, Gisele was gone, and our studio workshop ended with a disastrous presentation of the Crucible for Lee Strasberg, who burned us all at the stake, particularly our director. To put it mildly, school was out. I gave myself two years to be a 'movie star'. A reasonable goal, I thought, or it's back to the Goons. Getting an agent was my daily hunt. Countless phone calls, dropping photos with bogus CV credits at Agents and Casting directors' offices, and no one cared that I could fence in tights – thank you, Academy! This was real life, and it's hard out here.

I got the lead in a student film, a non-paying NYU student film called *The Unicorn*, directed by a student film director named Martha Coolidge, who would go on to make films such as *Valley Girl*, *Lost in Yonkers*, *Angie* and *Real Genius*. (Martha recently asked me to speak in her directing class so it's nice to think back to beginnings.)

My roommate, Walker Daniels, played a great part in a new musical performing in Central Park. It was Joseph Papp's production of *Hair*. Walker was one of the leads, and the show, hugely successful, transferred to an Upper West Side musical theater on the border of the theater district. Walker did the first album recording of the musical, but when it transferred to Broadway, the authors, Rado and Ragni, took over the lead roles and dropped Walker. That's showbiz, baby!

I made some money playing a background extra in *Love of Life*, a daytime soap. It wasn't acting, unless you call fake talking to someone without making any sounds acting. I think it's called Rhubarb. You sit in the background just mouthing the word 'rhubarb'. It only came up a few times a month, but it paid the rent. Well almost. Not even almost.

My first real audition came from an ad I read in the showbiz paper *Backstage*. A Barn Dinner Theatre tour of *The Rainmaker*. I saw the film, so I went in doing my best Burt Lancaster imitation.

"Mista, you're in a parcel o' trouble, ya need rain."

The director just stared at me. "Yes, we know Burt Lancaster did the movie." Then he asked me to read the part of Jimmy Curry instead.

I got the gig. I signed my first professional contract *Michael Brandon* in deference to Marlon Brando, my favorite actor. *I'm a professional actor now!*

I was happy flying to Roanoke, Virginia, in the Blue Ridge Mountains, until I found out what dinner theater really meant. Every evening before we performed, the cast – yes, the actors – served dinner and booze setups (ice and mixers) to the audience who brought their booze in paper bags. The audience was in the round and usually got loaded over dinner and asked, while you were serving, "Would you mind singing 'Happy Birthday' to my wife?"

Tips were half our salary, so ... *Happy Birthday...*

After serving dinner, we changed into our costumes while the stage with the set on it was hydraulically lowered into place for the start of the play. Well, you hoped it was, but it wasn't always the case.

During the performance, an audience member yelled out, "Hey can I get some more ice?"

Another hooted, "Can I get some more coffee over here?"

Hey, I'm acting now Dickface! But you couldn't say that, although Jesse Vint, an actor playing the sheriff, walked off stage and sat down at the offending table and delivered his dialogue right at them and shut them up. We performed every night but Sunday, and for $35 a week (twenty pounds) living in the back of the theater, sharing rooms with bunk beds, toilets down the hall, and cooking our own meals.

Next venue on the tour, the Barn Dinner Theatre in Kingsport, Tennessee. Yes, all of them shaped like a barn and stuck fifteen miles out of town in the middle of nowhere to keep the sinners (us) from town. It was the Ozarks; think "dueling banjos".

During the run, I saw a girl who had seen the show three times that week. She was so pretty, an apple pie, poster-sweet smile, and a Doris Day hair-flip. A shiksa, (very non-Jewish) goddess! While serving her dessert, she fluttered those bright blue eyes at me and asked if she could visit me on Sunday after church. I nearly dropped my tray!

She came on Sunday with a guard-dog ugly girlfriend who walked ten feet behind us as we strolled along the country road. Her chaperone barked if we stared at each other for more than a second. But it only took a second to have me thinking what amazing children this girl and I would have together, living together on a farm. I could teach acting and direct plays in the local theater, and then as if she was reading my thoughts, she suddenly stopped and turned to me. She shushed her bulldog and when she smiled at me with those big blue beamers and all those perfect white chicklet teeth, I swear I could hear the "Star-Spangled Banner" playing.

Instead, she said, "My daddy would shoot you if he knew I was with you."

The words didn't match the face. I was smacked back to reality. "Why would he shoot *me*?"

She laughed. "B'cuz, silly, you're a Yankee-slicker and a Jew." She leaned in real close. I thought she was going to kiss me, but she whispered, "Can I see your horns?"

"Horns?"

"All Jews have horns, just like on the statue of David, and you're my first Jew. Will you show me, pleeease?"

I may have been horny before, but I certainly wasn't anymore. This wasn't worth getting shot for. Get me back to New York City!

I mailed my first reviews to every agent in New York: "Brandon was the show stealer". My picture was in all the local papers. Okay, so it was Virginia, Tennessee, and Texas. To agents in New York, these were third-world countries. They didn't count except to my parents.

I was back pounding the streets of New York City hunting for an agent. I met one on a crosstown bus, a nice Jewish girl without horns (I checked). She got me a job in a film. Tiny problem, another actor was signed for the same role. Me and a guy named Al Pacino. It was a bit part, one line, but nobody knew either of us then. His contract was signed in the morning and mine in the afternoon, so he got to dance with Patty Duke in *Me, Natalie* instead of me. I did get to have lunch with Patty Duke and told her the story of *the Giving Tree* (Shel Silverstein).

The next thing this agent got me was being a stand-in for Kirk Douglas on *The Brotherhood*. A movie with real movie stars!

One day on location at the Toscanini Mansion, in New Rochelle, upstate New York, a big Mafiosi scene was filming. I watched everything very closely. How did Kirk remember to do the exact gestures in the exact same place every time? I was learning about continuity; matching what you did in each take so the editor could fit different takes together. I was sponge-man, soaking it all in.

Then suddenly Kirk got angry because some crew members were talking and ruined a perfect take. He smashed a pool cue over the table and his voice rasped loudly. "Movies can be made anywhere, and this one is going to be made in Hollywood unless I get some damned quiet around here!" Kirk Douglas was an amazing and scary movie star. I was very impressed.

Years later, my friend Michael took me to his house to have lunch with his father, Kirk. When I told him my first job was standing in for him on *The Brotherhood*, Kirk thought deeply and said, "Marty Ritt directed that. How was it for you?" I told Kirk my stand-in story.

"Well, they just did the focusing on me. But there was one scene when you pull up to your house in a limo, you get out and turn back to the Mafiosi sitting in the back (Val Avery) and say your line. You left your script on the back seat. I read the scene and when the limo pulled up, I got out and turned back and said, 'He's my brother, not yours, you *camorrista* bastard!'

Marty Ritt smacked his head and said, 'Holy shit, the stand-in knows the lines and the actor doesn't!'"

Kirk grabbed my shoulder and burst out laughing.

1968. I came home exhausted and half frozen standing in for Kirk in a butcher's freezer all day. My roommate was using my bed, bartering with the Chinese food delivery girl for a meal deal.

I should have bought stock in lice shampoo that year. I was fed up. I grabbed my suitcase, dumped my drawer into it, tied a frayed rope around it, and stormed out without a destination.

I had no money and couldn't afford a train ticket to my folks' house on Long Island. I called several people, including Geedee and Andy, to find a place for the night, but no answer, and I was running out of options.

Finally, one girl from the Academy, Evette, said, "Sure, the key is behind the fire hose in the hall. I'll be home after my dance class."

I found the apartment, located the hidden key behind the fire hose, and went in. It was disgusting. Filthy mattress on the floor, partially covered by stained sheets and dirty underwear. The kitchen alcove was worse, with a sink full of moving roaches on food-covered plates and garbage overflowing underneath. I couldn't do this!

I was heading for the door when Evette bounded into the apartment sweating in pink tights (a soft-porn version of *Fantasia*), holding one long agonizing moan as she rushed straight into the toilet, pulled down her tights, and gushed with the bathroom door OPEN! It happened before I could close my eyes. Evette pulled up her tights and came straight at me for a clammy hug. I was still frozen in place, trying to utter some lie about why I had to leave, when she ordered me to get the oranges from the kitchen.

I heard deafeningly loud Pavarotti coming from the room as I flicked cockroaches off the netted sack of oranges under the sink.

Evette demanded again, "Bring the whole sack."

I dragged the sack into the room, and Evette was stark naked against the locked front door.

She said, "Throw an orange at me!"

This was turning out to be a very unusual day. I tossed an orange, and she snatched it out of the air and hurled it back at me. I ducked and it smashed and slid down the wall.

She yelled, "Throw the oranges at me, harder!"

I was beginning to get nervous now.

She was splayed across the front door and there was no other way out. I threw another orange, but she didn't try to catch it. She let it hit her body. It bounced off her breast.

She kept yelling, "Harder, throw it harder!"

I had no experience to call on here. It was kind of a learning curve, forgive the pun. Okay, she liked it when I hit her in the gazookas? This was totally bizarre stuff for me in my little life so far. I pretended it was the World Series, and I was pitching for the Yankees. The crowd was cheering, and I could hear the Gutter Confucius yell, *don't throw like a girl! Come on, son, put one in the pocket!*

I pitched the oranges with everything I had. Finally, in juicy orgasmic pleasure, Evette slid down the door. Then the Gutter Confucius yelled in my head, *what are you waiting for asshole, run for home, get moving!* I yanked the door inwards (rolling Evette forward) and ran for my life. On the street, I could still hear Pavarotti blasting from her apartment.

I used to love fresh squeezed orange juice. I lugged my suitcase forty-four blocks to Andy and Geedee's. They were home. Their phone was out of order. I told them how I left my apartment after discovering Walker having a buffet party in my bed and winding up at Pavorotti's orange opera. We were in hysterics as we sat down to a mound of pasta and slabs of garlic bread. I said, you won't believe this but while I was throwing oranges at Evette, I heard my father yelling, *Put one in the pocket, son.*

Andy choked on his pasta. You shouldn't laugh while you're eating. He slowly started pulling a strand of pasta out of his nostril. Geedee and I just stared at him as he kept pulling using both hands like a handkerchief magic trick. He even hummed a magical theme. We thought we would die before he'd get the whole thing out.

They wouldn't let me go back to Walkers' apartment, so we unfolded their creaky sofa bed. It was an early Spanish Inquisition model. The matzoh thick mattress would have me converted by morning.

CHAPTER 5

Pedal To the Metal

I was a background extra in *Midnight Cowboy*. I was wearing a raincoat and walking down Fifth Avenue in fake rain. I had to get a proper agent. This one only got me extra work and stand-in work. I strongly complained and she came up with a real audition for a movie.

I went in and read for the lead in *Goodbye, Columbus*. I was on the money with my reading. The director, Larry Peerce, was extremely impressed with me. He had me back to read again and again, but with different actresses for the leading lady. I talked to my agent, and she confirmed that the director and producer, Stanley Jaffe, were thrilled with me. This is it! I got the lead in a movie and well within my two-year goal.

Every day I showed up at the production office and read new actresses for the female role. They were long days and very emotional for all the actresses. I tried to give my best to each one. And every day my agent replied, "We're waiting on the contracts." Until one day, they told me the girl was chosen personally by Bob Evans, the Paramount Studio boss. Her name was Ali McGraw. I was fine with whomever they chose but the next day my agent told me that because of Ali's height, they had chosen a taller actor to play opposite her. A guy named Richard Benjamin. I'd never heard of him. I was told I had the part. Jesus! How tall was this girl?

I was livid and despite what my agent said, I went to see Dir. Larry Peerce at the production office. But you said....

Larry said, "Sorry, kid, it's out of my hands. I'll find you something in the picture." What can you say? I was stunned. That's the business!

Then, my agent asked me if I would do stand-in for Richard Benjamin. I was speechless. This experience had been humiliating. I was young and it was the first of many lessons to learn in this business. One thing I did know, I couldn't be with this agent anymore. Director Larry Peerce gave me a role and it had one line, "Dartmouth". One word.

William Morris was the talent agency in New York. I walked in the door and there was the directory on the wall. A long list of agents in white letters on a black background. I picked two and called one from the lobby payphone. When the agent picked up, I said, "This is Michael Brandon," and told him that the other agent said he should see me.

It worked – he said he would. I nonchalantly added I was in the area and could come straight up. He agreed to see me. I ran up the stairs to get there before he talked to the other agent.

As he sized me up, he had inspiration and wrote an address on a piece of paper. "There's a Broadway show casting right now. Last day so get straight over to Philip Rose's office. Go now. I'll call over and say you're on the way. What was your name again?"

I was in Philip Rose's office, facing the casting director, a guy holding a yellow pad and pencil. He was tapping the pencil on the pad. I was sweating and panting from running to get here on time.

Finally, I said, "You want me to start, huh? You want me to say something? Okay, fuckface, I'll tell ya, I found my father. That's right, I found him. After nineteen years, I finally found my old man. You want to know what he was? A barber. That's right, after nineteen years, I finally found my old man and he's a fuckin' barber! Then as he puts that barber apron over me, but then he puts his hand under the apron in my crotch, I hit him. I hit him hard, and I hit him again and I hit him, I hit him, and I hit him."

I screamed and smacked the yellow pad out of the casting director's hands. I was shouting lines at him as I climbed over the desk to get him.

He jumped out of his chair. "Okay, that's fine, thank you. Send in the next actor."

I was hugging his legs on the floor. I smiled up at him.

I think I really scared the casting director. He thought I was going to hit him. But that was the gist of the audition scene for *Does a Tiger Wear a Necktie?* It was October 1968, and callbacks went on for months.

Meanwhile I auditioned for movies like Dalton Trumbo's *Johnny got his Gun*, an antiwar film. I had callbacks and I was offered several plays, but I didn't want to get naked. Since *Hair*, theatre nudity was rampant.

I got called back on *Tiger*, a few times in November and again in December. Finally, it was down to me and one other guy for the lead in a Broadway show. That guy again: Al Pacino.

During the last week of call-back sessions, Al won the Obie for his off-Broadway performance in *The Indian Wants the Bronx*. On December 17, they told me Al got the part and offered me the smaller part of Prince and the understudy role of the lead. From the lead to the understudy? Well, it was a Broadway show, and I didn't have to serve dinner. *Hey, I'm on Broadway*!

One hundred and seventy-five dollars a week, and they told me everyone was getting the same. What they didn't tell me was that was only during rehearsals. Everybody's salary went up but mine. The Gutter Confucius said, *use your head, you got shit for brains? Smuck.*

It was about three weeks into rehearsal, and I was thinking this guy Pacino was a dud. Boy, did they make a mistake. This guy's got nothin'. Then that afternoon, Al let it out. Holy shit! It was amazing. I had chills. I didn't know how to do what he just did in that room and in every performance thereafter. He built it slowly from within, and when he was ready, he let the Tiger out.

I learned a lot from Al. It wasn't all acting, either. Al was done at the end of the second act when his character drowns. Aside from being Al's understudy, I was in the first and third acts playing Prince, a smart-ass juvenile drug dealer.

One day, Al says, "Let's have a drink in my dressing room."

"Hey … you're dead, but I'm still in the third act."

He put his hand on my shoulder. "A tiny one, c'mon, please?"

Okay, we were having a tiny drink, and Al was really laughing it up. I should have smelled a rat when he said, "Please." Then I heard singing from the stage, and Al cocked his head and smiled.

"Holy shit, that's my cue," I said. "I'm supposed to be on stage!"

He'd set me up! I leaped down three flights of stairs and flew past the stage manager who was trying to get my jacket on. I was heading up to the gangway where I shouted to all the cast, "Bickham, (Pacino's character) is dead."

The stage manager handed me the jacket. "No time to get up there – just get onstage!"

I ran onstage and yelled, "He's dead, he's dead, he drowned, Bickham drowned." The entire cast looked up to the gangway above where I was supposed to be, so I yelled, "Here I am, here I am!"

They all turned at once to the stage left and stared at me in silence.

I went to everybody's dressing room after the show and apologized.

Al thought it was hysterical as we walked to Jimmy Ray's, the bar all the actors went to after their shows in New York. He got a lot of mileage out of that little trick. We had become friends these last few weeks, and I went to his apartment and had dinner with him and his girlfriend, Jill Clayburgh. Al wanted me to hear the play he wrote called *Rats*. He also hinted that after three months running, he might catch a cold and if it was a bad one, I would get to play the lead for a few days.

It was at Columbia Pictures/Screen Gems, which was based at 711 Fifth Avenue, where I made a true friend. Her name was Shelley Ellison. Shelley was the assistant to Renée Valente, the head of casting for Screen Gems. Shelley arranged for Renée to come see me in a workshop at the Actors Studio. I was doing a William Saroyan play called *Hello Out There*. I did the play as a vehicle to invite people to see my work, along with my friend and Academy classmate, Katherine Burns, who only a few years later got nominated for an Oscar for her performance in the movie *Last Summer*.

Here's how a career goes: First it's "Who is Katherine Burns?" Then, "Get me Katherine Burns." Then, "Get me a Katherine Burns type," then "Get me a young Katherine Burns," and finally, "Who is Katherine Burns?" Sing: *There's no business-like show business!*

Renée Valente was impressed with my work and told me to see her at her office and bring a scene, a monologue if I had one. I had been to 711 Fifth many times to hang out with Shelley. She was a port in a storm.

I arrived at Renée's office and did my audition scene from *Does a Tiger Wear a Necktie?* Renée recorded the scene and told me to sit at her desk. On the top of her desk was a Screen Gems contract, the television division of Columbia Pictures. Think of the Columbia Pictures' logo with the lady holding the torch like the Statue of Liberty. The torch was my burning desire to get that contract on Renée's desk.

She said, "Michael, you're good, you're very good." Her red fingernails tapped the contract as she finally said, "All I have to offer you is a player's contract at Screen Gems." Renée picked up the contract and put it in her desk drawer. "Michael," she said, "you're better than this. You're not a contract player. You'll do better on your own."

What was I going to say to that? *I'm not better; you're wrong, Renée.* I wanted that contract. A Columbia Pictures Studio contract meant a weekly salary from a studio that would hopefully supply me with TV and movie work to make me a star. It probably meant more dancing and fencing lessons as well. I walked down Fifth Avenue poleaxed over what just took place. It only fueled my purpose and strengthened my goal. I was going to be a movie star in two years.

The *Tiger* was dead; the show had closed February 1969, in its first week, all due to the New York Times critic Clive Barnes. And Al Pacino won the Tony Award for his one-week of performances. He earned it and was terrific! But I never got my shot there. Thanks, Clive!

I had conquered Broadway, right? *So Hollywood, here I come! That's where they keep the movies, right? Time to get movie bound on the Hollywood highway. Time to put the pedal to the metal.*

CHAPTER 6

Hollywood –Whupp Whupp

The wheels touched down and I was in California. Shelley, the Screen Gems casting assistant, had moved to LA to keep her job with Renee Valente, after Columbia had moved their offices to the west coast. Shelly picked me up at the airport. She was driving me to her house in Studio City and had offered me her sofa. I nodded off during the drive. When I woke up, she was still driving.

"What's up?" I said, checking my watch. "I thought you lived in LA?"

"I do, but I don't want you to see Los Angeles first. There's a lot of beautiful country in California. We're meeting some of my friends up in Yosemite and we'll camp out for the weekend."

"Shelley, I'm a Jewish boy from Brooklyn, and I don't like to camp."

"One of the guys we're camping with is an agent I wanted you to meet."

Did this lady know me or what?

"Hey, Shelley, you must be tired. I'll drive."

I'll skip the shivering in a bag on icy cold ground in the woods bit.

Monday morning. Los Angeles. May 1969. Shelley had a very comfortable sofa, and you can trust Sofa Man – I know my sofas.

Shelley yelled, "C'mon, *we're going to Columbia*!"

My first Hollywood studio.

Shelley drove her blue Chevy Camaro named Sage – yes, people name their cars in LA – up to the studio gate. The security guard waved and lifted the entry bar. She drove to a space with her name on it and parked. Very impressive. We had coffee in the studio *commissary* (that was a new word) and went up to Renee Valente's posh studio offices.

Renée Valente was very happy to see me. She asked Shelley to invite me to dinner at her house on the weekend, and then looked at Shelley, held up a red fingernail, "Get Bob Sweeney on the phone."

Shelley winked at me as she dialed the extension.

A minute later, I was told I had a meeting with the producer of *Mr Deeds*, a Screen Gems series filming on the studio lot. I was given a script and sent to a ranch-style office deep within the Columbia Studio. Sound stages and cottage-like offices were interwoven by landscaped pathways with palm trees. Like in the movies. I found my way to Bob Sweeney's office and sat in the waiting room.

The secretary said, "You can go in now."

I got up from the leather sofa (pretty comfy, I have to say) and walked into the office. Bob Sweeney was thin, slightly graying, with round glasses, and dressed smartly.

I was to read with Bob Sweeney, the producer himself. We read the scene, and he stood and said, "Thank you," indicating the end of the meeting.

I was walking toward the door when I turned and said, "Did I get the job?"

Bob waved me off. "We'll call your agent."

I replied, "I just got out here. I don't have an agent yet. Did I get the job?"

Bob looked up at me. "No, I'm sorry."

"Why not?"

Bob, perplexed, said, "Look, that's why we don't do this. We call your agent, and since you don't have one, I did you the courtesy of answering your question."

I just stood there. "What was wrong with my reading?" Bob looked exasperated. I didn't want to get Shelley or Renée in trouble, but I didn't understand why I didn't get the job. "It's a simple thing, Mr. Sweeney ... Why didn't I get the job?"

Bob Sweeney stood up. "OK, listen, you just aren't right for the role. What we're looking for is a street kid who's raw, explosive, unpredictable..."

It was at that point something inside of me snapped. I grabbed Bob by his jacket lapels and put him up against the wall and bear screamed in his face, "Who do you work for? Who do you work for?!" I Pacino-ed him. (It was lessons from the *Tiger*.)

There was a moment of heavy silence, I thought he'd call security. Bob smiled and gave me an appreciative nod, "OKAYYY, you got the job."

I don't recommend this approach for actors starting out. Today, I would be barred from the studio or even arrested. I had my first guest lead in a network television show, thanks to Renée and Shelley and, yes, even Al. Especially Al.

I worked the week at the studio. It still wasn't the lead in a movie, but it was a start. I had makeup and wardrobe, and I even had a little dressing room trailer. I was dancing in it when the director came by and asked if there was anything I didn't eat.

"Don't eat? Why?"

He said, "Tomorrow, we're shooting a scene where you and Monte Markham, the lead actor, are eating over a campfire."

I told him, "Eggs. I can't eat eggs without throwing up. My mother used to sneak them into my malteds when I was a kid. She would drop the egg in raw so I couldn't taste it. But the solid yolk would go sliding down my throat and make me throw up."

The next morning, the campfire scene was all set. It looked like we were in the woods on a deserted cabin porch, all created on a soundstage in Hollywood. I took my place at the campfire, the director called, "Action!" and Mr Deeds turned from the campfire and shoveled a pile of eggs onto my plate.

Eggs?

Monte Markham, playing Mr. Deeds, was saying his lines as he gobbled the gloopy eggs. I was staring at the eggs, thinking, *What the fuck? I can't eat this*, but the camera was rolling and so I said my line and pushed some eggs around the plate with my fork. Monte carried on slurping up the eggs with great relish. I shoveled some eggs onto my fork, but I was starting to feel a bit queasy.

Now it was Mr. Deeds' line to say, "How's the breakfast?"

I was supposed to swallow a big forkful smile and say, "Not bad." I pushed the eggs around the plate about as much as I could get away with, and then I slowly lifted the fork to my mouth. I looked at Monte, who was patiently waiting with a huge smile on his face. I put the eggs into my mouth, nodded and mumbled, "Mmm, not bad."

The director yelled, "Cut!"

I could hear whupp, whupp, whupp cheers all around the stage, including Monte and the director. The prop department guy held out a bucket for me to spit the eggs into, and then I realized the entire crew was laughing.

The director said, "That was great acting, son. I really thought you would upchuck. Well, done!"

Everybody was in on it. It was a good laugh. Jokes on a set are crucial. Lots of people take themselves too seriously. That was a valuable lesson, even if I was nauseous the whole day. Whupp, whupp!

I was now meeting agents as a working actor. A whole different ball game. I met one through Shelley named Chris Shiffrin, of the Shiffrin Agency. It was just him and his father. His father was known as Shifty Shiffrin after a few big deals, which earned him one of the best views sitting on the mountainside over the Sunset Strip. I asked him about the size of the agency and whether they had access to all the studios like the big agencies.

Chris said, "If someone is willing to knock down walls for you, access is secondary." He was the man.

Shelley gave me the keys to Blue Sage, and I drove around learning the neighborhoods. I was intrigued by the Hollywood sign that hung on the side of the mountain just about a mile or two north of the studio. It was originally Hollywoodland and put up by a real estate company in 1920, but by 1940 they took off the "land" part and it became "Hollywood".

I drove up into the hills toward the sign. From the top, I looked down at Hollywood and saw this odd-looking structure below. It had huge round windows and a pool and a strange dome on the roof. A statue of Jesus stood at the front of the building, holding out his arms toward Hollywood. I found it searching as I drove down the hill. The entrance was arched, and apartments surrounded a fountain with big colored fish. I think they were koi. An overgrown cactus pathway led up to the monks' dorm. This was on Vista Del Mar, almost straight up from Columbia Studios toward the Hollywood sign.

I found the manager, and he told me the Monastery of the Angels was founded in 1924 but there hadn't been monks living in the dorms for decades. I said I was interested in the one with the round window. He told me everybody was interested in that one; those were the monks' cells of the Monastery of the Angels. The cloister of Roman Catholic nuns lived below the wall and still baked bread there. Since there were no longer any monks, the monastery sold off the monks' dorm. The manager rented the dorms just as they were. However, the waiting list was over a year long. I left my number anyway.

I was at Shelley's house and answered the phone. The voice said, "It's Wisch". Jeffrey Wisch was a friend from New York City. He became an advanced mathematics professor to escape the Viet Nam War. Teachers were exempt. He would start each new semester by writing on the black board, I AM GOD. He would explain to the class that this was mathematics, and he would always be right. No arguments understood. Wisch currently owns a mountain café in Colorado. A while back a few friends of Wisch made an agreement; if Wisch calls you must drop your life and do what he says. Wisch created adventures and you could be certain that no matter what, it would be memorable. You could. not refuse or argue, or you were off the list forever. That was the point. Wisch said, "paper and pencil". I said, look Wisch, I just relocated to LA, and I just signed a new agent, and I am beginning a new career…. There was a silent pause, Wisch repeated, "Paper and pencil".

I wrote down a dozen different things starting with a large rubber duffle bag. Forty-eight hours later I walked out of an Arizona airport into burning sunshine. I had no idea what I was doing there, I was just following instructions. I looked around and noticed a guy with a rubber duffle bag. As I walked towards him another man approached me shouldering a big duffle bag and then another appeared. They all had the Wisch call. One guy was a chef, another a physical trainer and pro athlete, another with white beard and top hat said, just call him the white rabbit, he was a pot grower from Florida.

An old VW van with a bubble top pulled up at the curb. Wisch waved us all over and loaded our duffle bags and us inside and drove off. We drove for hours, finally arriving at a rustic camping site along a river. Wisch welcomed us and thanked us for coming with a BBQ full of steaks.

Wisch introduced Clear Quist, our bearded raft guide for the next week as he took us white water rafting down the Colorado River through the Grand Canyon. It was 1969 and way before organized tour guides took you safely on approved water trips. This was more like the Burt Reynolds movie, Deliverance. That night, we drank and ate and laughed like warriors. The next day would take us on a no-frills inflatable raft with two ice coolers for drinks and food and set off on the fast-moving Colorado River between the Grand Canyon walls.

Each night we set up camp when we found a bit of land along the river. While the chef prepared dinner, the athlete chopped wood and pulled the raft out of the river and tied it up. I made jokes as I built our custom-made toilet to avoid getting bit in the ass by rattle snakes. I became good at it. One day I challenged my vertigo and jumped off a boulder into an icy pool. It began to rain on the fifth day, and it went torrential. We saw the canyon walls moving as the water poured down bringing mudslides towards us. Quist was trying to keep us center river.

Quist told us to hold on to the ropes because it was turning into a flash flood. We were flying down the river out of control bouncing hard off the canyon walls until the raft hit flooding rapids and bent in half flipping us all into the air.

Much gratitude goes to Mr. Quist for pulling us all together like little chicks. We held on to the upside-down raft as it cascaded down the river. Then suddenly as it started the rain stopped and the river quieted. We slowed to a calm drifting and under Quist's instructions we got the raft right side up, but the outboard motor was gone. So were the coolers.

We drifted down river and Quist untied paddles and handed them to us. We got control of our direction and found one cooler, the food. The drinks were gone but white rabbit had powdered tear open packets of Grape flavored Kool Aid so that we could make the muddy river water taste better. We were exhausted but otherwise miraculously unbroken. We paddled to find a beach. What a day!

We sat around a tiny fire, not much dry wood around now. We boiled water to put the Kool Aid in. Quist studied his waterproof map and said, according to his map the rapids were over. It would be paddling from here to Lake Mead, our journey's end, as we had no outboard. Quist reckoned that if we slept on the raft, it would be a calm drift down river and save us a day of rowing. He looked around at each of us and we all agreed, let's do it.

Aboard, each of us stretched out across the raft. It got dark quick in the canyon. The huge canyon walls framed the corridor of sky above. A billion stars twinkled above but afforded no light into the canyon or on the river below. The only sound as we floated along was the rubber raft gently bouncing off the canyon wall. Then the intermittent inhaling and exhaling of white rabbit's protected joints as they were passed along the raft.

That's when we heard the water. The sound was faint at first but steadily getting louder. We all sat up like prairie dogs sensing trouble. We all thought it sounded like a waterfall. Quist had his keychain flashlight on the map and said, "The map says no more rapids, it don't say nothing about a waterfall". We couldn't see a thing, and it kept getting louder and closer. We were all imagining going over a waterfall in the dark and drowning. We desperately reached out for the canyon wall whenever the raft got close, and the athlete grabbed onto a branch sticking out and grunted holding on and the raft stopped. Before we could cheer, the wood branch snapped, and we were off again. Quist felt his way to each of us and checked our vests and put a rope in our hands. He even said, "I'm sorry about this." We all held hands, as the water got louder. Then we drifted by a waterfall coming down off the canyon wall. Instead of going over a waterfall we just floated by one.

Back on Shelley's sofa, I answered the phone and Shelley said I'd got a call from Gary Schaffer, the casting agent at MGM. He went through my New York agent trying to track me down. This casting agent was there the one-week *Tiger* was open, taking copious notes of all the actors he saw. A casting agent who looked for talent.

I checked off my second studio in Hollywood: MGM, the roaring lion. Neither studio exists anymore. I got my second guest lead in a show called *Medical Center*. I now had two TV jobs and a week on Broadway under my belt. I was still sleeping on Shelley's sofa, but what I really needed was a car. Los Angeles means City of the Angels but it's really the city of automobiles and without one you are stranded. I walked into Hollywood VW and bought a blue VW Bug. Cars were cheap back then. I had wheels. I could find an apartment and get to auditions.

That night in September 1969, I woke suddenly. It felt like everything was moving. I thought I was dreaming but then I felt it again. Shelley's house was shaking. I walked outside. It was quiet and still. Then there it was again. I was experiencing my first earthquake; the ground was moving. But it was more – more like a reminder call. I was on a mission and the soft life of sunny California had distracted me from my goal – to star in a movie within two years – and that date was closing in on me. Where was my movie?

CHAPTER 7

Lovers And Other Strangers

I got an excited call from my New York agent, Marty Gage at the Fifi Oscard Agency. "They're doing a movie of *Lovers and Other Strangers*. Come back and audition for this one, you are so right for this part."

Now here is the wonderfully weird thrill. While I was doing *Does a Tiger Wear a Necktie?* I wasn't in the second act. I used to sneak out of the Belasco Theatre and go up to The Brooks Atkinson Theatre where *Lovers and Other Strangers* was playing. It was the exact time their intermission was ending, and I was able to meld in with the returning throng for the second act.

Standing at the back, I would only watch the first scene, the dinner scene with Richard Castellano (Clemenza in *The Godfather*). Castellano was brilliant, and he was nominated for a Tony that year but lost to Al Pacino. (hmm, wouldn't it have been either comedy or drama?) I must have watched Castellano a dozen times. You're not allowed to leave the theatre once a show is in progress. If "Tiger" production ever found out I did this, they would have torn up my equity card.

After Shelley dropped me at LAX airport, we hugged and high-fived.

"Believe in yourself Brandon" she yelled through the open sunroof as she drove my blue Bug to her house for safekeeping.

Now I was flying to NYC to audition for the movie of that play. I was excited! I borrowed $75 for a student fare to New York, can you believe how cheap it was then? When I got to the city, I called my agent.

Marty said, "I'm sorry to tell you this, Michael, but they cast the part."

"What, while I was in the air?" This wasn't fair. My thespian mind was trying to find a loophole that forbid casting while I was off the ground. I just flew over five hours across the country! I was broke, but I owned a car in California. This opportunity to achieve my goal turned into a dead-end. What happened?

The Gutter Confucius says, *Trust in God, but tie your camel to a tree.*

Marty said there was a part in a soap opera casting if I wanted to go meet. The last thing I wanted was a soap opera. I sat in an all-night laundry eating a stale sandwich as I watched clothes tumble in the dryer. They weren't even mine. The laundry goes to the top, then freefalls for a second before it dives to the bottom. I was in that freefalling moment, just before diving to the bottom.

It was an awful night. I felt like crying, but I didn't know how. I've never cried in my whole life. My mother once naseled at me, *"you never cried. You fell down the stairs in your little kiddie car and you didn't cry".*

In the morning, I called my agent Marty from Andy's apartment, and he screamed, "Thank God! Where have you been? I haven't been able to reach you. They fired that actor. They want to see you. Get over there!"

The meeting was in David Susskind's office in the Newsweek Building. I was standing in front of Cy Howard, an old-time pipe-smoking director. He was puffing and staring. David Susskind walked in, very dignified in a nice suit and his white hair. Now they were both staring at me. I was standing there being stared at.

Cy Howard exhaled his pipe smoke and said, "You're really Italian, right?"

(I'm not, I'm Jewish, but I love pizza and I have Italian friends and then there's Flemighetti, the kid who left his Italian impressionistic work on me every day with his fist.)

My mind wouldn't shut up, so my mouth took over. "*Si! Si! Mia Madre es Napolitano. Eh verro!*"

I think what I said was, "Yes, yes, my mother is Italian from Napoli. It's true."

I was sweating this one out. If either spoke Italian or talked back to me in Italian, I was screwed.

Cy Howard took a long puff (how could he hold that much smoke?) and exhaled, turning to David Susskind. Then he nodded and said, "He's authentic."

"Okay." David nodded back.

Cy said, "You got the part, kid. You start filming on Monday. Learn your lines."

Thank you, Flemighetti, and thank you, Goons! Thank you, Rita Cepf, and even the little hole at the base of my spine that kept me from Viet Nam. I did it! I did it! I got a major role in a movie within two years! Not only that, I got a five-picture deal with ABC Pictures and an extra bonus; the brilliant Richard Castellano was playing my father!

Yes! I was exploding out of every pore of my body. I could have flown like the elephant in Dumbo. I was floating down the sidewalk, and I could feel the energy of New York coming through the cement. If I could have bottled this moment!

Marty said they couldn't pay me much because the actor they fired had to be paid off, but I didn't care. I had to find an apartment immediately, which I did, upstairs over the Dover Deli, complete with roaches so big I was afraid to spray them. *What if it only pissed them off?* I moved in the day after the landlord sprayed. A few left, some stayed.

Okay, the money was shitty, but I got the lead in a movie. No matter how many times I kept saying it over to myself, I never got tired of it. *I got a major role in a movieeeeee!* I celebrated with Geedee and Andy over spaghetti, eh verro! I even spent the night on the Spanish Inquisition sofa but having a movie lead, I confess, made it heavenly.

I showed up at the studio on Monday to see Castellano pinning the director up against the wall screaming, "Why didn't you hire my girlfriend?" Castellano wanted the part of my sister-in-law to go to his girlfriend, but they hired another unknown for the part, a girl named Diane Keaton. She was cute, and during the shoot I asked her if she wanted to grab a bite after work, but she said, "I just started dating this guy Woody."

It was Monday, my first day, my first scene, in my first movie, and I got into bed with Bonnie Bedelia, my leading lady

(Bruce Willis's wife in *Die Hard*). I had to strip down to my underwear in front of hundreds of people and I was nervous. I got into the bed, waiting for my leading lady to arrive. She did, in a flurry of makeup and wardrobe people, and an assistant brought her coffee. She noticed me.

I said, "Hi, I'm Mic—"

Bonnie cut me off. "I'm pregnant! Don't you dare tell anyone … I don't know where he is or how to fucking reach him! This script sucks, the director's an asshole, and I don't want a hard time from you, you understand?"

"I'm Michael. Nice to meet you."

Whoa! Wait a minute. What is this? This isn't in the acting manual! This is like getting into bed with Flemighetti.

The director came over and gave me a direction. As he was walking back to the camera, Bonnie whispered, "If you do what he just told you, you'll look like an asshole."

The director yelled, "Action!" and I stuttered out the line, totally flibbitzed by what she had said to me. The director screamed, "Cut! What's the matter, cripple, can't you remember your lines?" That's what he called me – "cripple". It was his term of endearment for me, a new actor. I think he liked me, but I was young, and I endured it.

After a lifetime of sailing across the ocean of life, I now realize that my little boat makes a wake, just like everybody else's – all our boats make wakes on the sea of life. Tiny or mighty, we all make a wake. Things were bumpy in Bonnie's boat; she was pregnant with no way of reaching her man, a writer off working somewhere unreachable. (Mobile phones didn't exist.) It was my voyage of understanding.

Each time I arrive on a film set or at a theatre rehearsal, I take a deep breath, because as they say in *Forrest Gump*, you never know what you're going to get.

Gig Young was a charming chap and a brilliant actor. He only murdered his wife and killed himself years after the movie, but at this moment, he'd just won the Academy Award for best actor in *They Shoot Horses, Don't They?* By the late afternoon he was loaded. We were doing a scene together and he was leaning his entire weight on me while we waited for a lighting adjustment, cheerily mumbling about a play called *Under the Yum-Yum Tree* that he did forty-five years ago.

I honestly didn't know how he would finish the scene. The director called, "Action!" and Gig snapped sober, tapped me lightly on the shoulder and delivered his line. "No gap here, son." He strode off, and I was left with my jaw open. How did he do that?

Then I heard Cy saying, "What's the matter, cripple, forget your line again?"

We got to the last week of shooting. I'd been taking subways and buses to every location. But the entire next couple of weeks would be shot upstate New York in the Tarrytown Hilton Ballroom. It was the big Italian wedding scene.

The first assistant director, Lou Stroller (great guy and still friends), came up to me and said, "Mikey, you mind riding up tomorrow with the atmosphere?"

"The atmosphere?"

"Yeah," said Lou. "The extras' bus."

I did a Bonnie on him. "Yeah, Lou, I mind. I'm one of the fucking leads in this movie, so how come I don't get a limo like everybody else?"

Lou chuckled and patted my shoulder. "Hey, kid, all you gotta do is ask."

Bonnie did have something to impart to me – *Stand up for yourself.*

The next morning, I was standing outside the Dover Deli, holding my coffee. I didn't want to be late for my first limousine. The snow was coming sideways in the wind as the limo glided up to the curb. The rear door opened, and Gig Young stepped out, holding the door like a chauffeur. Gig Young, the Academy Award winner, was holding the door for me. I slid in and there was Richard Castellano on the other side. I was in the middle, holding my takeout coffee.

I jovially said, "Good morning, guys."

Nobody responded. Absolute silence.

Then Castellano leaned forward and said, "Morning Jig," – not Gig, but *Jig*.

Gig leaned forward and said, "Fuck you, Castellano."

I was thinking, *Maybe I'll take the bus tomorrow. Better atmosphere.*

Then they both cracked up laughing. I looked at each of them.

Gig said, "Welcome to the club, kid."

Castellano added, "It's about time!"

The entire cast was there for the wedding scene, including hundreds of extras, even Sly Stallone playing a waiter. Sylvester used to go to my father's garage in LA and they got on very well (ex-Easterners). Pop gave Sly credit when he couldn't afford the repairs and asked me if there was anything I could do to help his career. I wish I had helped, but he did all right on his own.

Lots of cameras, cranes, and rehearsals. The set decorator and props departments were preparing a huge wedding right before our eyes with tables, plates, food, musicians, kids, and actors. It was chaos. This would take weeks to film. There were scenes in the bathrooms, at the tables, outside on patios, in hallways, and on the wedding dais.

The last day of filming and everyone was ready for the big shot. It was all in one, meaning no cuts; everything took place in one big take. The cameras swung on overhead cranes panning across the room and stopping at every table, filming vignettes of Beatrice Arthur listening to Diane Keaton confessing, "His hair just doesn't smell like raisins anymore," and Anne Meara saying, "You guys in the corps just can get it up," and Harry Guardino defending, "Don't ever talk about the corps," and Richard Castellano asking my brother, Bob Dishy, for the hundredth time, "So what's the story?"

Finally, the camera came to rest on Bonnie and me, the bride and groom for the grand finale to the whole scene – the wedding kiss. Balabusta!

Twenty-eight takes later, we'd still not gotten to the kiss. Focus went wrong, someone forgot a line, an extra accidentally blocked the camera, or a light bulb exploded. Normal movie stuff, but frustrating.

Finally, it was all going right. The camera was panning over the last table vignette and turning toward Bonnie and me for the kiss.

Bonnie whispered, "Don't kiss me."

I turned to her. "What?"

She said, "Don't kiss me. I don't feel like kissing."

I was panicking. "What do you mean, you don't feel like it? That's what this shot is about. We're supposed to be kissing." I could feel the camera coming toward me.

"Well, don't kiss me, that's all."

"Why didn't you tell the director that before he said *action*?"

She said, "He's an asshole and I don't feel like kissing."

The camera turned onto us.

I took Bonnie into my arms and kissed her. She bit down on my lip like a Rottweiler. I held in a muffled scream, but I couldn't believe the pain. I grabbed her by the jaw and neck to get her off my face. That was the pose when Cy yelled, "Cut!"

Nobody moved. Everything stopped.

Cy walked up to us, the pipe still in his mouth. He looked at each of us. He nodded, which meant he was at the end of his rope, but he was smiling. Taking the pipe from his mouth, he said, "Fix her makeup, clean up the blood on his lip and we'll go again. This time we'll be kissing, yeah?" He looked at Bonnie.

Bonnie, with her most innocent smile, said, "Of course, Cy."

Cy put the pipe back in his mouth. "Okay, everybody, we'll do it again."

As Cy walked off, Castellano came and put his arm around me and held out his other hand like a fat claw and said, "Mikey, this time, finish the job."

The last take was a thing of perfection, and we wrapped the film. All the actors were scrambling to get into limos to go home.

Lou, the first assistant director, said, "Sorry, folks, but the limo company screwed up and there's only one limo. The others will be about forty minutes."

All the actors looked at him and then dived into the one waiting limo. Nobody wanted to wait. Nine actors who would rather squish themselves into a tuna can than wait forty minutes.

The limo was riding low back to the city with the backseat filled with Diane Keaton by the window, then Bea Arthur, Bonnie Bedelia, and Richard Castellano pressed against the other window. I was sharing one of the little limo fold-out seats facing them with Harry Guardino, with Anne Meara and Gig Young on the other fold-out. Jerry Stiller and Bob Dishy were sitting up front with the driver. It would have made a great poster for the film.

That was the moment Bonnie decided to take out a pomegranate and began to peel it.

Beatrice Arthur slowly tilted her head to Bonnie, and in her deep bass voice said, "What are you doing, dear?"

"Eating a pomegranate," Bonnie said.

"You know, dear," Bea said, "pomegranates leave the worst stain of any food. You can never remove a pomegranate stain."

Bonnie sucked her pomegranate with relish. "If you eat two pomegranates a day, you never need to use toilet paper."

A beat later, there was room for another person on either side of Bonnie.

A couple of years later, on a TV anthology series of *Love Story*, I walked into rehearsal and there was Bonnie Bedelia, my wife-to-be, again.

She jumped up to greet me. "Michael!"

I said, "I'm pregnant. Don't you dare tell anyone. I don't know where he is or if he even gives a shit. This director is an asshole and the script sucks, and I don't want any trouble from you." Bonnie nodded obediently and burst out laughing, hugged me tightly, then stepped back and smiled proudly at me. "You've grown up!"

I had indeed, and I had the good fortune to work with the professional, talented and inspiring Bonnie Bedelia many more times.

CHAPTER 8

A Monk in Hollywood – January 1970

I could see the LA smog layer from the plane window. I left my little VW bug at Shelley's, and she picked me up with a message – the manager of the monk's dorm had called. I dropped her at the studio and drove straight there.

The monk's cell was mine if I wanted it. The monk's cell with the big round window. It was much cooler than I thought and much smaller than I could have imagined. It was like a shoebox turned up on its end. You walked in the door, and you were halfway across the room. One very tall room with a staircase going up the left wall to the open bed space. Straight ahead was the magnificent window, and below the window, there were two paned window doors opening to a tiny balcony facing the mountains and the Hollywood sign.

Under the staircase was a door to the bathroom; a toilet, sink, and a shower you could barely turn around in. There was no kitchen, so I put a bar counter under the staircase with a toaster, mini-fridge, and a water cooler. The wood staircase took you up to the open bed area overlooking the room below.

It was only big enough for a small chest as the bed was built into a wall under two small windows that led out to the roof.

The bed was small, but they were made for monks. Are monks always small people? In *Robin Hood*, there was fat Friar Tuck. Are Friars monks? Monk Tuck wouldn't be able to tuck in this shower. It was perfect for me, my pied-à-terre. There were ten cells along a narrow hallway, five on each side, that seemed to have music coming from behind each door. Most residents were actors, writers, and musicians.

I was dating a lovely actress named Brooke Bundy, who I had met on the *Medical Center* show before going to New York. We had been going out and spoke often while I was in New York filming. Brooke had a young daughter named Tiffany and we were all getting on great. And I mean great. Dinners and movies, picnics, and Disneyland excursions.

One day, I was picking Brooke up for dinner, and she bolted from her house and leaped into my arms overwhelmed with happiness.

"What's up?" I asked.

"This is so great; I can't believe it!" she screeched with elation. "I got you an appointment with my shrink. He's booked for years, but I got you in. You have an appointment to see him tomorrow."

I didn't want to rain on her parade, but I finally said, "And why do I want to see your shrink?"

She calmly took my arms and looked me deep in the eyes. "Are you happy all the time?"

Wow. Wow! This was big. "No, I don't think I am happy all the time."

She smiled with knowledge of the universe. "See, you're going to love Dr Pong."

I didn't love Dr Pong. I found him kind of cold and pompous, and I felt decidedly unhappy after seeing him, so I didn't want to see him again, which caused an irreparable riff that led to the end of our relationship. Gutter Confucius said, *when an irresistible force meets an immovable object, shit breaks.* That was a real shame, because I really felt deeply for both Brooke and Tiffany. I thought it was a package deal.

My second picture option on the five-picture deal came up in the form of a Western called *Zachariah*. I met George Englund, the director. He was the husband of Cloris Leachman, who played my mother-in-law in *Lovers and Other Strangers*. We got on great, but I didn't like the script. I did a screentest with the actor who would co-star with me, a newcomer named Don Johnson. Don and I got on great as well. In the end, the script didn't work for me. That was a shame too.

I should have done this movie. I was right about the script, and *Zachariah* failed at the box office, but I should have done it for two reasons: Westerns are rare and playing the lead in a Western would have been such fun, and more importantly, it would have kept my momentum going. A *working actor* is very attractive to producers.

My main regret was that George Englund who was Marlon Brando's best friend had said, "Michael, I know Marlon Brando is your favorite actor and if you say yes to doing my movie, I'll take you up to Marlon's house for dinner."

Boy, I kicked myself over that one. I'm kicking myself right now. I was young and stupid. My dream was to make a film like *On the Waterfront,* my favorite film. It's what inspired me, but I didn't realize how rare these films are. Almost as rare as a cowboy lead in a Western.

I needed professional guidance but didn't know how to get it. I had my monk's cell, my VW, my new LA agent who called with a job offer. It's a very popular series; big male star and they want you for the guest lead. I wanted to work, and it was one episode, a seven-day job. I said yes.

Everyone was so nice, and the producer was very welcoming and invited me to a party at his house on the weekend. I decided to go. Checking the address on the printed invitation, he left in my dressing room, I drove up to a house with red carpet rolled up the walkway and torches lighting the way from the valet parking at the curb. There were Ferrari's and Lamborghinis and vintage cars I'd never heard of. I felt embarrassed to give my VW bug to the valet. Even he was better attired than me. I pulled out of line and drove up a bit further and parked my car myself and walked back down to the house. This was my first Hollywood Bash. But it wasn't in Hollywood, it was Beverly Hills so do you still call it a Hollywood party?

At the entrance I squeezed by Burt Reynolds, who was hugging hello to Angie Dickenson. I walked past a waiter, who offered a tray of drinks. I didn't see any Coca-Cola, so I grabbed one that looked like lemonade, but it made me gasp when I sipped it. Then the producer was there next to me with an arm on my shoulder. You made it! C'mon I'll give you the ten-cent tour. He walked me through a gauntlet of celebrities who all greeted their host warmly as he led me into a paneled library. He was welcoming me just like all the big names.

It was an amazing room, like out of one of those mystery movies. Book lined walls and leather sofas. I said, "It looks like a movie set," and he laughed, saying it was one. All of it came from various productions over the years. He told me he wanted to show me something unique. He pulled a thick leather-bound book and the whole shelf section opened like a secret door. Behind the door was a cozy apartment with a bedroom, sofa, chair, TV and kitchenette. He led me in and walked to a door near the kitchen and said, "This is the best part". He opened the door and there was a Porsche parked just on the other side. I laughed, it's like the Bat Cave, you can walk right out to your car without going outside. He said "It's your car, it goes with the apartment. When can you move in?"

I stuttered, "Huh? I have a car and an apartment, I'm good". He leaned on the wall behind me, very close and said, "You can phase it, stay a couple of nights a week at first or a weekend until you're comfortable".

Then someone was calling him, and he smiled and said, "Speech time. Listen, try it out. Kit, car and caboodle, it's all free. Have a think". He left me there and walked back to his party. I needed air, and maybe a nurse to take my pulse.

I snuck past the Porsche, out through the garage to a side street and found my way to my car. I was thinking about it alright; I couldn't stop thinking about it. This was a first for me. In my bug driving home, I could hear the Gutter Confucius saying, "*Nothing is for free, son*".

Not much sleep that night. I didn't know what to do. Oh, I knew I was not moving my caboodle anywhere near his house, but what about Monday on the set? Maybe I was reading too much into this whole thing?

The work was good, and the show was over and the director, who was a talented man, thanked me for my excellent contribution to the show and said he was having a BBQ lunch at his beach house on Sunday and to bring my bathing suit.

I drove out to Malibu, to the Colony as it's called. The stars weren't in the sky, they lived here on the beach. This enclave was host to many people I would work with over the years. This was my first exploratory trip. All the houses were behind a gate and on the beach. You walk out your back door to the sea. I knocked and the director showed me in and straight to a dressing room where I could change into my bathing suit and come back to the beach. I rolled up my pants on top of my shoes and found my way back. There wasn't much beach between his house and the sea, but it was empty of people. I thought the whole cast and crew would be here, like a wrap party. Maybe I was early, I looked at the BBQ on the deck and no sight of food. He exclaimed, "Take a look from up here, on a clear day you can see Catalina Island". I climbed the wooden stairs to where he was standing, overlooking the ocean. The view was phenomenal. He stepped back into the room, saying "This is why I bought it". As I turned taking in the vista, he pushed me back onto his bed. He was on top of me, had my wrists under one of his big hands and was trying to rip off my bathing suit with the other. I was taken completely by surprise. He was a big guy and at least twice my weight. I was having a real struggle getting him off me. He had me pinned under him.

Was this really happening? Was I wrestling with this man on his bed?

"Get off me! What the fuck are you doing!"

He was strong, and he was trying to kiss me. I kept turning my head while bucking to get him off my body. I really thought I had it when I heard a kid's voice calling from outside the room, "Dad? Dad?"

He was off me in a flash. His kids were standing in the bedroom doorway. He was standing in front of them to block them from seeing anything and while he was blabbing, I had my suit pulled back up and jumped off the deck to the beach. I ran around to the front and fortunately the kids had left the door open. I poked my head in, coast clear, I grabbed my clothes from the dressing room and galloped for my car.

I was lucky. His kids saved my ass, literally. Was it me? Was I putting out some vibe that made these guys come on to me? What a week, What an eye opener. This is what women go through all the time. You need to have that extra awareness. No, I never told anyone. There was no *#MeToo* kind of consciousness. Yes, I believe it was a part of the business. Not just show business, but anywhere people aspire or have desires, it gives other people power over you, if you let them.

I was breathing deep on my balcony watching the colors of the sunset. I needed my good friends to chat with, so I called Geedee and Andy in New York. They got me laughing and happy when they revealed their plans to move out west to Los Angeles. It had been about year now.

Andy and GeeDee had found an A-frame cabin up Laurel Canyon in the hills though contacts. When they moved in, we filled it with laughter like the old days. So good to have friends you can share everything with. We talked late over pasta and garlic bread and wine about how to survive in a no walking city. I had got stopped by police walking in Beverly Hills one night. The Police wanted to know what I was doing walking at night. Walking is suspicious behavior here. NYC is a walking city, a theatre town. People about anytime of the day or night. Los Angeles is a driving city, and a film town. Early to bed and early to rise. Dictated by the hours you can shoot film in daylight, and the same weather conditions daily.

I told them about the film Zachariah and missing dinner with Marlon Brando. They moaned along with me. I know. *Smuck!* I could hear the Gutter Confucious.

Instead, I did this little art picture for United Artists called *Heir*. It was a well-written book based on the true story of Walter Annenberg's son (Annenberg of the publishing dynasty), who overdosed his girlfriend, killing her by accident. It was a touching love-gone-wrong story directed by a young hot director, Noel Black. {Academy Award winner for short film} After I signed up to do it, Paramount replaced Roger Simon, the original author, with Erich Segal after his smash success with *Love Story*. It was a mishmash of ideas from the studio, the book, and Erich Segal's script. Paramount even changed the title to *Jennifer on My Mind*, because the girl's name in *Love Story* was Jennifer. To me, the whole movie went sideways. I should have done the western and had dinner with Marlon!!

However, I did meet this guy named Robert DeNiro. He was playing the small role of the gypsy cab driver. We got on very well. We had dinner at this Chinese restaurant in Needle Park and I remember confessing to him, "I don't know what the hell I'm doing in this film."

Bobby said, "How can you know what you're doing when nobody else knows what they are doing? One day it's a comedy and the next it's a tragedy." He shrugged with the smile that would become his trademark expression.

Bobby did me a good favor one day during filming. I was dying of pain from a toothache, and when they called lunch Bobby drove off the gypsy cab with me in the back.

I said, "Where are you going?"

He said, "I'm taking you to my dentist, man. You can't work while you're in pain like that."

His dentist did an emergency root canal. I didn't go early enough to save the tooth. I was a young actor, and I didn't want to complain. Bobby was a good guy to take me. Director stared at my swollen face and sent me home.

The filming in New York temporarily stopped to shoot a few sequences in Venice, Italy. This was my first time leaving the US. On the way to Italy, I stopped in London to visit Carnaby Street and then went to Amsterdam to visit Dam Square, where I bumped into this huge man with a beard wearing tie-dye overalls. He stood about six foot, six inches tall and leaned over me and talked down to my face in a very slow manner: "Do-you-know-of-any-hotels?"

I replied, "Do you have a speech impediment?"

His eyes went wide. "Far out, you're an American! There are no hotel rooms in the city." Oh no, I didn't make any reservations.

It took me three hours to find a room. I was starving, and the desk guy pointed to the clock and shook his head; it was too late to eat there. I ran to Rembrandt Square, which was the closest place with restaurants. The lights were going off as I approached them. There was one place left with lights on but as I got to it, the waiter locked the door. He waved *Closed*.

Inside, I saw the guy from the airport, the tall guy with the beard, eating at a table with a pretty woman. I pointed to them and indicated I was with them. The waiter turned to the bearded guy and when he saw me, he nodded, waving to the waiter to let me in.

They shared their food and wine, and we laughed about the whole situation. They were on their honeymoon in Italy and decided at the last minute to visit Amsterdam, like I did.

We walked back toward their hotel, which turned out to be the same hotel as mine. We spent the next two days hanging out together and laughing almost the entire time. Stella, his wife, a Brooklyn girl, got into one of the windows in the red-light district and pretended to be the occupant hooker while her husband tried to pay with his American Express card. A crowd formed as he knelt and asked her to marry him in lieu of payment. It was hilarious street theater and earned applause.

I had to get to Venice. I said my goodbyes to these extraordinary people.

Richard said, "Here," writing his number and address on a napkin. "Michael, if you're ever in San Francisco."

I was hesitantly poised in a gondola in the middle of the Grand Canal. The producers voice squawked through the walkie-talkie, "Water's clean."

"Yeah, I heard it's a sewer."

"Used to be a sewer. They cleaned it all up. It's fine."

Never trust these guys! I jumped in the Grand Canal and got typhoid.

By the time we got back to New York, I was so ill I thought I was dying. But I was the lead in the movie, so I hid being sick and lived on aspirin. They had to call a doctor when I collapsed during filming in Central Park. I was in bed for two days, engulfed with high fever and guilt. Young actors are like that. There are older actors who would rather die on stage than take a day off sick, like a Viking holding a sword to get into Valhalla or a Jewish mother holding her winning bingo ticket. *Tradition*!

We finished filming in New York but there was damage to some of the film shipped back from Italy. My heart clutched but thank God my jump-in-the-canal footage was okay. I had to return to Venice but no swimming. This time I was able to experience Venice, the city.

There was one day left of filming in Venice when I bumped into Michael Douglas and Brenda Vaccaro at Harry's Bar one evening. I knew Brenda from New York, and I knew Michael from L.A. The three of us bonded after a New York screening of Michael's first movie, *Adam at Six A.M.* some months earlier. Michael was deeply upset about his performance. We were young artists and so ultra critical of ourselves.

They asked me to lunch at San Giorgio Maggiore, the elegant island where they were staying, a short boat ride away. I loved those mahogany water taxis they used there. I arrived while they were having an argument. Brenda's agent had called and said she had a job offer and Brenda was on the phone booking a return flight to the States.

Michael shouted to me, "Brenda insisted we don't take jobs so we can take a romantic holiday and recharge our relationship. I agreed, and now she's going to take a job! Sure, just go and change the rules!"

This is an occupational hazard in relationships with actors. Read the label! If an actor is out of work, book a holiday and watch what happens.

Michael said, "I didn't come all this way to go home two days later."

"Then stay," Brenda said. "Michael is here to keep you company."

Yeah, it wasn't the same.

Well, it turned out I was finishing my film the very next day, so I suggested to Michael that we go visit Norman Jewison filming *Fiddler on the Roof* in Zagreb.

Okay, Americans think of everything else in the world as smaller, so if you're in Europe, everything must all be close by.

Michael said, "That's a great idea. Where's Zagreb?"

I air pointed saying, "Yugoslavia's around the corner from Italy. You go up, turn right at the top, and head down."

Michael and I rented a car and drove to Yugoslavia. It was a bit farther than around the corner, but we were having a good time until we got to the Yugoslavian border. The guard asked us for our visas.

Michael looked at me. "You didn't say anything about a visa."

I shrugged. "What am I – a travel agent?"

The guard pointed to a little cement shed to the side and lifted the gate, instructing us to drive there. We looked at the little cement hut, Michael and I looked at each other and I made a snap decision. I stepped on the gas and hauled ass.

I think this is where Michael learned a lot of the expressions he used in *Jewel of the Nile*. He was hunched down in the front seat, screaming, "What the fuck are you doing? You're going to get us shot!"

I said, "C'mon, that's only in the movies."

Nobody chased us, but we kept an anxious eye on the road behind us. A couple of hours later, we arrived in Zagreb.

I knew where they were staying because Paul Michael Glaser of *Starsky and Hutch* is a friend of mine. The role of Perchik, was between Paul and me until we got to the song audition. I didn't sing and Paul did, and he got the part. Then they cut the song out of the picture!

We were at the desk, registering, when I saw a van pulled up in front of the hotel with the actors returning from filming. I waved Michael to hide behind the column.

As Paul came to get his key, he saw me. "What the fuck are you doing here?"

I looked at him sheepishly. "Oh wow, they didn't tell you?"

Paul's face dropped. "What, I'm fired? Oh shit, man!"

Then he heard Michael laughing behind the column and got it. A moment later, it was big huggee time.

Michael and I were having dinner when this charming woman, very pretty, sat down with Michael and me and asked if we were Americans. When did we get there and were we working on the film? What did we do? Michael joked, saying we were a couple of spies on holiday.

Later that night, around 3 a.m. our rooms were entered by men with guns who went through our stuff simultaneously. A second later, they were gone, like they were never there.

Michael stood in the open doorway to my room, rubbing his head. "In the morning, remind me never to travel with you again."

"Excuse me, but who said, 'We're spies on holiday?'"

Michael flew back to LA from Zagreb. I just finished a picture, and I wasn't ready to go home. Turned out I had a friend working as a set photographer. Billy Hassell was finished on *Fiddler* and going to Berlin to see the wall. Sounded good to me. Germany is just straight up from here, right?

The long and winding road took us through amazing places, like Bled in Slovenia. There was an eleventh-century castle overlooking a lake that was right out of a storybook. We drove up to the castle to find a wedding in full costume dress. They were very welcoming, and we danced and drank local beer. Billy took lots of photos of the bride and groom and gave them the film as a wedding gift. When we arrived at Checkpoint Charlie separating East and West Berlin, I pulled over.

Billy said, "Why are you stopping?"

"Well, there's this thing called Communism. The other side is Communist East Berlin and being Americans, we're not allowed in."

"So what? Let's go for it."

I pulled up to the East German soldiers at the checkpoint and they asked for our passports.

A soldier leaned over the car and said, "Hassle," and Billy nodded. "Brandon." I nodded. He said, "You are red, yes?"

Billy and I looked at each other and nodded to him. Boom, boom, he stamped our passports and handed them back to us.

We drove quietly for a bit.

I asked Bill, "How did that happen, Comrade?"

"I figure," said Bill, "my last name is Hassle, and yours is Brandon. Hasselblad and Brandenburg are mighty names over here. Who cares? We're in."

We had a 12-hour visa allowing us to arrive at Warnemunde Port for the ferry to Denmark within that time. East Germany in 1970 was the real deal. Cobblestone streets and regimented trees along the roadside. It felt surreal to look at life we only knew from newsreels. Then three factory girls waved, and we stopped. They were hitching a ride home from work. They saw the license plates on the rental car and gestured to us and asked, "*Italianis?*"

Billy said, "No, Americanos," and the girls jumped from the car while it was still moving. They ran away from us as fast as they could. Bill laughed. "It's that charm of yours, Michael." But it gave pause to the reality of things here.

We took a wrong turn or two and wound up lost on the outskirts of a village. We were desperately trying to get back on the main road. We had a time limit over our heads, when Billy shouted, "Holy shit!" I looked up and there in the field was a huge missile. We sat there staring at it like we were at a drive-in movie. A real fucking missile, aimed at the sky – or maybe Brooklyn?

Billy whipped out his camera and I grabbed his arm. "I don't believe that's a good idea, Comrade."

"Are you crazy, there's a fucking missile in front of us!"

"Don't do it, Billy, they could fuck us up badly."

Billy said, "I got to, you know I got to. I promise I'll be careful."

While he was shooting pictures, I listed all sorts of bad things they will do to us like being hung upside down pouring hot gruel in our asses.

We got to Warnemunde Port, but they directed our car into a shed. The floor was all mirrored and they asked us to step out. They opened the trunk and looked through everything. Billy was keeping the camera over his shoulder tucked behind his arm. They found his bag of film rolls and put it out on the table. Then one soldier talked to another and a third came out, an officer who really looked the part. He demanded to know why Billy had so many rolls of film.

Billy explained he was a professional photographer and worked on movies. They kept me separate, but I was close enough to hear Billy being questioned. This was no game. This could go very wrong. I heard Billy yelling and I was sure they were inserting the gruel funnel into his ass. Billy was freaking because they were taking his film to develop it, and he was shouting, "You're going to ruin my work." Then suddenly the soldier noticed the camera tucked behind Billy's shoulder and demanded to have it.

I peeked into the room and Billy looked at me. A scary moment of truth. The soldier held out his hand demanding the camera. Billy slowly took the camera off his shoulder. As Billy fumbled handing it to him, he deftly opened the back of the camera, exposing the film to the light. He let the camera fall to the ground gently, as he still had the strap in his hand while making a big show of catching the lens.

He acted frustrated that his film was now ruined. "Oh shit!" he exclaimed, pulling the rest of the film out, angrily demonstrating the damage, as he held it up to the light exposing any pictures. It worked.

They developed a few random rolls and were satisfied Billy was who he said he was. The clock struck midnight. They escorted us to the last ferry to Denmark. We were both drained, stretched out on benches.

Billy sighed. "Should have got one of you smiling in front of the missile."

I used Michael Douglas's line: "Remind me in the morning never to travel with you again."

Our adventures weren't over yet. I told Billy how great Amsterdam was and he said, "Let's go". "OK, it's only one country over to the right".

It was a different city. The city fathers had issued a clean-up of all the hippies in the city. They had had enough and ordered police to arrest and detain any individuals who were without hotel rooms. No backpackers or sleeping bags in Dam Square from that moment forward.

Billy and I were innocently walking down a street on our way to check out one of the famed hash bars of Amsterdam when the police vans closed off the end of the street. Police units jumped into a line with helmets, batons, and wicker shields. We thought, *Let's go the other way and* quickly started to head in the opposite direction when more police vans closed off the bottom of the street and formed into a line facing us. Billy and I now realized it was us they were hunting.

"Is this a photo opportunity?"

He looked at me, "Run, Michael, run!"

We ran as fast as we could up the only side street we could see. It shortly came to a fenced dead end. The police, with their shields, closed off the street and were marching toward us. We started climbing for all we were worth, but they were on us and hammered us with the batons. We were fighting for our lives.

It was one of the most bizarre moments in my life. I felt like I was at Thermopylae with the three-hundred Spartans, except two-hundred-and-ninety-eight of them were late showing up. I really was fighting for my life. They were out to beat us to bloody pulps. Billy somehow grabbed my arm and hauled me up the fence and over, holding onto my aching elbow. We were just running in the night.

Back at the hotel, we applied ice to the welts on each of our backs. Billy was bleeding from his nose and over his eye. We took care of each other's wounds, then looked at each other. *Did that just happen?* Together we said, "Remind me never to travel with you again," and burst out in painful laughter.

We caught the first flight to New York. My elbow was swollen like a grapefruit. We lowered our aching bodies into our seats. Michael Douglas would be delighted he missed this trip to Amsterdam.

I was back in my rented apartment on the Upper West Side. I rented a furnished one bedroom for the entire filming of *Jennifer on My Mind*. The minuscule garden, which wasn't really a garden, was surrounded by tall apartment buildings. You had to look straight up to see the sky.

I was sitting on the chair still icing my elbow when I got a call from my agent. He said David Susskind, the producer of *Lovers and Other Strangers*, wanted me to fly to San Francisco for a test premiere of the film that weekend. First class all the way. This got me an airport limo, first-class lounge, flights, and a hotel suite for my first movie premiere. And I was going to fly to California anyway. Well, the economy way.

I checked into the elegant Mark Hopkins Hotel on Nob Hill. Looked a bit fancy for me and I knew I wasn't fancy enough for them. They looked at my long hair and my bellbottom jeans. They wouldn't allow me to eat in the restaurant tieless, but I didn't own a tie at the time. They said I could dine in my room. Middle finger to you, sir! I checked out straight away but now I was at a loss as to where the hell I was, and I couldn't reach production until morning. I was a lover and a stranger in a strange land.

I pulled the folded napkin from my wallet and called Richard, the guy I met in Amsterdam. The big guy with the beard who was on his honeymoon. I called over and over and it was busy, busy, busy. I tried for a half-hour, and it was still busy. I had his address on the napkin, and I asked the doorman, "Which way to Sausalito?" He pointed over the bridge. I could see the bridge. You could see everything from up on Nob Hill. I decided to try the California method of hitchhiking and stuck out my thumb.

A couple of minutes later, a brush-painted blue VW convertible with stick-on flower decals stopped for me. I opened the door and there was Richard! The big, bearded guy from Amsterdam. No shit! I stood there staring at him and his mouth dropped open.

"Far out, man," he said.

I held up the napkin with his address. "I was hitching to your house."

"Very far out!"

We were heading for the bridge to Sausalito. We drove by the Metro Theatre. On the marquee, big letters said: *Michael Brandon and Gig Young in Lovers and Other Strangers.*

I yelled for Richard to stop the car. He pulled up and I got out and walked up to the front of the cinema. A man was coming down a ladder, having just put up the letters. He saw me staring and said, "Premiere's tomorrow night," and took his ladder away. I just stood there, staring up.

Michael Brandon and Gig Young. Gig Young, who this year won the Academy Award for best actor and me, and I was first billed. *This is it, baby! This is what I've been waiting for. There it is, up there in lights!*

I felt empty. No gong moment like with Rita Cepf when she said, "You should be an actor." No *bwonggg*, no bells, no whistles here; just quiet emptiness, very empty. I was expecting something more. Numb.

Richard walked up and looked at the marquee. "Is that what you do?" (We had never talked about what we did. No small talk interrupting our laughing in Amsterdam.)

"Yeah," I said. "Michael Brandon, actor."

Richard nodded and put out his hand and said, "Hello, Dr Richard Louis Miller, director and founder of the Gestalt Institute of Multiple Psychotherapy. Pleasure to meet you."

I couldn't have been with anybody better for this marquee moment. Richard said, "There are no accidents, Michael. Meeting in Amsterdam airport, the restaurant in Rembrandt Square, staying in the same hotel, a premiere in San Francisco … and sticking out your thumb as I drove by." He nodded, eyes wide, pulled his beard. "Michael, we gotta look a bit deeper here. There's some amazing shit going on."

CHAPTER 9

Redwood To Rome:
Neil Young/Dario Argento

1971. Life at this time seemed to have a lot of elasticity. I had finished a film, traveled to Europe, been to my first premiere and found a friend for life. I had no obligations to be anywhere. I stayed with Richard (Dr. Richard Louis Miller), and I observed his life and the gestalt process. It was a life rewarding experience.

Back in the monk's cell in Hollywood after the test premiere in San Franciso, I was feeling pretty good. The reaction to *Lovers and Other Strangers* was euphoric. The premiere audience, including Richard and his wife, Stella, were standing and applauding. It was a very funny movie. I was proud that my first film was a quality effort.

I got a call from my agent about a Universal movie for television. An MOW, he called it. This was the beginning of the Movie of the Week era. I was skeptical about a "movie" made for TV, but I was assured it was a real movie, just shot in three weeks, written by Alvin Sargent, award winning movie writer, and directed by John Badham, who would direct

Saturday Night Fever, and produced by Paramount's Emmy award-winning Bill Sackheim. My co-star would be Carrie Snodgress, currently nominated for an Oscar for Best Actress after winning the Golden Globe award for *Diary of a Mad Housewife*. In movie poker terms, *The Impatient Heart* was a good hand to be dealt.

I was playing a fishmonger working on the Santa Monica pier, a few doors down from the old landmark merry-go-round. Above the merry-go-round there were apartments in the turreted towers. Well, in the movie they were. One such apartment was occupied by a social worker played by Carrie Snodgress. On the pier boardwalk our paths crossed. She was someone who helped people change their lives, and I was a guy who hated my life but hated change even more. *We meet, fall in love, she changes me, and I leave her, but she is feeling rewarded.*

During the shoot, Carrie and I became friends. Some dialogue in a crucial scene wasn't working for us, and the director took us to screenwriter, Alvin Sargent's house to meet with him.

"Okay, so you don't like my words?" Alvin smiled from his desk. "What would you say?" He wrote down what we said, rubbed his chin, "Yeah, that *is* better." No ego, just making a picture as good as we could.

One day Carrie asked me if I liked Neil Young.

"Very much."

"There's a concert tonight, wanna go?"

We finished filming and were speeding downtown in my yellow '64 Cabriolet Porsche toward the Dorothy Chandler

Pavilion. As we got out of the car and ran toward the venue, Carrie broke right and ran around the building.

I went after her, yelling, "You're going the wrong way and we're already late!"

She didn't listen and I chased her around the side of the theater. She banged on what looked like a solid wall, but it was a faux concrete door, Neil Young opened his dressing room door. He invited us in and did some tuning up as we got introduced. He hit a few chords and hummed a bit of a song, and someone knocked, saying, "Ready, Mr. Young." He got up with a guitar pick in his lips and indicated for us to follow him.

I felt like a handheld camera at one of those rock concerts, walking between the roadies and sound crew. Neil walked us to two chairs in front of a curtain. We sat down, and he said, "See ya later." He took three steps away from us, and the roar of the packed auditorium made my heart jump. I didn't realize if we leaned forward the audience could see us onstage with him. Neil walked straight to a piano, center stage, sat down and began to play and sing. If we were any closer, we would have been on the piano bench with him.

After the concert, the three of us squeezed into my Porsche with Carrie on Neil's lap. They were in love! We headed back to Santa Monica to the Holiday Inn where we were crashing during the shoot. It was a handy hotel across from the pier where we started each filming day, with dawning California skies and fresh fish deliveries.

Neil crashed in my trailer to escape the wardrobe and makeup rituals in Carrie's trailer while I practiced wrapping fish at the fish stand rented on the pier for the shoot, while the film crew were at another location. It was a good time to apply my fishmonger skills. I was behind the fish counter wearing an apron covered in fish blood from many fish head-chopping attempts. I was dismayed as my slimy fish wrapping wasn't going well. This was, in a word, disgusting. That's not to say that my character Frank Pescadero didn't find wrapping fish disgusting as well, but he certainly wrapped them better than me. I was ready to pull my hair out except my hands were bloody.

Then this girl walked up and said, "Pound of shrimp, please?"

Without looking up, I barked, "Try another fish stand, down the pier."

"I beg your pardon. I would like a pound of shrimp, please!"

"Hey, I don't work here, and these fish aren't real fish." She gave me this wide-eyed look and pointed to the refrigerated counter full of shrimp. I said, "Listen, you don't want to eat that shrimp. They're not real shrimp. They're movie shrimp."

"Movie shrimp?"

"Yeah, they're just here to make this look like a real fish stand."

"Oh!" she queried, "This isn't a real fish stand?"

"No, we're making a movie and I'm an actor practicing how to wrap fish, as you can see."

She looked around, seeing hardly anyone on the pier. There were no trucks, no crew, no movie lights. She said, "Why don't you take those movie shrimp and shove them up your delusional ass?"

I realized how stupid this all sounded about the same time I clocked how good-looking she was. "Wait," I called after her. "I'm an actor trying to learn how to wrap fish, and in about an hour the movie crew will be back, and this place will be buzzing."

She flashed me a quick smile, flicked her middle finger and walked off. Her long hair bouncing off a great butt.

By the time we finished filming the scene, I had a perfect fish-head chop and three-fold paper wrap and roll, down with the speed of a rodeo cowboy tying up a calf. The director told me to stop throwing both arms in the air when I finished wrapping and yelling yeehaw; it wasn't a rodeo. Then I saw the shrimp girl sitting on the railing on the opposite side of the pier, smiling. Her long hair and big eyes were ready for my full attention.

We went out for a bite (not fish), and she was a smart, sassy New York chick. I made a quick decision and told her Neil Young invited me up to his ranch in the Northern California redwoods. I asked her to drive up the coast to Neil's with me for a week. She looked at me incredulously, but I could tell it wasn't an absolute no. Next morning, I asked Carrie, who asked Neil if I could bring Susie Shrimp along.

I rented my dressing room trailer and drove the huge motorhome up the California coast to the Redwoods. Susie and I were singing along to a Neil Young eight-track as we entered the darkening forest, where we immediately got lost and stopped at a small bridge with a big sign that said *Cattle Crossing*. This was my first cattle crossing. I didn't see any cattle crossing and then noticed the huge gaps in the bridge surface. I figure a cow can't walk across the gaps.

Susie asked, "How does a cow know not to walk across the gaps?"

I pointed. "The sign, of course."

That's when we heard Woody Woodpecker. *Ah ha ha ha-ha* was coming from the woods. We held hands over the cattle gaps and walked toward the forest with the darkness coming on fast. Huge redwood trees surrounded us, and the road disappeared. There he was, Woody Woodpecker, hammering a tree, giving that famous laugh and zooming off. We walked a little further on and came to the charred frame of a recently burned-down house. Sitting amid the rubble a long-haired man sat in a reclining chair, holding a beer, smoking a cigar, and watching Woody Woodpecker cartoons projected onto a ten-foot screen.

This was no made-up hallucination. This was Elliot Roberts' house. He was Neil's manager at the time. His house had burned down, and he was enjoying what was left of it. There was no door to knock on, so I politely asked if Neil lived nearby. I told him I was at the bridge crossing. Elliot took a pair of old gloves and dragged out some boards from the bridge roadside and laid them over the gaps so the camper would be able to drive over them. He pointed me in the right direction, and ten minutes later I was talking to Louis, the old man Neil sings about, "Old man take a look at your life, I'm a lot like you."

We parked the motorhome near Neil's house by a little lake. I felt our first date was going well. Susie did wear all her clothes to bed the first few days. But finally, she trusted me enough to take her boots off.

Carrie was a woman in love (with Neil) and happy in her new surroundings. Neil was a generous host, showing me his amazing recording studio in the forest and his vintage car collection. He played me his recent recording of *Heart of Gold*, from his new album.

One morning Neil came by, frantically banging on the trailer door, and asked if I had seen his notebook. I said, "No," and he hurried off toward his studio. I made a couple of coffees and walked to the lake where I found Susie drawing. She held up her pencil sketch of the lake.

I said, "Where did you get the sketchpad?"

"On the piano."

"Can I see it?"

She said, "Okay, but it's not finished."

I turned the pages and there were all the handwritten lyrics to every song on Neil's *Harvest* album. "We better go find Neil".

When Susie and I got back to LA, we stayed in the trailer in the monastery parking lot for two more days. Our cocoon.

We walked up the overgrown aloe vera pathway to the monk's cell, which if you turned it horizontally, was the same size as the trailer home. I asked Susie to move in with me and she accepted. She did, eventually, take off her clothes.

Susie Simons was a great girl. We were easy together and had fun going to concerts and making trips down to Palm Springs with Andy and Geedee and up to SF to visit Richard Miller and Stella Resnick. Our friendship was a growing one.

We used to visit a hot spring about two hours from SF with Richard and the longstanding couple who owned it, Mildred and Merle, who charged us two bucks a night to sleep on the floor of an old cabin and soak/bathe in springs. A couple years later, Richard bought the hot springs called Wilbur, when it went up for auction. It had hundreds of undeveloped acres and old gold mines from the gold rush days. It was a lifetime decision for Dr. Richard Miller. Wilbur is a thriving health sanctuary to this day.

CHAPTER 9A

Four Flies on Grey Velvet

There was a knock on the monk's cell door. A charming white-haired gentleman started speaking Italian.

I said, "The pizza goes to Mort, nine at the end of the hall."

He said, "No pizza, no pizza! My name is Salvatore Argento. My son, Dario, want you for new picture in Rome."

I should have known; Two Guys from Italy, pizza guy doesn't come in a suit. But producers don't normally knock on your door. How did he find me?

He handed me a script on onion paper. "Beverly Wilshire Hotel, numero..." He pointed to a phone number on the script. "You read, you call, okay? Ciao." I called my agent, Chris, and told him what had happened.

He said, "Dario Argento is the biggest cult director in the world. His pictures make more money than Fellini and Bertolucci together. Read the script and call me."

I read *Four Flies on Grey Velvet* by Dario Argento. The violence was extraordinary, and the story dark and fascinating. Chris and I went to the hotel to meet with Salvatore. I apologized profusely for mistaking him for the pizza delivery man. He laughed, kindly asking if I liked the script. I said yes, but I had reservations about the violence.

Salvatore listened and nodded. "No problem, we change, your part, no violence. Now, excuse me, if I may speak with your agent."

I stepped out of the room. When Chris came out, he did a Groucho Marx Walk straight pass me to the elevator. He was bursting and waved me away from him till he was ready to speak. We drove to McDonalds and as I sat munching a Quarter Pounder he said, "This is a lot of money." It was. More than I had ever made in my entire life all together up till now. We packed for three months in Italy. I took Susie Scampi to Rome.

I was given the top-floor suite of the Parco Dei Principi Grand Hotel fronting onto the Via Veneto and overlooking the Roman Zoo from the back. I had one room devoted solely to my film drums to practice. My character was drummer in a rock band. At night on my balcony, in the middle of Rome, we listened to the lion's roaring. Next morning, while drum practicing, I gave Susie 20,000 lira and told her to go shopping. I'd never seen her eyes get so wide.

She was back in twenty minutes fuming. "Twenty thousand lira is ten bucks, you fishmonger!"

When I met Dario for the first time, he looked at my face and he freaked out. He was ranting in Italian. I thought he hired the wrong actor, but it was because my eyes weren't blue. The script girl, Patrizia, had trouble translating this, but it seems Dario was upset because he believed the actor he hired was a light-eyed actor. Once I understood what the commotion was about, I showed him that if you highlight my eyes, they turn green. Dario had a flashlight sent up immediately and after aiming it into my eyes, he was finally happy. The shit you go through! (My eyes do change color because they're hazel or chestnut as they are called in Italy.) Dario hugged me, "Mi scusi". He was so sorry for the confusion. After that, we got on famously and even though he spoke no English and I spoke no Italian, we communicated fantastically. That's what *sympatico* is.

I was leaving Susie on her own most of the day. Being on set gets boring quickly, especially if you're not there to work. After an exquisite dinner on our terrace serenaded by the lions, Susie told me she would see me back in LA.

Midway through the film shoot, Dario took me to a private club for lunch. Italian lunches were at least two hours in length. The driver took us to Il Club on the outskirts of Rome. It was a huge villa belonging to an Italian Prince. The pool was phenomenal. It started out with a very shallow slant so you could lie in the sun with water just covering your body like being at the seashore. There was a white linen-covered patio with tables covered with every Italian delicacy. The fruit was fresh and colorful; the vegetables were lightly oiled and heaped in artistic mounds around assorted fish, meat, and antipasto.

I loved it there and went whenever I had the time from filming. I often dined with the prince, who was a charming man and a good friend of Dario's. He took this silver bracelet he wore and gave it to me for luck and I wore it in the film.

I was treading water in the gorgeous pool, and came face to face with Francis Ford Coppola who was filming *The Godfather*.

We smiled at each other like two happy frogs in a pond, and he sighed, "This is living the life, Michael."

The filming went well. We were in magnificent locations like the old theater in ancient Spoleto and the streets of modern Turino. Dario had this magical ability to add a certain texture to his visions which he took from dreams and nightmares. Filming with him was watching an electrical spark come to life. He reached for the hand camera, (machina mano) and ran around like a lizard being chased by a cat. Then clapped his hands. "Okay." He was like a painter envisioning his painting to an audience of technicians.

I had a bad tummy during the first weeks of filming. One day, Bud Spencer, who was a big man as well as a huge Italian movie star, invited me to have lunch with him in his trailer. Bud was an ex-Olympic swimmer turned actor. He became a big star in Spaghetti Westerns. Do they call them Spaghetti Westerns in Italy? Bud had a personal chef cooking all morning and it was going to be fantastic. I told him my stomach wasn't good.

"*Mal,*" he said; sick. "Okay, my chef, he fixes special for you."

He gave me *aglio e olio*, which is garlic and oil on pasta. It really helped … it still does. Then the table was pulled away for sleeping divans.

"Now we sleep," he said.

I asked for Fiuggi water, which was the delicious, bottled water that I had been drinking since I arrived in Italy.

Bud said, "Why do you drink Fiuggi water? It's for cleansing the body. It's a diuretic not for just to drink." End of troubled stomach.

Another day, Dario said "Surprise!" and put me in a car. The driver took me to Cinecittà Studios to have tea with Federico Fellini on the set of his new movie, *Roma*. These studios, like Studio De Polis in Rome (where we were shooting), had dressing rooms that Sofia Loren and Elizabeth Taylor used, with marble bathtubs the size of swimming pools. I arrived at the Fellini stage where the circus scene was being shot. It was like watching one of those movies about making movies, with people walking about wearing all sorts of outlandish costumes. It's what the public imagine about film studios, but this was for real.

I was taken to see Federico, who welcomed me as a friend. Immediately, two chairs, a small table with an umbrella and a pot of tea appeared. We had a lovely afternoon. I'm a big fan of Fellini movies, *La Dolce Vita* being one of my favorites. What I truly appreciated about Mr Fellini was his respect and warmth and how actors were treated as artists in this country. In LA, you get more money but less respect. I'll take a little less money for a dash more respect anytime. Well, I did, didn't I? I moved to Europe.

That day we were filming in the studio – a bathtub scene. Francine Racette was the beautiful girl in the bath with me (she married Donald Sutherland). I was in the studio café having a bite and Dario saw me and screamed, "*Smetti di mangiare, non mangiare!*" I dropped my fork only because it might have meant my food had been poisoned.

The next thing I knew, Patrizia, the script girl, came and said, "No shooting today. Canceled."

I asked why?

She said, "Because you ate food."

What Dario was saying was, *stop eating, don't eat!*

"Actors are not allowed to eat food?"

Patrizia said, "You have the bath scene today. You cannot take a bath after you eat."

Ah, an Italian thing. The Jewish version of my mother yelling, "Don't go in the water after you eat, you'll get a cramp and die."

I said to Patrizia, "Tell Dario that in Brooklyn we always take a bath after we eat."

She smiled and winked at me, and the bath scene was saved. But not the piece of tape over my privates or Francine's; they floated to the top of the bath. It was more embarrassing having them put on than being naked. We gave up the modesty and just filmed the scene.

Dario and I really connected. In fact, many years later in Hollywood, at Raleigh Studios, there was a Dario Argento film retrospective, and I was invited to be a surprise guest speaker. Dario grabbed me and hugged me for five minutes in front of the packed audience. Then said that aside from the wonderful experience of filming together, I had changed his life.

Really, what did I do?

Then Dario said to everyone, "Yes! He changed my life. He gave me the first marijuana I ever smoked."

Working with Dario was an amazing experience. One night he set up a private screening of one of his favorite films, *The*

White Voices (*Le Voci Bianche*). It was a black-and-white Italian classic. We watched it privately in an old movie theater. It was one of my favorite times with Dario.

Sadly, the filming came to an end. While I was packing in my hotel room, there was a knock and a driver I didn't recognize said I had to come with him to the set. I said *finite, fine,* finished, done, over, no more. He wasn't listening to a word I said. I must come! Dario, forget a close-up! I didn't want to miss my plane, but I wasn't going to let Dario down. I was sitting in this Citroen driving for hours. I fell asleep and woke up, it was dark, and we were still driving.

I said, "Hey, where are we going?"

Now the guy didn't speak any English. He went deaf on me. Nothing I said got a response. Maybe all that money I was going to get paid wouldn't have to be paid if I had an accident. There was a story about two actors in a witch film and they were both 'accidentally' burned to death, unknowns, but still.

The car finally pulled up to a very large estate. It was dark and I couldn't see much except a huge door in a castle-like building. The driver waved at me and said *"Andare"* (Go, Go). He grunted, "Get out," so I got out, and as I looked around, he drove away. I was standing in the dark a hundred miles from my hotel in the middle of nowhere.

I walked to the big door and lifted the round metal knocker. The banging echoed and my nerves were on edge. Finally, after banging for a few minutes, a caretaker who looked like Quasimodo's uglier brother pulled the huge door open. He was holding a lantern. A fucking lantern, I'm not kidding. If that wasn't bizarre enough, I was now inside the door, but it was outside in a huge park. I followed Quasimodo's brother down a path that had hedges twelve feet high. Every time he turned the corner, I was left in the dark. I was starting to get seriously worried.

I started thinking things like, *I hope it's not a stabbing. I hate stabbing; all that sticking … That's how Julius Caesar got it. Shit, we're in Rome! Should I run?* No, I walked, following this man who turned a corner and stepped to the side of the path. This could be it. I looked out and it was just darkness.

Then the lights came on, hundreds of fountains erupted, and a full orchestra began playing. The cast and crew cheered and applauded. It was Dario's surprise wrap party at the Villa d'Este, Lake Como. Six hundred fountains lit up and exploded to orchestral accompaniment. It was overwhelming, especially when I thought I was going to die. Dario and I hugged till we hurt. Salvatore' had two men carry in a model ship with triple sails. It was an enormous goodbye gift. What a wonderful night, what a wonderful experience.

Fantastico! Un milione di grazie.

Top left: Miriam Tuman – Ma!, Top Right: Mom & Pop (Miriam & Sol) in their twenties, Middle left: Me with Elliott age four; Middle Right: With my family in Oldsmobile Super 98 the way to my Barmitzvah, Bottom Left, Me aged 13 with Elliot age 9 and Debra aged 4, at my Barmitzvah, Bottom Right: Me with Mom & Pop at my Barmitzvah.

Top left: Ma - "*Just eat it!*" Top Right; Pop at work; Middle Left; 1962 age 17 High School Year Book Graduation; Middle Right: Me (Valmor), with friends Kerry (Ox), Gary (Gaa), Frank (Frankie) & Dennis (Piper) in my chameleon days; Bottom: Valley Stream High School.

Top Left: American Academy Dramatic Arts School, Madison Avenue, NYC, where it all started, Middle: The Barn, Dinner Theatre Tour, Virginia; Bottom Left: On stage performing in Tiger 1968; Bottom Right: poster – Belasco Theatre, *Does A Tiger Wear Necktie?*

Top Left: Monastery of the Angels; Middle: Mellow Yellow; Bottom Left: Riding in Tennessee, Bottom Right: On the balcony of my monk's cell.

Top Left: Chris Shiffrin my first LA agent, Top Right: Andy Rubin in my monk's cell. Bottom Left: Reading a script in Acapulco, Bottom Right: Leaping naked into an Acapulco pool!

Top Left: In Carnaby Street before heading to Venice; Top Right: Dr Richard Lewis Miller; Bottom: My first Name In Lights, Premier San Francisco Metro Cinema 1969.

Top Left: Candid shot of Michael Douglas in Venice; Top Right: Me getting typhoid In the Venice Grand Canal, Middle left; Running with Erich Segal author of *Jennifer On My Mind*, Middle Right, Neil Young; Bottom Left: Andy, Geedee and TR6 in California, Bottom Right: Susie Shrimp at Neil Young's piano.

Top: Cinecitta Studio Roma, Top right Dario
Argento with cinematographer on set on *Roma,* Middle Left: On set of *Four
Flies On Grey Velvet,* Middle Right: Poster of *Four Flies On Grey Velvet,*
Bottom: Me with Bud Spencer on set.

CHAPTER 10

Kim Novak

I arrived in Los Angeles Airport late the next evening arms loaded, carrying the huge triple masted ship that Dario and Salvatore had given me. Thank goodness Patrizia, the script girl translated to the stewardess, perhaps with a little Lira, and the crew helped me place the ship into two empty seats for the journey.

Andy pulled up at arrivals curbside in his triumph convertible. He stood up behind the steering wheel and bowed. "Welcome Home Christopher Columbus, how was your voyage?" Andy laughed, "let's take a drive. Tell me about Italy and why you are carrying the Santa Maria?" We climbed into his battered TR6, with the ship's prow aimed between our shoulders.

Andy offered me a doobie, which we smoked en route to Malibu Beach, where we raised a mound of sand to place the ship upon. We settled down on the sand behind the ship and watched the ocean waves rolling behind the wind filled sails. It was incredibly lifelike, and dramatic as waves white tailed in the ocean. We smoked, talked and laughed all night. Morning was upon us, and we remembered a friend, Rhoda, who lived on the beach. Maybe we could get a coffee? We sailed the ship up like two Gulliver's with the ship under our arms to her porch door and peeked inside to see if she was awake. Just inside the sliding porch door, a couple was asleep on the floor in a sleeping bag. How sweet. We were tip toeing away when it hit us at the same time, that was Susie Shrimp in the sleeping bag. We tiptoed the ship backwards for another look and leaned our faces against the glass. That must have looked very freaky to the guy who woke up and started pulling on his pants.

That's how Susie and I broke up and how I met my friend Richard Baskin in the same moment.

FELIZ NAVIDAD IN MEXICO.

It was just past sunrise, and my agent was leaning on the gate to the Mexican villa, panting and sweating through his linen suit. He started rattling the old, rusted gate and yelling my name. Chris Shiffrin had come from Los Angeles to deliver a script personally. The mobile phone was decades away from being invented and the remote hilltop villa I rented on the cliff over the sea had never had a telephone. You just can't escape Hollywood or my agent.

Chris was the agent who said, if someone is willing to knock down walls for you, access is secondary. We had been together almost a year, and it had been an exciting partnership so far and he would knock that gate down if I didn't get out there.

After flying through the night to a third-world country, he had the distraught look of a soldier who had seen more than his young years. He shoved a script into my hands and ran, leaping into the pool with his suit on. When he surfaced, an agent reborn, I handed him a beer, which he downed empty with his eyes closed.

Chris finally said, "*The Third Girl From The Left*, starring Kim Novak and maybe you too, if you can get your hippie ass up to LA for a meeting with Kim Novak and the director this afternoon." So that's why he'd come down. My agent stripped naked, spreading his soaking-wet suit over a plastic chair, and reached for another beer. "Read the script. The flight to LA is in four hours." He cannon-balled into the pool.

Dr. Richard Miller, the director of the Gestalt Institute of Multiple Psychotherapy and living in the now, had, spontaneously come down to Mexico to join me. Reclining in his floating chair behind a copy of Fritz Perls' Verbatim, he uttered impressively, "Kim Novak," like he was tasting the name. Then he exclaimed, "Picnic."

Chris, floating on his back like an otter and opening another beer on his chest, said, "The Man with the Golden Arm."

Miller responded like it was a tennis match of film credits. "Pal Joey."

Chris' return was, "Bell, Book and Candle."

This was worthy of a double nod from Richard, who then proudly exclaimed, "Vertigo," like he was serving an ace.

Chris returned with a curveball. "Jeanne Eagles," a 50s gay iconic movie.

And Miller was out of balls.

I shouted from the balcony above, "Strangers When We Meet."

They both looked up at me and gave me a fuck-off gesture.

I walked inside the villa where it was cooler to read the script. After reading, I came out onto the hacienda roof.

"Okay, I'll do it, let's go to LA." I leapt into the pool and my next adventure.

The Mexican sun had dried out Chris's suit, but his shoes were still squelching as we boarded the flight to Los Angeles. They don't make agents like him anymore – or waterproof brogue shoes.

On the flight, we ordered tequilas, and my agent filled me in on *Third Girl from the Left*.

"A Playboy Production. Yes, Playboy is producing it, because Hefner wants to move into the legit film market by making *Macbeth*, directed by Roman Polanski, followed by this TV movie premiere, *Third Girl from the Left*, written by Dory Previn." Chris slugged back the tequila and muttered, "It's not an offer."

I swallowed my shot and looked at him. "You got me on this plane and it's not an offer?"

He shrugged. "I couldn't get you an offer. They want you to read with the director. Kim Novak makes the final decision. But you'll get it!"

Chris dropped me at my monk's cell with just enough time for a quick shower and change. I hopped into Mello-Yello (yes, I'd gone LA.; I named my car), my '64 Porsche Cabriolet, and roared up to Mulholland Drive. I cut across the top of a mountain with views of the valley on one side and the ocean on the other. It was a great drive in that car and a faster route across town. I dropped down into Laurel Canyon toward Sunset Boulevard, and my adrenaline was pumping as I stopped for the red light at Laurel and Sunset.

There was a café on that corner at the light, with tables of people talking over coffee. This attractive girl stepped over the low wall of the café to the sidewalk, in a short skirt revealing a good bit of leg. She walked straight up to my car.

My top was down, so she just leaned on the doorsill and said, "Can you give me a ride?"

Before I could say, "Sorry, but I'm turning here," she dropped over the door and was sitting next to me, and the horns from waiting cars behind forced me to go forward.

I made the right turn onto Sunset and pulled to the curb. I said, "Look, I'd be happy to give you a ride, but I'm only going up the street."

"I don't mind," she said.

I laughed. "No, I'm going to a meeting, so I can't give you a ride."

"I'll go with you."

"With me, where?"

"Wherever you are going."

"But I'm going to a meeting down the street, so I can't take you anywhere. Please, you'll have to get out."

"No."

"What?"

"NO, I'm going with you."

"You can't come to my meeting; you have to get out of my car."

She was smiling by now. "I'm going with you."

I reached across her to open her door, and she screamed. It was a short loud scream and scared the shit out of me. I pulled my hand back from the handle and looked at her still-smiling, lovely face.

Okay, fact is, I had a nutjob in my car, an attractive nutjob, but nonetheless a nutjob. Why was this happening to me? God decided, "Hey, let's give Brandon some bizarre aggravation today." Or was this being filmed for some crazy TV comedy? I didn't know what to do. A bit of madness was taking place in my car. I couldn't leave – it was *my* car!

"Sorry, but I'm going to be late for my meeting. Would you please get out?"

"I am going to spend the day with you. Wherever you go, I'll go with you." I contemplated the idea for a millisecond.

"That's not going to happen. Look, get out or I'll drive to the police station."

"Go ahead, I'll tell them you hit me [she smacked herself hard, making a mark] and raped me [violently tearing her blouse out of her dress and mussing her hair]."

Oh Boy! I should have stayed in Mexico. This just cancelled out all that holiday chill.

I pulled the car into the parking lot adjacent to the café. I turned the steering wheel all the way to the left and kept my foot on the gas pedal and the car in gear.

I asked her one more time. "Please, would you kindly leave my car now?"

She turned to me. "I told you; I'm coming with you."

But before she finished the sentence, I popped the clutch, floored the gas pedal and, at the same time, pulled her door handle open and the car lurched to the left. The sudden motion caught her by surprise, and she was out of my car! I turned the wheel sharply to the right; the door slammed shut and I screeched to a halt.

I looked in my rearview mirror to check she wasn't hurt, but she was already up and running for the car and reaching for the door handle. She was quick and coming fast, so I floored it before she could climb over the door. I left burning rubber and smoke as I squealed out onto Sunset.

I could still hear her screaming, "You bastard, come back here, you bastard!" I glanced in my rearview mirror and could see her jumping up and down, hammering the air with her handbag as I put more distance between us. *Wow! Did that just happen?*

I finally got to my meeting with *The Ruling Class* director, Peter Medak. I was blown away by that film, so I was very pleased to meet him.

After a lovely chat, Peter said, "I've got to go meet Kim at Universal Studios. We are screening your last film, *The Impatient Heart*." That's the one with Carrie Snodgress on the Santa Monica Pier.

"Wow, I haven't even seen it yet," I said. "Can I come?"

"Kim asked to see it," Peter said. "I would love to take you with me, but it might be a little awkward. I think it's better if we see you after."

Ron Roth, the producer, asked if I'd like to wait in Hef's office. It was comfortable and there was a bar. I said OKAY, but this was an already awkward situation. What if they didn't like the film or my work in it?

As we walked to Hef's office, I told Ron about the girl getting in my car. He stopped and got this weird look on his face like he didn't believe me and then said, "She did it to me, too. I drive that route to my office every day. She came out of the café and got into my car. I thought she was a hooker at first, but then it got so weird, I pulled up next to a parked police car. She screamed *Rape*! They finally figured out she was the fruitcake, but not before they had me bent over the police car in handcuffs. Cost me two hours of my life."

"What are the odds, Ron? We're part of a secret club. I wonder how many cars she had taken hostage. The roadside pirate."

Ron assured me he thought this all would work out, but he had to leave for a dinner engagement. I was bored twiddling my thumbs, sitting in Hef's leather chair for hours. The walls were covered in huge, framed pictures of famous Playboy centerfolds. I was thinking I could do more than twiddle my thumbs, medicinally it would make me more alert, when suddenly the door opened, and Kim was poking her head in.

In the most amazing whispery deep voice, she said, "There you are! Been looking all over the building for you."

I stood staring at her. She was like a sunlight tsunami bursting into the room. I really had no idea what to expect and, to tell the truth, I had no expectations. When I saw *Vertigo*, I wasn't even an actor. All I remembered was she was a mysterious mirage of someone searching for herself.

She was very alive, and pulled open Hef's personal fridge, taking out a bottle of his best champagne. "I don't think he'll mind, do you?" She handed me the bottle. "Would you?" She picked up a couple of glasses and after a brief inspection of the office walls, said, "Let's go up to the roof."

She was like the wind coming around a corner and catching you in its gust.

We went up on the roof of the Playboy building. The view was LA in winter, with the snow-peaked mountains to one side and the moon glistening on the ocean to the other.

She was breathless with excitement and said, "Open it, open it." I did, and the cork popped perfectly into the air and disappeared into the night. I poured, and she said, clinking her glass to mine, "You were wonderful in the movie. I loved it and I want you to do this movie with me."

I clinked her glass back and smiled. *Great!* The look between us was like a long closeup. We really looked at each other and took the time to enjoy it. She was gorgeous. Those eyes were islands of exotic colors you wanted to swim in, and I was jumping in.

We started talking about everything all at once. I held up the script and Kim snatched it, throwing it in the air, the pages snowing around us.

"Isn't the director nice?" she said. "Peter is so warm, and I think he'll make a special film from Dory Previn's story. Dory and Peter are at a production meeting, but they both loved your work."

Then I saw her shyness in her crooked smile. I was so happy my agent came to find me. Even the roadside pirate climbing into my car was okay – well…

I got back to the monk's cell and called my friend Andy to meet me in the Hollywood classic Musso & Frank Grill. I shared my news and bought him a celebratory dinner. I came back to the monk's cell to find a missed message from Kim: "Hi, it's me. I was thinking if you weren't busy, we could get a bite or something. Oh, well…" A long sigh, and the phone disconnected.

I hated myself for leaving the apartment. I missed having dinner with Kim. It was too late to call. I couldn't sleep.

I booked a session with my weekly acting coach Eric Morris (author of *No Acting, Please*) and he said, "Michael, you got this character." He took my script. "I'm giving you a little jellybean on one of the pages. If you need some motivation in a scene, just look for what I wrote." (A jellybean can be a motivational choice or direction. For example, if you don't find the actress you're working with sexy, imagine your favorite ice cream on her lips. The camera doesn't know what you're thinking but it sees desire.)

I found my seat in first class, and I was feeling pretty good. I could work on the script while flying to New York where we'd begin filming. Then I saw Kim across the aisle, sitting next to another woman. I thought that later I'd go over and say hello.

I was reading the script when her voice drifted over. "Are you busy?" I looked up and she was leaning on my seat. "I thought we could talk about a couple of things."

She took the empty seat next to me. We turned to each other and whoosh, it was that mesmerizing closeup again, just saying nothing and looking at each other and really enjoying it. It was so good just to look at her. My eyes were slowly drifting all over her face and back to her eyes again.

I broke the silence. "I can't ice skate."

"Doesn't matter," she said. "I can skate well, so instead of you teaching me how to skate, I'll teach you. Peter will be fine with that. It's more fun anyway." The whisper of her voice, and the closeness of her eyes, and then stupidity struck.

In my head, the Gutter Confucius was shouting, *Son, better to be silent and thought a fool than to speak and remove all doubt.* But who was listening? I was jumping into emerald eye-pools. I was young and stupid and confused by the wave of feelings I was experiencing for this lady, and the words just came out.

"I've heard rumors and I just want to run it by you. Are you gay?"

The emerald pools froze over. The temperature suddenly dropped, and the whisper of her hurt voice said, "Fuck you."

Kim got up and went back to her seat, leaving me to myself; the only person I didn't want to be with on this flight. I hated myself. *What an asshole I am! I didn't know they could fit an asshole as big as me on this plane. If I could turn my giant asshole inside out, I'd use it as a parachute.*

All I was thinking was that I'd ask her directly before I committed to those amorous feelings I was incubating. But it didn't come out that way. Was it possible that I'd just alienated my leading lady with whom I was about to begin a picture, and in that same moment, blown any chance of having any kind of relationship with her? *God, it feels like this plane is going fifteen miles an hour. Why do I say such stupid things? I am embarrassed writing this, can you imagine how I felt sitting there.*

In the suite of the New York Drake Hotel on Park Avenue, I was lying on the floor because a lowlife like me didn't deserve furniture. I was wondering if room service would bring up ten feet of rope when there was a knock. I crawled to the room door and pulled it open. She was barefoot, in jeans and a T-shirt, and then I saw she was holding a joint.

She looked at me. "You want to try that again?"

"Yes, please." *She forgives me!*

A short while later, we were hysterical, going over what happened on the plane. Explaining it and laughing made us very hungry. It was very comfortable and enjoyable with her. I offered to take her to the best pizza place in the Village. She suggested we call production to get a car, but we didn't know the number.

"It's faster if we just take the subway," I said. Kim had never been on a subway. "Never?" She shook her head, and her shy crooked smile appeared. "Come on. This is my town, I'll take you."

Kim was excited by her first subway ride but even more so by John's brick-oven pizza. After devouring it, we walked into the night. Cuddling her sheepskin jacket around her face, we talked our way uptown just past the Pan Am Building. We were staring at the lighted architecture while huge snowflakes quietly fell around us. We were watching our breath, waiting for the light to change when we realized there wasn't a car for miles in either direction.

We laughed, and Kim said, "Why are we waiting?" She took my hand to cross. "Your hand is so cold."

The light changed but we only moved toward each other. We kissed the cold away. Hell, we kissed the whole damn city away. We held onto that kiss across the street into the hotel and took a breath at the elevator door. "I think we should do that once more don't you?" "Yes" the husky whisper responded, "I definitely think so."

We worked, ate, and slept together. Kim and I had scenes to shoot where we were falling in love (Eric Morris again – *No Acting, Please*). *Hell, no acting necessary!* In our ice-skating scene in Central Park, I think everyone knew we kissed longer than the scene required. Our director, Peter Medak, was a wonderful and easygoing curmudgeon, who had left his honeymoon to make this picture and was missing his wife. We filmed in Times Square at midnight, and it was all magically surreal. I'm from New York but I'm seeing the city differently. The days in New York were rushing by, and Kim and I were feeling as if we'd known each other for a lifetime.

The word for this lady is 'Luscious', it means, *highly pleasing to the senses, delightful, delectable, delicious, lush, scrumptious, alluring, enchanting* and *yummy*. I think that says it.

One early morning, we were cuddled together in my room. I disengaged from Kim to shower and get dressed.

Kim sleepily asked, "Where are you going?"

"Well, since we have the day off, I thought I'd visit my grandfather. He has a tailoring shop in Queens."

"How will you get to Queens?" Kim asked.

"By train."

She smiled. "Can I come? We can get the limo to take us there?"

The limo cruised under the EL (elevated train tracks). There it was: Grandpa Hymie's tailoring store, with yellowed windows, a faded cardboard display of a man in a suit, cardboard neck bent forward leaning against the glass, and American flag lying crumpled on the floor of the window display. Kim pointed to an old candy store two doors up.

"I bet they have some of my favorites." Kim jumped out of the car. "I'll meet you at Grandpa's."

I thought maybe she was giving me a moment alone with him.

I walked in as a customer was yelling, "Where's the suit, Hymie? I brought it in three weeks ago."

Hymie responded, "You didn't say it was a rush. How's tomorrow?"

The guy threw his hands in the air and left.

I walked up close to Grandpa as he looked up from the man's ticket. "'Can I help you?" he said. Then his eyes welled up with tears. He hugged me, crying and patting me to make sure I was real.

Grandpa took my hand, leading me into the back, and pulled out a bottle of what he called "Schnapps". It was whiskey. He picked up two dirty shot glasses and an even dirtier rag and wiped them out. Then poured two drinks. I was hoping the alcohol killed the germs.

"L'chaim," he said. *To life.*

Down the hatch mine went! It ignited my throat like fire. When I could speak again, it was just in time to introduce Kim, who burst in the door with a huge smile and a big brown bag of sweets.

Hymie held up the whiskey glass, offering her a shot. Kim grimaced, offering up a chocolate-covered marshmallow twist instead. Hymie pointed to a glass containing his teeth.

Kim capitulated and took the shot glass, "*Dasvidaniya!*" and slugged it back.

Suddenly, we notice a cluster of old ladies in matching aprons, heads covered in huge hair rollers with big hairnets and aluminum spikes, peering through Hymie's dirty window. It looked like an alien invasion. They came from the hairdressing shop next door after spotting Kim walking by. They fluttered in like prehistoric pterodactyls.

"Hymie, Hymie!" they were all calling my grandfather.

He didn't like the interruption. "What do you want?"

They pointed to Kim. "Hymie, do you know who this is?"

Hymie shrugged. "That's my grandson's friend."

"Hymie, Hymie, this is Kim Novak, Hymie, she's a movie star!"

The wizened old owl lowered his chin. "So's my grandson." He shooed them out of the store.

Kim chatted to the flock, herding them out the door with her bag of sweets like a farmer with a bag of feed.

While Grandpa and I shared another shot, he gave me a tiny nod. "So, you and her?"

I nodded to his nod, then Grandpa and I talked about how my mother and all the rest of his children wanted him to give up the store and move to Los Angeles. I could still see the bruises on his face from the last mugging. Hymie noticed me looking, "Nobody came to help, nobody", he said, "not a person. When I was able to move, I crawled back in the store. I'm not going anywhere, they'll put me in an old people's home."

"The thing is, Grandpa, you were mugged three times this year. This last time they left you lying in the gutter."

He put away another shot. "I'd still rather be here." In my grandfather's mind, going into an old age home was like going back to Russia.

Kim came back covered in dust from climbing into the filthy front display window. She was carrying the American flag that'd been lying in that window since I was a kid.

She held the flag with reverence. "Hymie, this is an antique…"

"So am I," laughed Hymie. "You want it, take it."

He sensed we were about to go and wiped his teary eyes with the same dirty rag. We all hugged goodbye. The next time I see him, he'd be moved out to LA.

Back at the hotel, we shook out the flag on the balcony and gave New York City a patriotic dust storm. Then we unfurled the flag on the hotel suite carpet, after moving the chairs and tables.

Kim climbed onto the flag. "Love, look, it has forty-eight stars, it will make the most unbelievable quilt." It would, but at that moment we were feeling very patriotic.

After dinner in the room, I was watching football on TV when Kim asked me what scene we were shooting in the morning.

"I'm not sure – my script's on the table. There's a call sheet inside it." (The call sheet had info on the next day's work.)

Suddenly, there was a scream, and I got whacked over the head with my script and it hurt. It was followed by more whacks, making me get up off the sofa and defend the blows with my arms over my head as she pushed me backward, whacking me out the hotel door and into the hall.

The door slammed in my face! I was standing in the hallway in my underwear.

I shouted, softly, "Hey, what the hell's going on?"

Then, from the space under the door, a mangled piece of paper spewed out. I picked up the scrunched paper and straightened it out. It was a torn page from my script, the page on which my acting coach had handwritten his jellybean. Seeing it for the first time, I read what he'd written: *Make her fall in love with you.*

We hadn't gotten that far into the script, and I'd forgotten he wrote it and never needed his jellybean. Bash! A plate smashed against the door. Other things were crashing inside the room.

"Kim!" I said against the door, "you don't understand. Please, let me explain."

There was a loud scream like a wounded animal. "I hate you!"

I sank to the hallway carpet. This was impossible to explain. I leaned against the door; I could hear her crying on the other side. I understood how she felt. On the plane, I was an asshole; now she thought I was a despicable manipulating asshole.

My love believed my love was a lie. This hurt me more than anything in my life.

On my knees in the hallway, I told her the story of my acting lesson and my coach writing a motivational jellybean somewhere in my script. Please just look at the writing on this piece of paper. It's not my writing.

The door opened and we looked at each other. I held up the page, "I never saw this before, I swear, I know how awful it must have felt to read this, I'm so sorry."

I suddenly stopped talking because I felt this drop hit my hand, then another. I looked and saw damp spots on the script page and then on my hand. I felt my face and looked at my wet hand. They were tears. This was the first time I had ever cried in my life. There were times I wanted to cry, like at my grandmother's funeral, but nothing ever came out. My mother said she didn't remember me crying as a child.

"You're crying,". Kim touched my face. I laughed in disbelief, "I'm crying".

"I should have known it wasn't your handwriting; I can *read* it". We fell into each other's arms, in the hotel hallway.

CHAPTER 11

Brooklyn Buckaroo

We finished filming the New York exteriors of the film. The rest of the movie would be filmed at MGM Studios in California. We had a week before all the crew and equipment would get back to LA. Kim said, "You showed me your city and now I will show you mine."

Kim picked me up at the airport in Carmel, CA, where Clint Eastwood was the current mayor. She drove me by the Carmel Valley stables where she kept her horses, a quarter horse named Kingo, a young Arabian stallion named Nurjan and her Arabian mare, Shallee. Then we drove to her house in Big Sur – a most fantastic house with a stone turret overlooking the Pacific. A llama was peeking over the gate.

Inside, the view was just glass and the ocean. The waves crashed below on the rocks, and you could feel it. During big storms, the waves sprayed up to the living room glass. When we lay by the fire, it couldn't be any more cozy or romantic. Kim fed me raw lychees on Grandpa's flag, spread over the warm heated slabs of stone.

I met her family, the dogs, the goat, the llama, and the bird. Animals and nature were air to Kim. I could see it in all her paintings. Soon I was on a first-name basis with all the animals, except Creach, the goat (big horns with attitude). Cuddling up that night, I listened to the sea – and it did remind me of the highway traffic behind my old house.

Sunrise from the deck, watching whales swimming by, and otters playing in the sea, and I drank my first cup of black coffee with honey. It was fantastic, and I still drink this way fifty years later. I'm having a cup as I write this. After coffee, Kim drove me to a mountaintop overlooking the forest and Carmel Valley below. It was very still and quiet compared to the sounds of the wind and the ocean. This was where she was going to build her new ranch house.

Big Sur was a relaxing break, but then it was time to resume filming at MGM. Metro-Goldwyn-Mayer Studios, the one with the roaring lion. During its heyday, they said, MGM had more stars than there were in the heavens. Now it's Sony Studios.

I gave Kim a bit more space in LA so we could focus on our work. I slept in the monk's cell one night because she had an early call the next day.

When I arrived on stage, I went by her dressing room to say good morning. The dressing rooms were boxes on wheels so that they could be moved wherever they were needed. Kim's was on one side of the stage for privacy. Tony Curtis and I were on the other side. Inside the boxes depending on your status, were sofas, tv, carpeting, mirrored makeup tables, full bathroom and even a shower and telephone. I had a chair.

Inside her dressing room, we kissed, and it got away from us. As I left her dressing room, I was wondering, *does everybody know?*

One day my folks visited the set. Kim and I gave them a tour and passed the editing bay. There on the floor was a shot of Kim and me kissing from the ice-skating scene.

The editor said, "it's a great shot". Kim and I thought it looked fantastic. Kim said, "there's a crystal bridge of light between our lips'. The Editor said, "You say crystal bridge and the network sees spit."

"Yeah," my mother says, "spits not nice."

The editor said, "Keep it, it's yours."

I still have that frame of the film. It's the only existing copy. Kim went back to the scene she was shooting but the actor kept forgetting his line. The director said, let's take a break. Kim had a coffee break with us, and my dad leaned over and said the actors forgotten line, "Baby, when the face goes, you go!" Kim burst out laughing and said, "Sol, you should be doing this part!" My father really got a kick out of that. So much so, he has said the line, *when the face goes, you go* every time I saw him.

When I was passing Tony Curtis' trailer on the way back to the set, Tony called me in and offered me a toke on a huge spliff. Tony and I got on famously. I declined his offer saying, I'm in the next shot.

Tony exhaled, "Kid, I see what's going on. You don't know what you're getting into. Can I give you some advice?"

"No thanks, Tony," I said. "I may not know what I am getting into, but I'm going anyway!"

Tony fell back laughing, "Enjoy the ride, kid!"

Many years later, the last time I saw Tony was in Spago's Restaurant in Beverly Hills. It was shortly after Dodi Fayed's funeral in the UK. We had been there. Tony got up and grabbed me in a hug. A moment of memory for our friend Dodi and for Princess Diana.

When the filming ended, I drove Kim back up to Carmel in Mello-Yello, cruising up Highway One, top down, hair in the wind.

When the building commenced, Kim and I would have our coffee on the deck and head out to spend the day at the site with the builders.

We had our lunch sitting on top of one of the little mushroom tree rounds. From here we could discuss plans and changes. Kim could see her house coming together. It'd been an incredible process, and it was nearly a year and nearly done.

On one cleared piece of the property, Kim and I built the corrals for the horses. We dug post holes for days.

We took turns digging each post hole. Kim wearing her black rubber boots, black jeans, and a denim shirt. When we were done, we put scarves over our faces and applied creosote (smelly wood preservative).

The corral was done, and it was time to mount the gates, but we were arguing over which way the gates should open. We argued and laughed and argued some more until I mounted my invisible horse and galloped up to the gates, spanking my behind and pulling on the imaginary reins, demonstrating how I would open the gate. Kim asked me to dismount and borrowed my invisible horse. She mounted and galloped around showing me how she would do it and that's the way it's going to be. Then she galloped off. I yelled, "Come back here with my horse".

The Gutter Confucius said, *Son, walk the dog.* Meaning: *What the lady wants the lady gets, take yourself for a walk.*

Later I caught up with my Horsethief and as all the builders had left for the day, I took kindly to her. She got her gate to open her way.

One day there was a huge storm. No coffee on the deck that morning. No builders showing up either. The Big Sur house was like the prow of a ship cutting waves in heavy seas. This was dramatic weather.

Kim came into the room carrying some unusual wet gear like extra-wide raincoats and dropped them on the floor in front of me. We got suited up in the windbreakers and she said, "It gets really noisy, so read my lips if you can't hear me."

We walked out to the side of the house away from the ocean. There was a steel ladder attached to the wall going up to the roof. We climbed up most of the way. It got a lot noisier as we climbed. We weren't in the raw wind yet.

Kim said, "We go over the top and there's another railing that climbs along the top of the roof all the way to the mast at the very top. Stay flat to the roof as much as you can. When we get to the mast, there are two handholds on the mast. One on the right, and one on the left. I'll take the left, okay?"

I nodded.

She nodded back, looking into my eyes to make sure. We were now just below the rooftop ledge.

"This is very important," she shouted against the noise of the wind, demonstrating with her hands. "When you grab the handhold on the mast, grip it with all you got. Then go for it with the other hand and grab the hold with both hands and kick yourself up off the roof into the air."

I didn't say, *are you fucking kidding me?*

Okay, so how can you say to Kim Novak, "I have vertigo". Heights are not my thing. Climbing this ladder was a testosterone roller coaster but I was going to do this. My heart was in my mouth with fear, but I would do this with her. I trusted her.

When we were near the mast, the wind was a force to reckon with. I reached up for the handhold and my hand just blew backward like a piece of paper out of a moving car window. I didn't get near the handhold. Kim looked me in the face. Her hair was flat against her face in the wind; she looked like a she-lion, a puma. She demonstrated using more force to grab hold.

I did it. I grabbed the rail and held on. I could now see over the roof edge, and it reminded me I was on top of a house on cliff over the sea.

Kim shouted, "Okay, we do both hands next, okay?"

I nodded yes, and she nodded, one, two, three, and we reached out and grabbed for the rails. I grabbed it for all I was worth, and I didn't have to kick up; the wind lifted me into the air. The wide raincoat spread like a sail. I was blowing in the wind like a flag in a windstorm. I was flying!

I looked at her face and it was luminous. She was in her element. I was holding on for dear life. This was truly incredible. I could hardly open my eyes. The wind kept shutting them. I couldn't keep them open for more than a few seconds without having to turn my face to the side. I looked at Kim flying, and I was flying next to her with the whole world beneath us.

We carefully worked our way back down and hugged when we got to the ground. We held each other's faces, just standing there, taking in each other's joyfulness. Then we were shivering. Kim opened a door in the turret wall revealing a stone shower. Before we got into the shower Kim turned my face to see my reflection in a mirror. My long hair was standing straight out. I looked like Tarok the Wind Warrior.

In the morning, the sun was out, the sea was calm, and the coffee was hot. The months slipped into changing seasons, and Kim and I rode horses every day. The house was built. It even had sliding walls so all the animals could come in. Llamas, dogs, and even a raccoon (that's its own story).

We moved into the ranch. We brought the horses home from Carmel Valley Stables. Watching the horses exploring their new corrals and freedom was extraordinary. Kim found it much easier to communicate with animals and nature than most people. I would find this out every few weeks when we would be working in the barn and she would softly breathe, "What are you doing here?"

I'd smile and say, "In the barn?"

"In my life."

This cloud would come over her and it was time to hit the road.

At first, I tried to talk it through. "Is it me – are you feeling hemmed in?" But it still wears you down trying to reason without reason. Well, it wore this man down. It was easier to just walk in the house, grab my leather carpet bag, chuck it behind the driver's seat of Mello-Yello, slide in a Neil Young eight-track and put the pedal to the metal.

Kim had given me an old WWII bomber jacket. It was a beauty and the real McCoy, with worn cracked leather and sheepskin lapels. She said she borrowed it permanently from actor Stuart Whitman on a movie set. It was beaten up, but it felt good and kept me warm on the drives up and down the Pacific Coast Highway.

I drove south, stopping at the Nepenthe in Big Sur for a coffee with honey. I wrote on a napkin: *She taught me how to fly, then took away the sky, where am I falling?* Coffee done, I walked out to my car, the rain thwacking on the old leather bomber jacket. I put up the top and began four hours of missing her on the road to Neil Young's "I am just a dreamer, and you are just a dream".

The chauffeur within took over, letting my mind drift to one of our late afternoon horse rides. We had fallen asleep on the warm grass and woke to the full moon rising. We mounted our horses and let them lead the way home, side by side on the path they knew so well. Then Kim, in one graceful move, swung herself from her horse over to mine, like a ballet dancer in cowboy boots and sat facing me. She was fearless on horses. She took the reins from my hands, loosed them behind her and kissed me. We kissed and held each other to the gentle swaying motion of the horses walking home in the moonlight.

One day while taking a silent walk through the forest we found a baby raccoon. It was so small, the size of a thumb. Now we had a mission – get to the vet. We marked the tree, thinking if the raccoon wasn't dying maybe we could put it back in the nest after the vet checked it out.

The vet said, "When a baby raccoon disappears from the nest, the mother doesn't go looking for it. That's the nature of it, and the likelihood of him surviving without his mother isn't good. Sorry."

Kim wasn't having it. "How do we keep it alive? What do we feed it?"

The vet was shrugging. "Well, get an eye dropper for one. It's too small for a bottle."

We got all the fixings to feed the raccoon what we hoped would keep it alive. Every morning, the baby cried when it was hungry. Kim and I were doting parents and named our adopted son, Ume – you and me.

A couple of weeks later, we took Ume to the movies with us in Carmel covered in a baby's swaddling cloth. The ticket-counter girl even gave us that "aww, new baby" smile. Kim and I ducked into the theater before she peeked. We sat in the back in case Ume started to make noises.

Just as the movie was starting, two elderly ladies entered and stopped in front of us. Before we could do anything, the old ladies leaned down lifting the blanket revealing Ume's face. "Oh, look, a …" one said, and there was this moment: *Not only is your baby ugly, but it looks like a rodent.* The white-haired ladies were frozen, and Ume hissed, showing all his teeth and they screamed.

Kim and I ran for the exit. We couldn't stop laughing. We laughed the entire night with Ume cuddled between us.

The cuddling went on for months and Ume was getting bigger all the time. In raccoon, he was probably a teenager by now, and Kim and I talked about schools. Well, we did discuss how long he could continue to live in the house without turning our lives into a living hell. He opened everything, ate everything, made messes everywhere, snatched our food off our plates, jumped on the dogs' backs, and sat on their food bowls to tease them. Ume even brought home a girlfriend. He was very cute but very naughty. He was a raccoon!

The final straw came when Ume got jealous of me and his mom (Kim) in bed one night. He bit me in the balls. Let me tell you, there is nothing to compare with having your most delicate body part between the sharp teeth of a carnivore, even if it's your own carnivore. I had purple balls for a week. Kim convulsed with laughter watching me waddle around the house. I even had a momentary vision of Ume as a Davy Crockett hat. No joke, it was time for Ume to go back to the woods, or at least bar him from the bedroom.

Driving down the coast to Hollywood with two hours to go, all I could think about was Kim. *It's so good when it's good. Then, suddenly it goes strange.*

Kim came down to Los Angeles a couple of times. She stayed with me in the monk's cell one weekend, but it was too close for comfort. Kim was used to open mountain views and here from one room was one mountain that said Hollywood on it. We climbed the mountain behind the monastery to the top and had a picnic and decided after that to get hotel rooms.

I never thought about Kim being an international movie star unless she was sharing a story about someone like Sammy

Davis Jr, who told me the exact same story at his house years later. Sammy left Vegas between shows and flew to Chicago, where Kim was spending Christmas with her mom. Sammy covered the tree in her backyard with emeralds and asked her to marry him. Then a car showed up with the boys from Las Vegas. They took him back for the Christmas show.

The next week, Kim got a call from Harry Cohn, the Columbia Pictures Studio boss. He wanted Kim to come to his office. Of course, she went; he was the boss.

He said, "Do you know how much you get for a picture? Not what I pay you on your contract, but what I get for you to do a picture? A million dollars."

Kim was shocked. She never saw that kind of money.

Harry emphasized, "Nobody gets that much money. You know what you'll get if you see Sammy Davis Jr again? Zero! That's right, nothing. Because that's what you'll be worth in this business. This doesn't happen, do you understand? Don't see him again because I'll tell you what will happen if you do. They'll break his legs or blind his good eye. So, think about that."

In a BBC documentary, "Sammy Davis Jr – The Kid in the Middle", it was disclosed that Cohn had the mobsters threaten Sammy Davis Jr with exactly those consequences if he didn't marry a black woman in 48 hours.

Hollywood!

I killed the engine and stretched getting out of the car. I ambled up the cactus path to my monk's cell. The phone was ringing inside. I knew it was her. I dropped the bag and picked it up.

Silence, then a breath. "Hi, love."

"Hi," I said, "just walked in the door."

"I figured how long it would take you. Pretty good, huh?"

"Yeah, I drove down here thinking about you and me all the way."

"Want to think about us some more and drive back up? I miss you."

Sometimes I would just get right back in Mello-Yello and drive back up. I was feeling like a yo-yo bouncing between loving life with Kim and hating my life without her. Kim played me an original song recorded by Lori Lieberman; *Killing Me Softly with His Song*, it felt like our love song. Many meanings to this wonderful song over our time together.

The road was good for thinking and on this drive, I realized I couldn't just be happy when I was with Kim, I had to be happy when I was with me. I needed to find my own ranch.

CHAPTER 12

Fork In The Road

When I told Kim about looking for my own ranch her first question was where? She wanted to call her land agent to find me a place nearby.

"I need to be closer to LA if I'm going to get work. I couldn't drive from Carmel to LA more than once or maybe twice a week."

I'd just driven up and back and it nearly broke my ass bone.

On the next drive down to LA, I detoured to Ojai. A small town between Los Angeles and Santa Barbara, Ojai was known for its hot springs. A real estate agent had a ranch to show me. We drove to a ranch with a hundred acres of orange groves. Outstanding pretty but I started hearing Pavarotti. I imagined Evette pirouetting through the orchid while pickers pelted her with oranges.

Could I do this drive after working all day, come home, feed the horses, and go back in the morning? Add in traffic and mudslides. No.

I continued driving back down the coast. After forty minutes, I was at the northern-most tip of Malibu. On my right, the sun was beginning to set over the ocean, while something was catching the light on my left. A burning red light, coming from the hills. I took it as a sign and made a left onto a small country road. I followed the light up a road called Yerba Buena, which means "good herb".

I drove a few miles up this winding canyon road and it was getting dark. I found the source of the red glowing light I'd seen from the coast. My burning bush turned out to be reflecting sunlight from a metal sculpture at a children's summer camp. But I still I felt it was a sign.

I drove a mile or two further until I came to a fork in the road. There was more daylight coming from the left fork and I'm a go-with-the-light kind of person. I took the left, and the road started climbing steeply.

Another hundred yards, I passed a gate on my right. Above the gate a sign said *The Lazy J*. The *J* was tipped back to make it look lazy. There was also a tombstone just inside the gate. On it was written: *Here lies the last man who left the gate open*. I laughed out loud. Kim would love something like that at her place. Too often, workmen didn't close the gate, and animals went for a wander. I drove around a curve, back into the setting sun, because from higher up, the sunsets last longer. It was like driving into a painting of Austria. I expected to see Julie Andrews running through the grass singing.

A line of mountains ran along the right with a lush green valley at its base. Where I was sitting, on the top of Mello-Yello's folded convertible top, I was looking straight down the entire valley to the sea. Just below the hill I was perched on, there was a stone house overlooking the precipice to the valley. What a setting!

It looked like a windmill but without the Don Quixote blades. The roof of the stone tower had light blue tiles matching the ranch house adjoining it, and there was someone waving to me. I waved back and he waved me over. I let the emergency brake off and Mello-Yello silently rolled down the road and up the drive to the windmill. I pulled up the brake and that metallic cranking sound was remarkably loud in the quiet surroundings.

A kid with long hair said, "Hey man, nice car."

"Thanks, nice view."

"My name's Gabriel. I work here. Want to smoke a doobie and watch the sunset?"

Well, it was the 70s, after all. I climbed up and shared the sunset with Gabriel.

The sun hit the sea, making a seashell, and the sky got red. The sky went a deep red, painting the bottom of the clouds.

I looked around and said, "I could live here."

"Well, you couldn't live here, Annie Chamberlain lives here," Gabriel said. "I work for her, but you could live there," and he pointed across the road.

A hundred yards up, there was a wooden gate with white stone mill wheels on either side of it. The gate opened to a dirt road winding down through an oak grove up to a little white cottage nestled in the hillside.

I got chills. I stood up, almost forgetting my vertigo, and just looked at it. The red sky was lighting the windows of the cabin with that same burning red light I saw from the coast. I felt as if I'd been guided here.

I took the number from Gabriel, thanked him for the sunset and the doobie. I called Annie Chamberlain first thing the next day.

Annie had a face that was earned. Her deep lines weren't from age but from the life she lived up there. She told me the history of her ranch, built by her father. The ceiling beams were made from old telephone poles, and its walls all made from old railroad ties and stone. The house overlooked the drop into the valley below. Annie was born in this house and lived here alone on one-hundred-and-eighty acres. The exact size of the old Spanish Land Grants purchased from Mexico by her father. Henry was a doctor in Beverly Hills, which at the time was mostly just farmland. No Rodeo Drive then. He used to ride his horse and buggy up Pacific Coast Highway, which was a dirt road back then.

She asked how tall I was, and I told her I was 5' 11". That was odd and then she bid me to follow her as she walked down the road to the cabin.

The cabin had two bedrooms to one side with a small bathroom separating them. The biggest room was the kitchen in the center of the house. On the other side of the kitchen was a living room with a wood-burning fireplace. Get this, there was electric light in the kitchen and the bathroom, but oil lanterns for the rest of the house.

Annie pointed out the ceiling was only 6' 1" high, and if I raised my hand above my head, I hit it. Funny, but it didn't bother me because it was homey inside and had so big an outside.

There were forty acres to the house. A former ranch hand, Pepe Sanchez (obviously shorter than me), fixed up the tack room to be his house many years ago. Annie's father, Henry Chamberlain, was a doctor who found Pepe, shot and dying in the road. He loaded him into his buggy and took him to the ranch and saved his life. Pepe worked the ranch for Henry in gratitude till he could afford a place of his own.

Annie walked me down to the barn. I was so happy to hear there was one. It was also faded blue-and-white like her house, but the barn was run-down.

"I don't mind," I told her. "I'll fix it up to hold a couple of horses."

There were a few stalls behind a gate in a courtyard and a watering trough, and a corral out back of the barn for exercising horses. It was like an old western movie set that hadn't been used for decades. But Annie wasn't giving anything away yet. She wasn't sure if the barn was included in the rent or if she wanted to rent it at all. Did I know much about horses? Did I have horses? It occurred; I was in a tough negotiation.

Annie and I walked ten minutes back to her house, and she served homemade lemonade on the veranda overlooking the valley. Annie asked me personal questions about my marital status and whether I had a girlfriend.

As I sipped my lemonade, I decided to tell her my girlfriend, Kim (no last name), had an Arabian mare and paid for a very expensive stud to sire the mare. On a foggy morning in April 1973, my girlfriend got a call from the stable owner to say her mare was going to foal. We got there at first light, but the fog was thick as soup. We saw a creature in the fog. We looked at each other in disbelief. It was obscured by fog but we both just saw a unicorn.

The stable owner walked over. "You were going to find out sooner or later. That wild jackass, Foghorn, obviously jumped my five-foot fence and sired a mule, cause that's what you get when you cross a horse and a jackass. A mule. In this very special case, an Arabian mule".

The baby mule was pure white, standing sideways in the fog. With her long mule ears held forward, they looked like a unicorn's horn.

Annie slapped her knees, laughing, enjoying my story. She refilled my lemonade from the pitcher. My girlfriend saw how much I loved the little mule and gave her to me as a birthday present. That's why I need that barn.

Annie, who had been giving me a history lesson most of the morning, looked at me with an intense twinkle in her eyes. "When the Civil War ended, General Tecumseh Sherman offered each man forty acres and a mule. Here I am, renting forty acres to a man that has a mule. Well, gosh darn it, if that doesn't seem meant to be…"

CHAPTER 13

Deer Springs Ranch

Annie Chamberlain and I shook on it, and I could feel the hard-earned calluses on her hand. Deer Springs Ranch, Route 2, Malibu, California – not a bad address for this Boy from Brooklyn.

Annie asked, "When would you want to move in?"

I replied, "Are there sheets on the bed?"

She laughed loudly, "If you're intent on spending the night in the cabin, there's a bed in the back bedroom and clean sheets in the closet."

I was about to head back to the cabin as Annie added, "The nearest market is twenty-two miles away, so you may want to come to my place for dinner. My closest friend, Margaret, will be visiting me this evening, you're more than welcome. Come before sunset for an aperitif."

Annie waved and walked into her house. I drove the short distance to my gate and slowly rolled off the tarmac and drove down the dirt road bearing right at the oak grove up to the front of the cabin.

I walked to the front door. I looked back across at Boney Mountain. The largest mountain in the Santa Monica Mountain range was right outside my door. I felt kind of spiritual; I guess the way to say it is "overwhelmingly grateful". I did a slow turnaround, a slow eagle dance, my version of what I imagined to be a Native American dance of joy.

I wanted the earth to know I was happy to be on it. I walked down through the oak grove to the barn, just sitting there like a Pennsylvania postcard. It felt like a bunch of Amish people might come rushing out of the barn door singing, "Welcome Pilgrim – bring in the pumpkins."

I was looking across a field of wheat in front of my cabin, toward Annie's house. The sun was coming down, so I reckoned I would mosey over for that aperitif.

Annie's closest friend, Margaret, was, in fact, Margaret Hamilton, the actress who played the Wicked Witch in *The Wizard of Oz*: "You'll never see your Auntie Em again, hahaha!"

After a lovely dinner with these two delightful ladies, I excused myself to return for my first night in my cabin. Annie offered me a flashlight but the John Wayne in me said, "Thank you, ma'am, I got the stars to guide me." I may even have touched the tip of my invisible ten-gallon Stetson cowboy hat. What a schmuck!

As I headed out the door, I heard Annie say, "Mind the rattlesnakes. They like to sleep on the warm tarmac."

I stepped outside and thought I walked into a closet. It was so dark I couldn't see my own hand in front of my face. It was shocking. I was so used to the light of the city sky. Even in Carmel Valley, there was light in the night sky, but here it was pitch dark. Not being able to see your own body is quite disturbing.

I started out on the gravel toward the road doing a spacewalk. Then it came to me, what Annie said as I left: rattlesnakes like to sleep on the warm tarmac. My foot stopped in the air mid-step. I didn't want to step on a snake, sleeping or otherwise. I was on the tarmac and frozen. How stupid would I feel going back for a flashlight after my John Wayne exit? Fifty feet to my gate, then it was just dirt, and I should be fine, right?

Cold dirt wasn't warm tarmac, right? Does dirt stay warm at night? Those fifty feet felt like an entire Costco parking lot. *Do snakes have ears?* I was warning them I was coming. I wanted to kneel and scoop up a handful of stones to toss in front of me, but I was scared I might touch a sleeping snake. Where the hell was the gate with the big white mill wheels? Shouldn't I have reached them by now?

The mountain was out there but it was invisible somehow. Maybe because I just had dinner with the Wicked Witch. It made me think of the lion in *The Wizard of Oz* who just needed c–c–c–courage. I hummed my way to the porch, *we're off to see the wizard, the wonderful wizard of Oz.*

I was so happy to finally arrive. I found the light switch in the kitchen and, even though it wasn't a cold night, I built a fire in the fireplace. Who was I kidding? This city boy was scared shitless.

Next morning, I drove Mello-Yello to Hollywood accompanied by Neil Young's "Heart of Gold". Hard to believe I drove up this road yesterday not knowing where I was going. Now it's my road.

I was in time with my life.

Back in the monk's cell, I called Kim to tell her the news: I'd found a ranch. She was amazed. I'd only left yesterday. I told her the forty acres and a mule story, and she laughed, saying, "When Nubbin is ready, we'll take her down together and I can see your ranch for myself."

I took my last look around the monk's cell. It was four years since I arrived in this town. This place was good to me. All the friends behind each door – actors, musicians, songwriters, script writers, dreamers, and smugglers and Susie (Shrimp) Simons. It was a very special place.

Andy helped me pack a few things and the neighbors took the rest. I kept the Rock-Ola jukebox and the Prince Valiant armor I bought at the Columbia Studios auction. That day at the auction I'd accidentally scratched my head and bought a church pew from the movie *Nob Hill*. It sat eighteen people and wouldn't fit in my monk cell. The phone rang, and it was Scott Glenn asking if I could bring any extra chairs, I had to Thanksgiving dinner Thursday? That was meant to be, right? The Columbia truck was still unloading the jukebox, and twenty bucks made the boys happy to deliver the pew to Scott's house, where it remains. We loaded my *tupidanthus* plant in the back seat of Mello-yellow and Andy had the idea to wrap it with cling wrap to protect it from the wind. I put the pedal to the metal. *Bye, bye Hollywood.*

I remembered to stop at that grocery Annie told me about. My new home was not the kind of place you say, "Oh shit, I forgot to get coffee." It was twenty-two miles from the market to the big white mill wheels at the gate and forty miles from the monk's cell in Hollywood. As I drove up Yerba Buena from the coast, I was astonished at how far up I had ventured unknowingly the day I found it.

Once I put my plant by the front door, I unpacked the groceries and ate an apple as I stared at the mountain. It was so quiet; I wondered if Annie could hear my crunching. I decided to make a list of things I needed for the house, like more oil lamps and a telephone. In those days, it took two weeks to get one installed and up here, who knew?

Two of my best friends came out from Hollywood. Andy and Jay brought sleeping bags, tools, food, and grass. They helped me put some muscle into fixing up the barn to be a workable place. Fixed the water trough, installed some hay feeders, and hinged the gate and put some new wood on the stall doors. My friends were impressed that I gained some actual ranching knowledge. *Thank you, Kim.*

We had a good time laughing around the fire at night. Those were good days. As I write this, I realize they are both gone now. *Hey boys, I'm thinking of you. I gotta stop writing for a while now.*

Sometimes it was hard to be alone, but it was good for me to be able to hear my inner self for a change. Amazing what we take for granted. Here, there was no music from the other apartments, or traffic or airplanes in the sky. I read by the fire at night. In the morning, I made coffee and walked down to the barn and did some chores. I fixed the oven in the kitchen and painted the living room and even chopped some wood for me and Annie. The Gutter Confucius says, "*A man who chops his own firewood is twice warmed*".

I drove up to Carmel and spent my days caring for my baby mule and being cared for by Kim, who marveled at how attached I had become to this little creature. I stayed in the corral with her all day. Whenever I tried to leave, the mule brayed. Kim laughed when I asked her to bring me blankets and a sandwich.

I stayed with the mule the first couple of nights because she was nervous in her new surroundings. But the second night she slept on the ground next to me, showing she felt safe. I touched her legs often and she let me lift her hooves for cleaning without kicking out. As I brushed her, she brushed her head on me.

Kim brought a basket, and we camped out in the corral one night. We were having great days and nights. Kim bought a sandblaster and was going creative on the wooden doors. It was an artwork thing for her. Goggles on; blast away.

I was offered a TV show. *Medical Center* was a big hit series starring Chad Everett, whom everyone said was the new Clark Gable. I did one of the very first shows of the series, but I hadn't met Chad. I read the script and chucked it in the bin.

Kim said, "I thought you wanted to work?"

"Read the last line."

She did and made a face. "Couldn't you change it?"

"Sure, I could make those lines better—"

But Kim interrupted me. "Then call the producer and tell him! What have you got to lose?"

Hmm. I called and told him that I'd be interested in playing the rebellious Dr. Lensko, who ran a free clinic, if they could see both sides of the story with equal respect. Frank

Glicksman, the producer, was a terrific guy. He totally got what I was saying and told me to come do it!

I drove straight to the MGM parking lot and into my assigned space for the duration of the show. I walked in the stage door and was jumped by two or three big guys and pinned to the floor before someone said, "He's okay, he's an actor on the show."

Frank apologized after and told me, "Chad [Everett, the star of the show] was in some alleged palimony suit and they were trying to serve him a subpoena."

Okay. I brushed myself off and went to the wardrobe dept. This wasn't much better because they wanted me in hippie gear. I explained that I was a doctor who didn't wear a tie, but I did bathe. That done, I went to make up, and they freaked out when they saw my beard and wanted to shave it off. I refused. They called Frank, and he came down to the stage to explain that the network didn't think a doctor should have a beard.

Kim and I had a plan here. I had brought pictures with me of famous bearded doctors who won awards around the world. Okay, I was keeping my hair and beard. All this work to get to work, then...

Chad came in dragging the script by a rope, saying, "What a dog of a script." (It was in his contract that he got seventy-five percent of the dialogue.)

He obviously didn't like my twenty-five percent. Who would want seventy-five percent of the dialogue in a medical show? Saying all those creepy words like *metastasis and colonoscopy.*

Chad was unhappy with my changes. He wanted to be the good guy and for me to be the bad guy. He sarcastically asked me if I was from New York, and when I said yes, he kicked a piece of the set into the air and said, "I don't like New York actors. Maybe you should call your agent?"

"We have the same agent, here's a dime."

Every day the scenes with Chad were hard fought but every scene in my free clinic, was a joy. I would go to my car, but I would be too tired to drive anywhere. I slept in it. I was battle-weary trying to hold onto the integrity of Dr Lensko. Was it me or ego, and whose ego? Chad's show! It was the longest week of my life.

One morning a tap on my window woke me up, and it was Frank, the producer. He got in my car and looked at me and nodded and kept nodding until we both started to giggle, which turned into relieving laughter. He was willing to offer me a spinoff series of the character Lensko based on the film they had seen so far.

"This is unprecedented, Michael."

It was vindication that I did do something good. "Frankly, Frank, to be honest, I've had enough." I thanked Frank for his faith in me.

I drove slowly out to the Deer Springs ranch and climbed into bed. In the morning, there was a bunny rabbit outside my porch door. I opened the screen door, and it didn't run away. I picked it up and I noticed the bunny shivering.

"I'll take you to Annie, bunny. She'll know what to do." I carried the bunny down the road to Annie's and knocked on her door.

"Morning, dear, what have we here?" she asked. "Well, this little bunny needs some attention." I said smiling at her. "Just set him on the wood stump there, dear, and I'll be right back."

I placed the bunny gently on top of the wood stump. "See, bunny, you're in good hands now."

Old Annie came out with a wicker basket and opened the cover and pulled out a pistol and blew the bunny away. There was nothing but fur floating in the air around me.

I was frozen in shock. "Annie, Annie, what did you do?"

She said, "When they get like that, dear, it's the best thing for them. Want some fresh lemonade?" No wonder her closest friend was the Wicked Witch.

After the corrals were fixed, I put out word I was looking for a horse to buy. I needed a horse that would be a mentor to Nubbin, and that I could ride. Kim and I would be bringing Nubbin down to my ranch soon. I needed a gelded horse who would look after her and teach her some horse manners. That's when I met Patricia, the horse lady. Patricia was a professional horse jumper and trainer, and she had a horse for sale.

I drove to Patricia's stable, and she showed me a horse that was so huge I didn't know how to get on it. Sinbad was a thoroughbred, standing seventeen hands high. Much taller than Arabian horses. Sinbad was almost pure white and quite beautiful, but he had no saddle on.

Patricia said to take him for a test ride. Test-riding a horse was a new one for me. Patricia flew up onto his back barefoot, in cutoff jeans, a plaid shirt tied just above her belly button, and long blonde hair that caught in her mouth. She galloped Sinbad around going by me and then leaned down and pulled me up behind her, and we cantered gracefully around the corral. She was talking to me and letting her thighs do all the steering. I wanted them both. That would have worked but I still had Kim's saddle, if you know what I mean. My saddle was custom made for an Arabian, and this was a thoroughbred. Patricia helped me get Sinbad settled in at Deer Springs. I had a new friend and a big horse.

After a week of practicing, Kim and I loaded Nubbin and Kingo, a gelding, into Kim's horse trailer. Geldings keep the younger one's calm, so it was always good to have another horse for their first trailer ride. Kim also brought baby goats. Horses like goats and it's calming for the horses having them around.

Old Annie's eyes twinkled a bit brighter, realizing that my girlfriend Kim was Kim Novak. I did enjoy watching that happen.

Kim couldn't believe there was land like this so close to L.A. "If I knew about this, I might not have moved to Big Sur." I think she said that just to make Annie happy.

Annie was elated. "It's the last valley opening to the sea at the end of the Santa Monica Mountains." She had a new history pupil.

Kim and I rode the zigzag path climbing to the top of Boney Mountain. We stopped to take a drink by a natural stream and water the horses. We were up high enough to see the entire valley below and the sea beyond. I could feel Kim taking it all in. She was happy for me to get it so right. That crooked smile said it all, and that little shaded area by the stream was a perfect place for a perfect moment up here on top of the mountainside.

The next morning, Kim paused her Jeep at my gate to look back at me, standing on my porch, holding my mug of coffee with honey. We exchanged a long look, a nod, and a wave as Kim pulled out of my gate.

CHAPTER 14

Meanwhile, Back at The Ranch

1974, Deer Springs Ranch. It was my first rainy season and mud ran down the hillsides, flooding the canyons. I realized it was time to retire Mello-Yello. She couldn't drive the little dip from my cabin through the oak grove to my gate. The water was over her doors.

I was about to start filming *Hitchhike,* a movie of the week. I couldn't get to the studio because of the torrential rain. I went to the Jeep dealership and took the Gutter Confucius with me.

Pop said to me as we walked in the door, "Be ready to walk out." I had no idea what he was talking about. The salesman wanted to know my needs. My father cracked up. "He doesn't want therapy; he wants to buy a Jeep."

I described Kim's Wagoneer model, and the man said, "You know those Jeep Wagoneer's are very popular with the UN."

My father looked at me and gave me the "Here it comes" smile.

The salesman said, "It's extremely hard to get hold of one of these. There's a huge back order."

My father stood up. "Okay, Let's go!"

The salesman panicked. "But I think we can pull some strings. Let me check with my manager".

After the salesman left, the Gutter Confucious laughed, "This salesman is so full of shit, if you gave him an enema, you could bury what's left in a shoebox".

The salesman returned, "I think we might be able to get our hands..."

My father said, "Have you got a car to sell him or not?"

The salesman spluttered, "Yessir."

"Okay then," said my father, "let's talk numbers." Pop winked at me. "This is when money talks and bullshit walks". These were the times I enjoyed most with my old man.

A half mile up the road passed Annie's house, there was an outlandish double gate with giant wolfhound statues on either side. It belonged to Tony Duquette; a movie set designer. Tony bought Quonset huts; the half-circular metal structures used by the navy in 1941 and put them out on the end of his property to build an artist's community. That didn't happen, who wants to live in a Quonset hut? Over the years Tony Duquette acquired movie set pieces. Movie set fountains and gazebos, trellises and beautiful statues stood about the grounds. Annie Chamberlain and other local ranchers considered it Sodom and Gomorrah. The good news was, my best friend, Andy moved there and rented one of the trailer houses on Tony's property. Having my best friend so close was great. When I went up to Kim's, Andy enjoyed caring for Nubbin and riding Sinbad. It worked out for both of us.

Before the rain came drought and then the fires. There was a big fire in Malibu that 1974, and it was burning through the mountains. The horizon glowed red, like Mars. Fire trucks came up my road and parked in front of my porch.

I made coffee for the firemen, and they warned me, "Fire's just beyond the ridge. It's all up to the wind now. If it comes over, we won't be able to save the house. Put what you want in the field, and we will tarp it and try to keep it wet."

Annie stormed up. "Let the house burn if you must, but don't let those oak trees burn. You save those trees, hear? I can build a house; I can't build a tree."

Those firemen bowed their heads with respect to Annie and nodded *yes, ma'am.* Luckily, the wind died down, and the trees and firemen survived.

Kim came down to visit, and my family came up as well. My father threw up after the drive up the winding road. Grandpa came along and he and Kim had a remembered moment. *Dasvidaniya!* After a few toasts, she even got him on Sinbad at almost ninety years of age.

Mom asked Kim what that animal staring at her was? Kim told my mom it was a cow.

My mother said, in her nasal tone, "Does it bite?"

Kim laughed and told my mom that her mother was at her ranch in Carmel, taking care of all the animals while she was away visiting me.

My mother was amazed. "Does she like taking care of animals?"

Kim confessed, "She hates it!"

They both had a good laugh. It was a big hug for Grandpa and Kim as we all said our goodbyes. Kim and I loaded Kingo into her trailer and I watched her drive up my road to the gate, waving all the way.

I called Kim to make sure she arrived safe, and her mom answered, "Kim was at the vets with Ume (our raccoon son), who got in a fight and lost his tail."

Kim picked me up at Carmel Valley Airport and we collected Ume from the vet. It was serious but he would be all right, except now he'd look more like a Russian hat than a Davy Crockett hat.

Kim said, "He's just too tame for the wild." My testicles twitched.

He was drugged up with bandages all over his bottom. Raccoons have amazing hands and can undo anything. We were busy parents. After a couple of weeks, Ume was walking around pretty much like I was after he bit me on the balls.

Kim and I had drifted into a different space since I had my own ranch. I had wings of my own. It just kind of happened one day as we were leaning on the corral gate. Didn't feel like the usual time to leave, it had more gravity to it. I pulled off my work gloves and we just looked at each other. She shrugged with that crooked smile. The same smile I saw on the roof of the Playboy Building when she wanted to work together. We recognized and acknowledged the moment without words.

"I'll hit the road," I said, and I was about to put the pedal to the metal when I remembered I didn't have the metal to put the pedal to. I had flown up. Kim whispered, "Can I give you a lift?"

We hugged goodbye at the airport. Kim hugged me and gave me a card and said open it later, gave me a lengthy kiss, a look at each other, I nodded as she handed me my saddle bag and I walked to the plane.

The card from Kim was goodbye. It was a long goodbye because she wrote it in a concentric circle. All the words going around and around, getting smaller and until it got to the center. It took the entire flight to read and much, much, longer to ingest.

Our wonderful time had ended. I think I knew it had but my heart didn't.

PRINCE VALIANT

My friends Jay and Andy and I drove down to El Cajon. It was close to the Mexican border. There was a horse-trading sale. Jay bought an Appaloosa stallion, a real beauty, and named him Snort. We trailered Snort back to my ranch. I kept Snort in my barn for whenever Jay could make it out to ride him. Andy and I rode almost daily now, letting Nubbin gallop along behind. The three amigos: Andy, Jay, and me.

Below Annie Chamberlain's house, there were three thousand acres of green valley that lay stretched below Boney Mountain. There was a herd of cattle that grazed there and only one person was living in it. The foreman (forewoman) was Maisy. I heard she was a tough ranch woman who herded the cattle and took care of the entire estate single-handedly.

When I bought Sinbad, I asked Annie if I could ride in those three-thousand acres and she said, "Absolutely not. No one is allowed in the valley, and we respect that. No trespassing, Mr. Brandon."

That was almost two years ago. I was feeling more a part of this landscape now.

I hauled out all the Prince Valiant gear I bought at the Columbia Studios auction. I put Knight's blue saddle pad and horse armor on Sinbad and Prince Valiant's armor on myself, lifted the shield, raised the lance, lowered my helmet visor and rode down into the valley for dragon.

I was charging up a hill with my lance tucked under my arm when an old army Jeep came chasing me. I rode through trees that the Jeep had to go around, but eventually I was cornered. I pulled Sinbad up at the top of a hill.

Maisy, whom I had never met, climbed out of the Jeep and walked briskly up the hill. She stood, arms on her hips, and sternly said, "May I help you?"

I raised my helmet plate. "M'lady, it is for the knight to ask, 'May I be of help to you?'"

She laughed, thank God, and said, "You must be that actor that moved into the Chamberlain place?"

"Guilty as charged. You, Milady must be Maisy of the Valley and it's my pleasure to serve you."

She smiled. "Why don't you follow me to the cabin, and I'll serve you some coffee?"

It was a lovely afternoon and well worth dressing up for. Maisy gave me permission to ride the valley, and the only rule was not to chase the cattle, so no rodeo shit. Fair enough. In gratitude, I offered my services if she needed any manpower, come storms or cattle rustlers. We clinked mugs. Maisy was a bona fide working ranch woman.

There was film work over the next several months, so I had to leave the mountain. I made some good films: a remake of the classic Civil War film *The Red Badge of Courage*, playing the part of Jim Conklin with my longest dying scene ever. The director asked me to find God and, believe me, I did thorough search as my character was JC.

Richard Thomas (John-Boy, *The Waltons*) starred, and we shot on location in Nogales, New Mexico, near the Mexican border. There was one scene when the Yankee army (this Yank included) charged the advancing Confederate troops. The production had hired hundreds of gung-ho local college students and dressed them as soldiers to charge behind us as the Union army. They were all pumped up shouting and stabbing the air with metal bayonets on their mock rifles. Richard and I inquired to the props dept. "Yeah, we know but the rubber bayonets wiggled and looked phony, so we used the metal bayonets". Richard and I shared a wide-eyed look just before they called "Action!" We ran for our lives. A real moment in the film.

Another good film was *Queen of the Stardust Ballroom*. The Broadway and London musicals were based on the film we made. Charlie Durning and Maureen Stapleton were award-winning wonders in this piece. Maureen was playing my mom and acting with her was what I imagined it would be like working with Marlon Brando. She gave me chills with a simple hand gesture. She was an absolute hoot when hanging out on set with Charlie Durning and me. This was just a good working environment. One of the good ones – no egos here, just talent.

One night after filming, the director, Sam O'Steen, took me aside and asked me to do him a favor; would I please drive Maureen back to her hotel and get her there without any stops. Reluctantly I agreed to take Maureen home. She did try to get me to stop at several bars and wine shops (like her real drivers), but I told her my horses were probably eating each other, and I had to get home.

When we got to her hotel, she asked me to walk her to the door. Okay, then she said, "Oh, do me one more favor, please; I can't reach the top of the dresser." There was a bottle of gin stashed on top. She said, "Pour me a drink; there's ice in the fridge, a little ice, a lot of gin," and she went into the bathroom to take off her makeup.

I was just slipping out the door when the phone started ringing and kept ringing. Maybe Sam was making sure I got her back. I answered and a voice said, "Maureen?"

I said, "No, who's calling?"

The voice said, "Mike Nichols."

Wow!

I said, "Look, she's in the shower, can you call back in ten minutes?"

"Who is this?"

"It's Michael Brandon and I'm working on the film with her."

Mike said, "I know, Sam told me everything. Sam is my editor, Michael. I got him this directing gig. Listen, Michael, I need you to do me a favor." (It was do me a favor day.) "Ask Maureen if she's doing my picture?"

"Mike, look, just call back in ten minutes, she'll be out of—"

"I can't wait ten minutes! I got producers on my case right now! I need to know; is she going to do my picture or not?"

Exasperated, I said, "Okay, hold on."

I put the phone down on the desk and knocked on the bathroom door. "Maureen!" I banged away. "Maureen!" I banged till I got a response. I told her, "Mike Nichols is on the phone, and he needs to know right now if you're doing his movie?"

Maureen yelled out one word. "No!"

I got back to the phone. "Hello, Mike, she said 'no.'"

I heard him regretfully say, "Shit," then he said, "Michael, doesn't she like the script?"

Again, I said, "Mike, call back in five and—"

"I need to know now; please ask her if it's the script?"

I went back. "Maureen, Mike wants to know if it's the script?"

She called out, "No, the script is beautiful."

I went back to the phone. "Mike, she says the script is beautiful."

"Then what is it? How can I get her to do this picture?"

"Mike, do you really want me to yell that through a bathroom door? Why don't—"

"Michael, I must decide now! Please ask her."

I put down the phone and went to the door. "Maureen, Mike wants to know how he can get you to do his picture?"

"Tell him to try greed!"

I picked up the phone. "Mike, she said try greed."

I heard him banging a table. "What does she want. What does she want?"

Really, was I doing this? "Hold on … Maureen, he wants to know what you want."

"I told him before!"

"Maureen, tell me what you want, please!"

"I told him, the houseboat on the Hudson."

I walked back to the phone. "Hello, Mike, she said, the houseboat on the Hudson."

Mike Nichols finished the last two words, *the Hudson*, with me. "Okay, okay, tell her if I get her the houseboat on the Hudson, are we good to go?"

"Maureen, you got the houseboat on the Hudson, are you good to go?"

"Tell him I'm quivering with anticipation. I can't wait to start the movie."

When I hung up with Nichols, I realized I should have said, "A houseboat on the Hudson and a small part for Michael Brandon." What a schmuck again!

Patricia - pushing my boundaries.

The filming was over, and I had been alone for months reflecting on everything when I noticed how much Patricia wasn't around. She was a free spirit. Besides I needed the time to absorb what had gone down with Kim. I reflected on how much I was missing her. Not Kim, Patricia. You know how you don't miss something till it's gone? I could smell the emptiness. I had treated Patricia as a part-time girlfriend, while having my relationship with Kim. She knew that and it was fine. Now I guessed it was not fine. Now I saw how not fine that must have been.

It seemed, Patricia had had enough and the realization that I had been a complete asshole hit me hard. She was an amazing girl. She could laugh raucously, passionate, natural and dress up to shame the biggest models of the day. I really did love Patricia, but I came to that understanding too late.

We just blended with each other's life. I would go off to film and she would go off to horse events, and I would go up to Carmel to be with Kim and she....?. I don't know what she did. We were together when we wanted to be. She would show up, spend a week and off she would go. We would ride every day, her Irish Setter, Shane jumping into puddles.

One night lying in front of the fireplace she resolved to pierce my ear lobe. She only had a safety pin handy. I said, it was kind of thick and she said "So is your lobe". I submitted but after a while I sensed something was wrong. She said, it's stuck halfway. I omit the gory details of the story. Okay, I ran around screaming with a big safety pin sticking out of my ear lobe and she chased me trying to shove it through. It was a frightening, funny night.

Once at a celebrity ski party at George Hamilton's house in Aspen, one of the guest celebrities (a singer/TV star) grabbed the little, stuffed bunny rabbit I had given to Patricia. He snatched it out of her bag and teased her. Patricia asked for it back please. He was twisting the head off in make-believe torture. She didn't find it funny and asked nicely for it back, holding out her hand. He wouldn't stop and made the mistake of pushing Patricia too far, so she decked him. He went backwards over the sofa. I was shocked and impressed at the same time. The asshole deserved it and the whole room knew it. They applauded Patricia. She skied better than me, rode better, and once, while I was sizing up a river crossing with my new Jeep, Patricia got behind the wheel and drove my jeep into the river. The very deep river. She was beautiful, fearless and maddening at the same time and had great thighs from holding onto horses for years.

I ran after Patricia when I knew it was her, but she was really gone. I tracked her down at this guy's ranch and went in and begged her to forgive me and come back, but she was done with me and was now with someone else. She was a rare beauty and a special person. She went through my heart like a hurricane. I was left in complete devastation.

I was broken-hearted over Patricia and hardly left my ranch. I would get up and have a coffee, feed the horses, muck out the stalls, make breakfast, saddle up Sinbad and ride up Boney Mountain. Alone on my mountaintop, I'd pull out a bottle of Southern Comfort and sip.

Annie Chamberlain stood in front of my porch door. She came to say that she had decided to sell the ranch. For the first time since I'd met Annie Chamberlain, her eyes were wet with tears not from laughter. My next thought was, *Will I have to move?* If I had thought about the future at all, maybe I would have taken more of the work offered to me. I was always living in the moment. Was the Gutter Confucius, right? Was I *stuck in the now?* I made Annie the best offer I could come up to.

Annie was determined to sell the ranch in one piece, the whole one hundred and eighty acres, and there was no way I could afford that. That's when I met Bob Dylan. He came to look at the ranch and Annie asked me to show him around. He out bid David Cassidy. Maybe I should have told him about the sleeping rattlesnakes?

As we walked down my dirt road from the gate, Bob saw Nubbin following me along the fence line. She wasn't easy to ignore, shaking her head and kicking her hind legs in the air.

Bob asked, "What kind of horse is that?"

We stopped and I petted her neck and said, "She's a mule. Her name is Nubbin. Her mother was Arabian horse and her father a wild jackass." Bob asked if we bred them. "Nope, mules are sterile. You can cross a horse and donkey, but that is where it ends. I don't know why, but it does."

Bob rubbed Nubbin's nose and stared at Nubbin, and I thought he was writing a song. "It's the end of the line, rubbin' nubbin, neigh, neigh, neigh."

Bob bought the ranch for his ex-wife, Sara. She was a lovely woman. After she moved in, she invited me for Thanksgiving dinner. After a great evening, she said she was deeply sorry, but she needed my cabin for staff, so I would have to move out. But in all fairness, she gave me plenty of time to do it.

Luckily, there was another trailer home on the property where Andy lived. No, not a Quonset hut. I worked a deal with Tony Duquette for the other trailer, but he wouldn't let me keep horses on the property. I had been keeping Jay's Appaloosa stallion, Snort, at my barn for a year and now I had to tell Jay, "Snort needs a home as well."

Jay and I galloped across the valley. It was exhilarating to let a horse have his head and let them run full out. Snort and Sinbad were flying over the grass, manes in the wind. It was super exhilarating! They loved the feeling as much as did. As we gave the horses a breather to cool them down, I told Jay, Deer Springs Ranch was *Blowin in the Wind* to Bob Dylan.

Jay nodded to the ridge above my cabin and told me he had just bought that piece of land. He pointed, "Why don't you build a barn on that little strip of land, at front of the property? It won't be in the way of where the house is going to be built, and you can use my architect."

Jay's builder was Cary Smoot. He was an alternative architect, building domes and geothermal dwellings. He was building a horseshoe-shaped house for Jay with horse stalls underneath the house, opening onto a big corral. Mr. Smoot's idea for my tiny barn was to build it in a carousel shape.

I said, "Listen, Cary, cheap and functional; a two-horse stall with a tack room at the back."

He pulled his long scraggly beard and nodded. "A round roof will look great and coincide with Jay's curving structure."

Okay, so we built a carousel roof. The horses were already up there when the Santa Ana winds came blowing up from Mexico. The hot blustery winds come September through May, and I could see the side of the barn being lifted by the force. The wind caught the overhang of the carousel roof.

I quickly wrapped wire around a bolt on the wall of the barn and was securing it to a fence post when a fierce gust lifted the barn straight up into the air with me holding the wire in my gloved hands. The whole barn was straight above me, hovering in the air like a kite! Holding on didn't seem an option unless Annie's friend Margaret, the Wicked Witch, came by on her broom.

I finally wriggled my hands free of the gloves and let go. It hurt when I landed, but I was in one piece as Andy came running over and grabbed me, pulling me out of the way. We just stared at the barn hovering in the air before it took a nosedive down, landing upside-down in the corral.

The horses were all okay, thank God. They huddled together at the opposite fence like they knew something bad was happening. Andy and I secured the horses and started clearing the upside-down carousel roof splayed on the hillside.

At that very moment, Cary Smoots's Mazda pickup pulled up and stopped. He looked at what happened as he pulled his beard, and whistled, "That's some nasty kind of wind you got up here," and drove off to Jay's building site.

Andy and I just looked at each other.

CHAPTER 15

My Bionic Marriage

I was reading when Andy walked up from his place. I now lived a whole minute walk from him. The small barn we built on Jay's land was done; well, redone, into a nice, square, two-stall barn. *No more carousel rides, Toto.*

I was alone except for Andy, who was also alone and broken-hearted after his recent split with Kathy Lloyd (lead actress in *Missouri Breaks* with Marlon Brando). Kathy was a great girl, and I missed her too. Andy and I were two broken-hearted buckaroos. Not heart break mountain.

After searching my fridge, Andy said, "You have even less in yours than I do in mine. We need to do a market run. You're not still reading that same script?"

"Yeah, I keep falling asleep."

"Yes, reading is taxing for you."

"So how are you doing with the heartbreak?"

"Well," said Andy, "I haven't got the energy to kill myself, although it does cheer me up to think you would be the one to find me."

This was how we laughed at ourselves and our miserable situations.

Andy said, "Hey, my agent called today."

I looked up. "Really, your agent called?"

"He was looking for another client who I worked with a few years ago, said the prick didn't show up for a job he booked. Asked me if I had his current number. I said, 'Marty, He died two years ago!' My agent said, "that asshole" and hung up."

"Wow, your agent booked a dead actor!"

"Well, I'm proof that he can't book a living one!" Andy gave up on the fridge. "Listen, Milton Katselas is doing a masterclass tonight."

I replied, "Oooh, a *master*class."

"Hey, Michael. You're stuck on this mountain and you're turning rancid. C'mon, let's go, we'll have a laugh. Should be some well-known people there ready to embarrass themselves."

"Andy, Milton's masterclass is a scientology recruitment cell."

"Milton's a good guy and a talented director," Andy argued. "Besides, you can't be talked into something unless you want to be."

"Like you're doing to me right now? I'll regret this, but okay, you're right, Milton is a good guy. Let's go master classing."

We arrived at the workshop, and I remember walking in the door and stopping short.

Andy piled into me from behind. "What's the problem, boy?"

"Andy, I'm looking at the woman I'm going to marry."

Lindsay was sitting in the first row. The ONE. She was it! I had been hit by the thunderbolt. I walked over and took the seat next to her. I could feel electric sparks jumping between our knees. Really, the feeling was so real I had to look at our knees to make sure.

After some acting exercises and an awful scene with lengthy silences, there was a break. I introduced myself and asked for her number.

She looked me in the eye, took a sip of her drink and finally said, "Ask Vern."

"Vern, who's Vern? Your boyfriend?"

"No, that's my phone number."

Duh! It was the letters for the numbers to dial; it was easier to remember and give out. But that appealed to me. I was always a fan of the 1950s New York prefixes, like Gramercy 1 and Plaza 9. Much better than just numbers; there was a style to it then.

I called Vern for two days, but Lindsay's answering service told me she was out of town. (In the 1970s, answering services were real operators.) I couldn't wait to see her again, so I said I was her doctor and needed to talk to her about some test results. They gave me the number she was staying at. I made a note never to use that answering service.

Lindsay was amazed that I found her. I said I wanted to see her. She told me she was flying back to Los Angeles that evening, so I picked her up in my '74 Jeep Wagoneer.

Lindsay and I were enjoying the ride up the remote canyon road to the ranch until I ran out of gas.

She looked at me. "Is this for real? I'm on a road in the middle of nowhere, with a man I don't know who's telling me he's run out of gas?"

I smiled back. "It's worse than that. It's ten miles to the nearest phone box and five miles to my house, and a car may not pass here before morning."

I was so excited to see her that I forgot about getting gas. Yes, my father owned a gas (petrol) station. But I didn't want to tell her that; it would verify my honorary shmuck status.

Luckily, two minutes later, my friend Jay pulled up next to us, dropped his window, took a good, long, stare at Lindsay, and said to me, "Do you want saving?"

We had a good laugh, and I introduced Lindsay to Jay. We squashed into his two-seater for a rescue ride to the cabin. Jay dropped us off and I didn't go back to get the car for days.

Lindsay stayed on the mountain for a month. That's a pretty good first date, I'd say. There was that life elasticity, making our own time. We laughed tremendously and, other than Andy and Jay sharing a meal, it was just the two of us. We took long rides up Boney Mountain and even rode down to the coast and galloped the horses along the beach. I jumped down off Snort to take her reins and, looking up at her face against the sky, I was stunned by the color of her eyes.

I said, "I can see the sky right through your head." I *meant*, "Your eyes are the same color as the sky." She slid off the horse into my arms smiling.

I eventually had to take her home. We took a half-hour to say goodbye. Lindsay had a studio apartment in Benedict Canyon. It was half of a half a house. The other half was rented by Stuart Whitman's brother Kipp (who resembled Rufus Sewell). They shared a common pathway from the street that split like a Y as it got near the house.

I was coming down one day and passed Stuart Whitman walking up. I happened to be wearing the WWII bomber jacket Kim had given me.

"Hey, Michael, that's an amazing jacket. You know I used to have one just like it."

"Sure you did, next you'll tell me Kim Novak stole it."

I walked on. I could hear Stuart bursting out laughing.

Several weeks later, Lindsay and I went up to visit her family in Oregon. I met her mom, stepdad, and stepsister. We rented a remote cabin and got to know each other better. We didn't put clothes on for days. We picnicked in the forest like elves. I had to leave a couple of days early for an audition in LA. Lindsay stayed and spent time with her family.

I really liked the script for *James Dean: Portrait of a Friend*, written by Bill Bast, who was Jimmy Dean's best friend and college roommate. This intimate story of Jimmy Dean's career meant I had to shave my beard.

My agent shrieked, "Cut your hair, shave the beard, and get the job!" I shaved and auditioned, and I got to play the author, Bill Bast.

I have had the privilege to portray many real people in my career and the honor of playing some who were still living, like Bill Bast. The ability to source living history is phenomenal. Playing Pulitzer Prize winner, Arno Penzias in *Hawking* and Jerry Springer in *Jerry Springer the Opera*, for which I was nominated an Olivier Award for best actor, to name a couple.

Lyndsay came home from Oregon and walked into the house while I was on my knees in front of the mini fridge, my back to her. She said, "Hi Babe", I turned, she saw me, screamed and ran out the door.

I chased her down the canyon, yelling, "It's me, it's me, I shaved!"

Slowly she stopped running and turned toward me. She just stared at me. "So that's what you look like? Not bad." Then she kissed me, and we walked back up the canyon. She tried out my new face to our mutual pleasure.

The filming of the James Dean movie was one of those unique times, when you feel like you're making something special. This wasn't just about a twenty-four-year-old actor who died at the peak of his career. This film was a very personal one, looking inside Bill Bast's relationship with James Dean, as they lived together and studied together in the early days of Dean's career, on way to him becoming a star.

I was able to spend time with Bill, his partner Paul Hudson and many friends who were the real people in Jimmy Dean's life. I asked Bill if I could explore the gay side of the relationship, and he told me this story was not an easy sell to a television network. We had to be careful how we represented things.

There was a scene when Bill and Jimmy go to Browns famous ice cream parlor in Hollywood. I wonder if it was famous before they went there. Over ice cream sundaes they talked about finding apartments. They decide to share an apartment to afford it. While this scene rehearsed, I took my sundae put it on the floor and used my spoon to share Jimmy's sundae. To me it was that little behavior that would blossom. The next day at the same set, Bill came to my trailer. He was upset. He said he had calls from the network, they were coming down to the location. A knock on my trailer door and I admitted three network executives, who were looking for Bill. They asked if I would excuse them, they were asking me to leave my own trailer. I listened at the door. They were concerned about yesterday's scene because homosexuality would not be appropriate on family viewing time in 1976. I excused myself into the trailer conversation, asking what exactly they were referring to? One exec exclaimed, "Why two men are eating the same sundae!" I said, "It's because they are students and can only afford one." They looked at each other relieved, "They could only afford one!" That's what the scene is about, sharing and getting an apartment together. Problem Solved. Bill was holding his heart.

One of the most difficult scenes was after the premiere of East of Eden, when it became clear to Bill, that Jimmy Dean was a movie star. All he dreamed and worked for was really happening. Bill ran home and hid in his bathtub. Jimmy broke into the house to console his friend. I wanted it to be right for Bill and asked if I could view the dailies. The footage we shot the day before, viewed by the production for network executives. He said, they were private, but he would arrange the projectionist to be there after I finished that day's filming. I walked in adjusting my eyes to the dark and found an appropriate seat, when I heard sobbing coming from the front row. I walked down to find Bill curled up in a seat crying.

Finally, he looked at me with huge tears. "You were me, Michael, you were me". (That's as good as it gets).

During our time on the mountain together, Lindsay told me Universal dropped her after her last gig, *The Six Million Dollar Man*. She told me she only did it because it was her stepsister's favorite show. Her contract terminated before the two-part episode aired.

When the *Six Million Dollar Man* episodes aired, they killed her character off in a parachute accident. End of story? No, the public were outraged, saying kids were traumatized by the killing of the hero's girlfriend in a children's show. The attention and ratings made Universal reconsider; they decided to recon Lindsay's character and give her a spin-off series (recon is when they kill off a character and must bring them back to life: *recon-struct*).

Can you imagine the legal department when someone noticed, "We don't have her under contract anymore." Then someone says, "Get her back." (This is the best place an actor can be.)

Lindsay and I were enjoying the calls from agents and Universal executives, holding the phone between our ears. One friendly call from Universal said she was very lucky, because he could get her contract reinstated and probably add a sweet little bump. This was when we hired our new manager, Ron Samuels.

Ronnie said, "You take no more calls from anybody. I do the talking."

We passed the ball to Ron, and he slam dunked it. They offered to double her contract salary, then triple it, and the phone calls kept coming, up to twenty-five times higher, a Tinsel Town lottery.

We were both working actors. Lindsay, on *Bionic Woman*, would pick up a bad guy and throw him, while I was playing a gay man who just picked up a guy... We were becoming a celebrated Hollywood couple, as the "New Two You" in town.

Lindsay was a gorgeous woman, but she had a guy's outlook that was equally attractive. I remember during her series, she had one director who was one of those misogynistic old boys, who kept touching her when sizing up a shot.

He would say to the camera operator, "Where are you cutting this shot?" and put his arm across Lindsay's chest. "Are you cutting here?" and he would rub his arm across her breasts and then move it up and down. "Here?" he asked, moving his arm, "or here?"

Lindsay grabbed him by the balls, "I think we are cutting it right here!"

The director doubled over with a groan and the crew applauded her.

One night at Lindsay's place when we were in bed, she said to me, "What would you do if a movie star asked you to fly to an island, this weekend in a private jet?"

"Well, it depends on what movie star, what island, and whether I was in a relationship at the time."

Lyndsay looked at me "I said yes."

I rolled over to look at her on the pillow next to me. She was smiling and beautiful.

I said, "You said yes to a movie star who asked you to fly to an island for the weekend?"

"Yes."

A moment later, I got up and pulled on my jeans and boots. She looked at me. "What are you doing?"

I looked at her. "What am *I* doing *here* is the question." I grabbed my shirt on the way out the door.

I drove back to Deer Springs. Yes, it was the 70s. No, we didn't own each other but, yes, we were falling in love. That's what I thought anyway. What a night! I put her out of my head; well, I tried.

A night later, I got the call, collect, from an island. She said she made a mistake, she was sorry.

I said, "Forget it. I mean it, I'm done."

"Please, it was a mistake; I'm coming back."

I told her not to bother.

She flew back commercially, and the customs officers looked at her passport and visa, seeing she had flown in privately the day before. They body-searched her as a possible drug smuggler. Had they had known it was the "Bionic Body", it would have made international news.

She drove out to the ranch. I didn't want to see her. Her actions had spoken volumes to me. I could hear the Gutter Confucius: *Remember, son, when you're looking at the ocean, you're only seeing the top of it.*

She cried and cried; it was a long night. I told her and myself that there was no going back. *We're done.* But morning had us hugging and in love again.

Life changed for us both the more famous she became. And she became very famous. The hottest female actress on network television. It got harder to find time to nourish our relationship.

Once, she had the limo driver take her all the way up to my ranch. The driver spent an hour on his knees throwing up after driving the limo up the canyon road. We tried.

Andy and Jay were taking more care of the horses, as I was staying in town. I was getting calls from Lindsay's friend, Linda, who became Lindsay's PA, calling me about dinner dates and restaurants and arranging our social life. The hours Lindsay was working, were overwhelming her. Playing the lead in a TV series is all consuming.

The Benedict Canyon studio apartment was just too small, and we had no real kitchen, so we decided to find a house together. It was late 1975.

One Sunday morning, we had a viewing of a house that came to us privately. It belonged to the 1950s rock star Ricky Nelson. He starred on the *Ozzie and Harriet* TV show (Ricky was a 1950s version of David Cassidy). The house was off Coldwater Canyon. We stopped by the iconic deli in Beverly Hills, Nate and Al's, and picked up food for brunch first, then went off to view the house.

We were heading up Coldwater with the top down on a sunny, Sunday morning, when the car took off, jumped the curb and hit a big tree. My head got caught on the convertible hook and slammed me back in my seat. I remember my hands floating up and down in front of me and I couldn't see out of my right eye from the blood.

Lindsay was hurt as well but she was more conscious than me. Her lip was split, torn and bleeding, and her arms were embracing her chest.

I looked at the tree and then the house set back off the street, and people were standing in their doorways, pointing at us.

A guy came from behind and took my hand and he placed it over my forehead. He said, "Hold this here 'till the ambulance comes. I'm a paramedic. You need to hold it in place." Then he ran back to his car.

I don't remember how long it was, but there was a doctors' strike at the time. They were protesting malpractice insurance, so when we finally got to the hospital, it was a long time waiting on a gurney parked in a hallway. A nurse was asking me insurance questions and all I said was, "Call Ron Samuels," and strangely enough, I could remember his number. "Tell him we were in a car crash and to come quickly."

Ronnie was in Palm Springs. He jumped in his Porsche and was at the hospital in forty-five minutes. Half the normal driving time. He got Lindsay a doctor and, once she was being seen, he hunted for a surgeon. I needed surgery; my head was torn open.

No doctors.

Ronnie grabbed a guy and dragged him over to me.

The man said, "I'm not a plastic surgeon. I'm a micro-surgeon."

"You're saying you can't do it?" Ronnie said.

Dr Selsby (wow, I just remembered his name) said, "That's not what I said. I'm a micro-surgeon. I sew cells together. He needs a plastic surgeon."

Ronnie said, "There isn't one, so what I want to know is, can you do it, and can you do it well? This man is an actor, and his face is his trade. We don't want a patch-together job that means lots of plastic surgery later. Can you do it right?"

Dr Selsby said, "Okay, let's get him to the OR."

I opened my eyes, well, eye I should say, and saw the entire agency of Creative Artists standing there around my bed. Now some people would like to see their mothers, wives, or children, but an actor wants to see his agents. There were five agents in the newly formed Creative Artists Agency. They were the entire agency, and they were all there: Mike Ovitz and Ron Meyer; Bill Haber; Mike Rosenfeld; and Rowland Perkins. The founders of what is today a three hundred agent, and three-thousand, four-hundred client, office – and the most powerful agency in the world. A moment later, Ronnie, my manager entered reassuring me, "Lindsay is fine, they stitched her lip and sent her home yesterday". Ron Meyer said, "The accident hasn't been released to the news. The police department thought you were Michael Landon. (*Little House on The Prairie*) They know he's married, so they squelched the story." (Old Hollywood – that would never happen again.)

I felt my bandaged head and said, "So, it looks like monster roles from now on, hey boys?"

They all laughed, and Mike Ovitz said, "No, I spoke to your doctor, and he said you'll be good as new." A comic-writer, Fred Allen once said, "If you took all the sincerity in Hollywood, it would fit in the navel of a flea and there would still be room for two caraway seeds and the heart of an agent'. However, due respect, these guys were the best of the best.

It turned out that Dr Selsby did get it right. I never needed anything further. I had a huge bandage over my head and one eye. I got up and read the report in the file at the foot of the bed. He rebuilt the orbital lobe surrounding my right eye. It collapsed three times in the process, but he got it right in the end. I owe him and Ronnie Samuels a load of thanks. The doctors believed the accident was caused by Lindsay developing secondary anemia caused by exhaustion from overwork. That was the most likely reason for her blacking out while driving. My father said "And you didn't sue? Schmuck!" I couldn't sue my wife pop.

I finally got back to the studio apartment in Benedict Canyon. Lindsay was moving about gently, as she'd severely bruised her ribs on the steering wheel. Her lip had been torn in half, and she had tape sutures across it. The most difficult medical instruction was not to laugh. We couldn't look at each other. We cuddled our way to wellness. But the studio kept calling to get her back to work and finish the episode because they'd had to keep actors under contract to complete it.

It wasn't easy going back to work, but she finished all the episodes. To help herself deal with the demands and stress, Lindsay said we needed to go see a shaman. A man named Oscar Ichazo. He had a school in New York city called Arica. We flew to New York. Arica was basically meditation and philosophy put in Oscar's unique way. I attended with an open mind, but I had trouble with certain aspects.

He sensed it and said, "What's holding you back?"

I told him it was all the religious references.

He was unfazed. "Okay. For you, I think you must substitute instead of Divine or Godly, it's Consciousness. This is okay with you?"

I said, "Yeah, that works."

We had dinner with Oscar at his apartment, and after, he served Cognac and lit up a cigarette.

I was stunned. "Here you are, a guru and meditation teacher, and you're smoking and drinking?"

"This relaxes me," he said. "Many people think I am the school, I am Arica. No, I am Oscar. So, I have a cigarette, but only one. I do it with consciousness. If you are conscious of your actions and in control of your actions, this is okay. The mind likes to make noise. In Chile, we call the noise of many chickens rubbing their legs together, chicharoo. All minds make this chicharoo. You must still the chicharoo in your mind."

Oscar was a wizard. I thank Lindsay for introducing us.

I asked Lindsay to marry me. She mulled it over and her response was "Let's go see *Snow White,* it's on at the Pantages Theatre on Hollywood Boulevard." As we sang along with the dwarfs Lindsay turned to me and said, yes!

Andy and his new girlfriend, Debra Winger, who was playing Wonder Woman's little sister at the time, gave us a gift of a personal reading by an internationally famous astrologist. We rolled our eyes, but it was L.A. The astrologer clucked her tongue and shook her head. She had never seen so many planets in conjunction; there was no choice in our paths crossing. Did that mean it was unpreventable or destiny?

The ceremony itself was Lindsay's choice, in a Church of all Faiths that had my mother's shitty smell expression working overtime. She had an allergic reaction to the word "church".

My brother picked up mom's look, "Mom's not happy you're getting married in a church, but hey, it's your wedding."

Everybody came back to the house for food and music, and my grandfather, Hymie, was my best man. *Sorry Bro, but Grandpa was 89.*

We went to Sun Valley, Idaho, on our honeymoon. Neither of us skied but we had a lot of fun playing in the snow. My friend Scott Glenn was living up there and introduced us to a realtor, who found us a special piece of land on the river. We bought it complete with an old rusty mining cart on a section of track from the mining days. We would build our cherry creek log cabin there.

Later that year we chartered a private jet to see how our cabin was coming along. We took Andy and Debra on a laugh-till-we-land jet ride. Lindsay lifting champagne, "This is why I do a series" Amen from us all.

Lindsay found a house she wanted to buy in Coldwater Canyon. It was on the valley side of the canyon, (closer to the studio) and mostly on a hill but very private. The main house needed to be torn down. We moved into the guest cabin painted a vibrant blue with yellow flowers on it. It wasn't much bigger than her apartment, but it had a kitchen.

Lindsay was nominated for an Emmy Award for Best Actress in a TV Series and won. I was very proud; she had worked so hard playing a double role and she really deserved it. These were happy times.

On a Sunday morning (very early morning, I might add), the buzzer on the intercom was blasting. We looked at the clock and each other. Who would dare ring the doorbell on a Sunday morning?

I staggered to the intercom. "Go away, whoever you are."

A bland voice responded, "Mr. Brandon, it's the FBI."

Lindsay got up, jamming her finger on the intercom. "If that's you, Bear [her motorhome driver], I will have you shot and stuffed."

The voice repeated, "It's the FBI, and we need to have a word with you. May we come in, please?"

"The FBI? Why are they here?"

"Do we have any grass?"

"I'll go to the gate."

I pulled on my jeans and zigzagged down our driveway to the gate (we were on a steep hillside). I was staring at three guys in suits standing at our gate. They were staring at me.

I said, "Can help you, boys? It's six-thirty on a Sunday morning."

They held up identity cards. "Mr. Brandon, we need to speak to you and your wife over a matter of some urgency."

Okay, I clicked open the gate, and we all hiked up. I took them into the kitchen, which was quite small. I sat them on the bench behind the table. I figured I could pin them in together if we needed time to escape (you can take the boy out of Brooklyn…).

"We're here in response to a conversation that was overheard in a restaurant, by the person who reported this incident to the FBI."

They told us a conversation had taken place between three men and a woman who were planning a kidnap that included Lindsay Wagner. They discussed plans to kidnap Farrah Fawcett and another girl from Charlie's Angels, with Lindsay being the third girl to be kidnapped. The plans overheard were deemed credible because these people had information on how the Charlie's Angels actresses entered the hotel on location and how they were picked up in the basement by vans that took them to the set.

Lindsay and I looked at each other. I asked what they were planning to do about it. This was all they could do for the time being. The investigation would be ongoing, but for now all they were required to do was inform us. Inform us at 6:30 in the morning that my wife was about to be kidnapped and *see you around*! They could have ruined our Sunday at 9:30 instead of 6:30.

Universal was arranging for armed security guards to be at our property. Three eight-hour shifts – starting tomorrow. We called Bear, who as well as being Lindsay's motor home driver was an ex-paratrooper and unofficial bodyguard.

He came straight over and dumped a duffle bag of guns on our table. "You need these. You gotta be ready." That put a coating of calm on the picture.

Lindsay decided on the derringer with the ivory butt handle. It was small and fit well in her bag. I put the 357 under my car seat and kept the 45 next to the bed. We were armed and ready. Bring on the nappers! This insanity went on for weeks. Nothing from the FBI!

Then one night in the early morning hours, a gunshot! A loud BANG outside the house, in the driveway, where the security guard was posted in his vehicle.

I pushed Lindsay into the closet with her derringer, and said, "Stay there", while I took the 45 and crawled out through the bushes to the driveway. From the foliage, I could see a big hole in the windshield of the security guard's car. *Fuck, I think they shot him.* Meanwhile, the bushes were shredding my penis.

I called out, "You hit?"

The guard was almost squealing with his reply. "I'm okay, I'm sorry, I'm very sorry about this."

"What's going on?" I yelled as I came out slow and naked from the bushes.

He said, "I'm so sorry. I was cleaning my gun, and it went off."

I told him to get off the property. *Just go!* I immediately went (carefully) to find Lindsay.

I called out, "It's me, baby, don't shoot, it's all okay."

When I told her what happened, she was angry and then looked at me standing there naked with my gun and burst out laughing. We laughed in relief, but we both agreed, we had enough of the guns for a while.

We decided to inform the press. If the kidnappers knew that we knew, wouldn't that sort of nullify the threat. That was our thinking anyway, and it's what we should have done the day the FBI informed us.

It proved correct. James Garner called. He was an old friend of Lindsay's. She had guested on *The Rockford Files* when she was under contract to Universal.

Garner said, "Did the FBI come to you with this story of kidnap?"

We said, "Yes."

"Call them and ask them if the person who brought this story to them was an Australian woman who overheard this plot in a restaurant."

He told us a similar event took place some years ago with him. Turned out to be some nutjob who made up the whole story. Sure enough, the FBI confirmed that she was a New Zealand lady, and they were going to pick her up for questioning. I believe she was later deported and that was that. the Gutter Confucius said, "It's the gravity down there, makes them crazy and their toilets flush backwards."

I bought Lindsay a golden retriever puppy for her birthday, and we named it Pooka. (Pookas are animal guardian spirits.)

Anheuser Busch was opening a new brewery and theme park on the East Coast and wanted Lindsay to open the park. They sent a private jet. Okay, a getaway for us but surprisingly, James Garner was aboard the flight. We watched tens of thousands of people screaming to meet Lindsay and then I was a captured audience on the return trip. He had a TV pilot to push called *Scott Free*. I agreed to make *Scott Free* based on a man who was a gambling rogue. Of course, by the second script he's pressured to work for the FBI. The opening was great, I bet an entire bar I could get any alley cat to pick up a beer on the floor and put it on the bar. They could pick the cat. It worked too! But the TV pilot *Scott Free* never reached the wondrous heights promised on the jet ride.

I was working on an original movie script called *Starman*. It was a Romeo and Juliet story in space. Love between a male alien and an Earth girl. It was a story of the power of consciousness and love from within.

I finished a rough draft of *Starman*, and I called my main agent at CAA, Ron Myer, and he set up a meet with Roland Perkins, the agency's literary agent. I gave Roland my pitch and he loved the idea, and in record time made a production deal with Universal Studios to develop *Starman* as a feature film.

I always wanted to be a writer and now I was official – a member of the Writers Guild West. I continued working on another draft of the script.

I got a call from Harve Bennett, the *Bionic Woman's* executive producer. He asked if I would meet with him. At the meet, Harve uncovered an easel-size painting of Starman. Yes, Starman, an illustration of me with a galactic backdrop. Very compelling art work.

"What's that, Harve?"

"The cover of TV guide, Michael. Well, it will be, if we make *Starman* a two-part *Bionic Woman* special during sweeps week [when the ratings are measured]. Then a spinoff series!"

I was stunned – where did he get my script? "Harve, *Starman* is a movie."

Harve said, "You know how many more millions will see it on TV, Michael? And there's a spinoff series here. You're Starman, and it's a big payday to boot."

"Thank you, Harve, but no thank you." I headed straight for Lindsay's trailer. I felt betrayed.

"You gave Harve my script?"

"Oh, honey, think about it," she said. "We've always wanted to work together and this way, not only do we get to work together, but you get a series out of it as well."

"I don't want to do a TV series, Lindsay." Touchy stuff because there was a stigma attached to television actors that they were less than movie actors.

"All we talk about is working together. Don't you want to work with me? Please, honey, be great." Gutter Confucius yells, "*Take the deal!*"

Love in the afternoon in a trailer and guess what? I was TV Starman.

My agent negotiated the deal with Harve, for me to write and star in the two-part *Bionic Woman* special of *Starman*.

I submitted my script to Harve, and he said, "Okay, it's good. I like his powers to change his molecular structure, and the love story elements are great, but we need a time clock, something to create tension from the get-go."

It was a romantic story, so I was joking when I said, "How about he comes from space to see the last Superbowl because the Earth is dying? We open on the Universal logo, which is the Earth alone in space, then it blows up. The Earth only has forty-eight hours left."

Harve leapt out of his chair. "I love it! I love it! Oh my God!" He was raving about the opening. He immediately called the legal department to find out if we could blow up the Universal logo. *Why not?*

He gushed, "It's a Universal project. Once the studio name is gone and the Earth is alone in space, it's ours to destroy!"

I didn't have the guts to tell him I was joking. I was numb when I left his office. I returned home to begin work on blowing up the Universal logo and watching the last Superbowl.

Okay, I began writing the two-part final draft with the time clock. But the amazing thing was that I was placing a lot of ancient and contemporary philosophy into the story without getting preachy. This was probably the noblest thing I had ever done. The power is within.

Lindsay and I took a break and went to Hawaii. On a remote island hideaway with private huts that nobody knew about. At the weekend luau (they cook a pig in the ground with hot rocks). At the place nobody knows, we met Rob Reiner and Penny Marshall, (*Laverne and Shirley*) doing the same thing. We got on great, so we all rented a car to visit a volcano. Lindsay and I were in the back laughing hysterically while Rob, who was driving, reached back with his hand to try to separate us like noisy kids in the back of a car.

"Don't make me pull over and come back there, you'll be sorry. I'm warning you."

At dinner, I told Rob and Penny my *Starman* story, and they loved the concept. Penny suggested I meet this guy who claimed he was kidnaped by aliens and given a body probe. One would think aliens have nothing better to do than traverse the galaxy giving colonoscopies?

Rob asked me if I played tennis.

I replied, "Not really."

He said, "Let me put it this way, have you ever held a racquet?"

"I've done that."

"Great," he said, "meet me at the tennis court at 10 a.m. tomorrow. "

I did, and there were banners stretched around the village that read: *Celebrity Tennis Tournament, Rob Reiner and Michael Brandon take on the Pros.* I was freaking out, but Rob was confident of winning.

"Just duck and stay out of the way," he instructed me, "we'll be fine."

We weren't fine, we were losing terribly, and he just smashed his second racquet. He was about to smash a third, but Penny's famous "Laverne and Shirley" voice echoed across the court: "Nice try, honeee." His arm froze in the air.

The audience laughed, we all laughed except Rob, not outwardly.

Whenever something funny happened, and lots did, Rob didn't laugh. He just said, "That's funny."

I asked Rob, a very funny man, about his not laughing. He said, "I'm a comedian. Comedians don't laugh; we just say *that's funny.*"

That holiday, I made it my mission to make him laugh. When I finally did, Rob lost it completely, on the floor, on his back, with his legs in the air. That's when he said, "You should do stand-up!" From Rob's mouth to God's ears, as my mother would say.

My agent called that week, with a TV movie special playing a stand-up comic! I accepted immediately. I love things happening like that.

The best part of the Comedy Company film was working with George Burns. A comedy classic. He went back to the black-and-white television days of George and Gracie. He was a living legend. He made the film *Oh God!* and the sequel. George arrived and looked like a small, old man climbing into his trailer. Then out came George in his tux and cigar.

"Hiya, kid, let's go to work." George told me he'd just come back from doing a Vegas stand-up. He said his dressing room was right next to all the long-legged chorus girls with the giant bazungas. "There was a hole in the dressing room wall, and you could see everything." George sighed. "I plugged it up. Why drive them crazy?"

I made another TV movie with Bill Devane (*Marathon Man*), working as a security team at a nuclear facility. A disgruntled ex-employee plants a bomb in the reactor. It was called *Red Alert,* filmed in Houston, Texas, at NASA Space Center. They have a gravity control container with a huge door that weighs ninety tons. You can push it with one finger, I did, and you feel like Superman. We were on location there for weeks.

I was living in a hotel near NASA. One night a bunch of us were in a local bar after filming. Anyway, I wound up in the hotel room of someone from the crew. I was back in my room an hour later, head in hands, guilty over what I had done. Nobody would know, but I knew, and it was tormenting me. Lindsay set the bar; she asked that we be completely honest with each other.

I told this to our friend Michael ("Mickey") Callan, who picked me up from the LAX airport. (Mickey had been under contract to Screen Gems/Columbia and because of the restrictions in his contract, he lost out on the film role of *West Side Story*, a part he created on Broadway.)

He said, "You're not going to tell her."

I said, "Mickey, I have to. I had a realization over this, and I never need to ever be with anyone but the woman I love, and she'd want me to share this."

He groaned. "Look, I've been married three times, okay? Please listen to me! Women say they want you to tell them the truth, but they really don't want to hear it. You just live with it. Trust me on this, Michael."

I said, "Lindsay is different. She made me promise to have a totally honest relationship. We have an agreement."

Mickey swerved to the roadside and stopped the car. "That is a crock of shit. It's a fucking trap! Don't do it! I'm begging you."

"Mickey, you don't know Lindsay like I do."

Mickey yelled back, "And you don't know women like I do!"

With true humiliation and shame, I told Lindsay what happened. I begged her forgiveness and understanding. It reminded me of the night at the ranch when Lindsay came back from the island. Now the shoe was on the other foot.

Lindsay didn't speak. She just listened. I assured her that the lesson I learned from this would last forever. Our love was truly the most important thing.

She looked at me as tears ran from her eyes. "You burst the bubble!"

Top: Between Takes with Tony Curtis & Kim Novak on *Third Girl From The Left;*
Middle Left: A Crystal Bridge -the network called it Spit! The binned frame from
Third Girl From The Left; Bottom Left: Kim on Granpa's Flag, Bottom Right:
With Grandpa outside his store in NYC.

Top Left: With Kim in Carmel, Top Right: With Ume; Middle Left: Grandpa on Sinbad, Middle Right: Duelling cigars Pop & Grandpa; Bottom: Mom meets cow!

Top: First Time Riding Nubbin; Middle: Deer Springs ranch gate; Bottom: Out for a ride up Boney Mountain.

Top Left:Harvest Season, working for my share of the hay;
Middle Left: The upside down barn, Middle Right: On Sinbad;
Bottom : Ranch talk with Jay.

Top: Taking a break form building Jay's ranch; Middle: My Jeep Wagoneer and Trailer at Pop's gas station; Bottom: Photo Shoot With Debra Winger (credit Jonathan Exely).

Top Left: With Balou, Andy & Debra's Dog; Top Right: Feeling at one with the world, Middle: Mountain Man, Bottom Right: Embarrassing Beefcake shot.

Top: In *Another Side Of Us* With Lindsay, laughing between takes, Middle Left: With Lindsay Wagner, Middle Right: Divorce Headlines; Bottom Left: Escape to Hawaii following my divorce and filming *Vacation In Hell,* Bottom Right: With my best friend, Andy Rubin.

Dear Mike,

    This past Oct. 2 fight was certainly a milestone in my career and an event that will go down in history. I'm blessed to be one to have accomplished my lifes goals. It takes a lot of hard work, dedication, and most of all, friends like you. Thanks for all your encouragement and support.

                Your friend,

                Larry Holmes
                Heavyweight Champion
                of the World

Top Left: As William Bast in James Dean – *A Portrait Of A Friend 1976*
Top Right: Playing James Conklin In *The Red Badge of Courage* 1974
Bottom: With Larry Holmes Heavy Weight Champion, His Brother, Don King and other boxers, (Above a signed note he sent me).

CHAPTER 16

Doomed!

I ruined the marriage. I singlehandedly burst the bubble. I killed us. I should have just kept my mouth shut and learned to live with my guilt. There was no reason to hurt her with my stupid confession. But I truly bought into the honest relationship agreement. Let me not diminish the fact that I burst the marriage bubble, and that's the bottom bubble. I should have taken Mickey's advice and sucked it up. But this was my first marriage, unlike him and his third. Famous words: *I thought I was doing the right thing.* The right thing is not necessarily the good thing.

A few weeks later, Lindsay and I were trying to get back on track. Easy to say a few weeks later, but it was like the earth being off its axis. Everything was so uncomfortable. Nothing said is taken well. I felt like I didn't deserve to breathe the same air. Walking on eggshells. We were still estranged as we cruised in the rare car I bought from our manager, Ron Samuels. He bought it for his new wife Lynda Carter (*Wonder Woman*). The Italia was too wild a ride for Linda to enjoy. We took Mulholland Drive with the twinkling lights of Los Angeles below. No romance up there, so we headed down to the Westwood Playhouse to see a new play, written, directed, and performed by Steve Martin. He's usually a hysterical performer, not that night. Maybe it was me.

I couldn't take it. I had to get out. It was torture. I fought my way over Lindsay's legs. She didn't want me to leave. She hissed, "You can't leave," but I was on my knees in the aisle and did a four-legged scoot out of the theater. In the lobby, there was a bar.

I climbed on a stool and said, "Corona, please."

A voice behind me said, "Make it two and I'm paying." Paul Newman took the stool next to me and said, "I was trapped. Joanne wouldn't let me leave. Then I saw you hop into the aisle, and I did the same." We clinked, "To freedom!"

As we drank, Paul saw my car out the window, parked across the street. "What the fuck is that?"

Paul Newman was a car fanatic and racer. I told him what only the owner could know; it was an Italia/Apollo, body designed by Ghia in Italy and powered by an American Ford Shelby Cobra engine. Boys and toys chat almost always trumps the theatre offering.

As we crossed the street for a closer inspection, Paul asked, "How does she ride?"

"Tricky," I said. "You step down too hard on the gas and it's like a jet engine on a broom stick. She'll go sideways on you."

He nodded. "How fast?"

I told Paul about the pre-dawn drive I made with three other cars to Edwards Air Force Base to watch the recent Space

Shuttle launch, maintaining speeds of 145 to 160 mph for hours.

Paul examined the undercarriage like a doctor and said, "You're lucky to be alive, my friend. Here's the number of my mechanic, let him look at it. Seriously, you are lucky to be alive." Paul's mechanic was an artist. Since there were no parts available, he was very inventive using airplane parts. Thank you Paul.

Lindsay was in Vegas shooting an episode of *Bionic Woman,* where she played an undercover beauty contestant and had to sing. She was out of her comfort zone and feeling nervous, so I called a musician friend of mine, Kenny Rankin (*Blackbird*), and he helped sort out what they wanted her to sing and how she should be recorded.

I was writing *Starman* in the kitchen, there was no one else around. I used the kitchen counter as my desk, papers, and notes everywhere (there were no computers then). All my writing was in longhand. I didn't use a typewriter. Every day I worked on the *Bionic/Starman* love story and hoped to restore our own love story. Our bubble was leaking love and losing altitude.

I got a call from Ron Meyer at CAA. He said, "There's this movie, *FM*, a rock'n'roll movie with Linda Ronstadt, The Eagles, Tom Petty, Eileen Brennen, and your friend Cleavon Little (Cleavon and I did an episode of *Police Story*. The Network loved our two-cop buddy relationship and wanted to do a series called Black and White. A take-off of us and what they call Los Angeles police cars. Good idea but neither of us interested.

"John Alonzo, the great cameraman, is directing, and they want to meet you for the lead." Ron hesitated. "One problem. It goes at the same time as your *Bionic Woman* thing." Then he added, "The movie can't change its start date, I asked, however, Lindsay's series is a big hit and pretty much guaranteed to be on next season. Put the *Bionic* thing on the back burner."

"Ron, the *Bionic* thing is my wife!"

Ron said, "I get it, believe me, I am your friend as well as your agent, but this is a lead in a movie. Let me call Harve Bennet and see if it's possible to move *Starman* to the opening of next season."

I love Ron Meyer. He's a great guy, a friend, and the best agent. But I think we got this one wrong. It was a particularly sensitive time and choosing to do *FM* was choosing the movie over her. I think that's how she felt about it. I put her second and I let her down. It's complicated.

I had a great meeting at Universal for *FM*. The room was mixed. The outcome was I would have to test for it.

I had to audition for *FM*. Some Universal exec wanted a contract player to star in the film. Other producers wanted me. It came down to a screen test between us. I was given three scenes, and the director would film the scenes on stage with the contract player first from nine in the morning till noon, and with me from 1 to 4.

I worked on the scenes in Lindsay's studio dressing room. She was using her trailer that day. It was after 2 p.m. and they were still working with the other actor. Then it was three and I was really sweating it.

"It's clear they don't want me," I told Lindsay when she came to see how it was going.

She hugged me to give me confidence. It felt so good. I was starting to hope I might get my girl back. I felt Lindsay was okay with this.

I got a call at 3:30 to go to the set.

John Alonzo (the director) said, "I'm really sorry about this, but I only have time to shoot one of the scenes with you." Before I could tell them the scene I wanted to do, John said, "We are already lit for the office scene. Let's get straight on it. See that dartboard? You throw a dart and the camera swish pans to you, and you begin the dialogue."

"John," I said, "I've never thrown a dart in my life, and it's not in the script."

John confided, "I know but I love darts, I'm a dart freak. I'll win half this crew's paychecks during the shoot. Just do your best. *Okay, let's shoot!*"

He called, "Action!"

I threw a dart. It missed the board, hit the wall, and sank to the floor, just like my chances of getting this job.

"Cut! We'll do it one more time and Michael, when you throw a dart, it's overhand, not underhand." John demonstrated the proper throw.

Why bother me telling me how to throw a dart, when the camera didn't even see me throw it? He had the camera aimed at the dartboard. I felt like walking out. The other guy got to do three scenes, and I get leftovers. I was burning. In my head, I heard the Gutter Confucius, *there will always be people who want to fuck you over, but you don't have to spread your cheeks for them.* You are so right, Pop.

I tightened my cheeks. "OK, Let's do this, John."

He called, "Action!"

I threw that dart like the opening pitch Lindsay threw for Tommy Lasorda at the Dodgers' World Series game, only much, much harder, and *whack*. I hit the bullseye! The camera swished at me and the expression on my face was for real! I felt like I just won the lottery! I waltzed through the scene doing imitations of Cleavon Little and Eileen Brennan, already cast as DJs in the film. I nailed the sucker. I remember one of the Roman novels I read. The centurion pulled his sword and called to his outnumbered Legion. "Let's do Honor by our standard men"

Late morning, a limousine cruised up our steep driveway and the driver opened the trunk and took out a huge, gold-wrapped package. I opened it, and it was the dart board with a note stuck to the bullseye with a dart. The note said: *Start Practicing! Congrats, John Alonzo.* The director sent me the dart board; I got the film.

Harve Bennet, the *Bionic Woman* producer, said he could live with the delay, and added that it would give us more time to prepare the episodes' special effects and get more publicity for the show.

I never felt worse about getting the lead in a movie. How weird was that? I was losing my direction, at odds with myself. Delaying *Starman* might be the best thing for us all.

The film, *FM*, was about a revolutionary rock station with eccentric DJs and managed by my character, Jeff Dugan. The Q-SKY radio station set was built on a soundstage with multi-tilting windows on every recording booth. Director/ Cameraman John Alonzo could get a reflection of Tom Petty giving a radio interview and then focus through the reflection into the next studio where REO Speedwagon was being recorded. One shot involved a very complex scene with multiple focus changes through reflections, and it worked so exactly that John Toll, the very quiet camera operator, who never said a word, jumped off the camera with a full backflip. My friend, John Toll went on to become a famous DP himself and shot *Legends of the Fall* and *Braveheart* and won Oscars for his work.

It was James Garner who was the bearer of bad news. I was in the first week of filming *FM* and, during a break, Bear, Lindsay's motor home driver tapped me and nodded for me to follow him outside. James Garner was waiting around the stage corner to where Bear led me.

Garner said, "We need to talk." He leaned very close and whispered something politically incorrect. Basically, the gist was that Lindsay was sleeping with a stunt man from her crew. "No one likes this, Michael," he said, "The tower is very concerned." (The Black Tower was the name given to the executive building) "Your wife is the biggest star on TV and the biggest female star Universal has got. It's a kids show after all and if the press finds out about this, the show will get cancelled. Her career will be over. Besides, everybody on this lot likes you and they hate seeing this kind of shit happen."

Bear whispered, "The Teamsters will take care of this."

"I will take care of this," and I walked to my car.

I screeched up to Lindsay's Bionic set, waving her into the car.

She said, "Michael, we're in the middle of shooting."

I pushed open the passenger door. Lindsay waved I need ten to an assistant and got in and I drove to the back lot. Bruce, the shark from *Jaws*, was sticking out of a dried-up pond with its wires hanging out. No metaphor there, right?

"How did you know?" she asked. I kept Garner and Bear out of it.

"Seems, I am the last to know, everyone on the studio lot knows. They're probably adding it to the studio tours."

"You're not going to get him fired, are you?"

I articulated, "Your friend has the prospects of losing more than his job right now. If this show tanks, the entire crew will lose their jobs."

She got angry with me over that; she loved her crew. No pun intended. I told her, "End this today. I mean it, tell him it's over and then we get ourselves sorted out." When she left the car, we seemed to have an understanding. We looked at each other, and I drove off.

I waited for her home. I called the studio and found out *Bionic* wrapped at 7 p.m. She walked in at 2 a.m. She sat, took a deep breath, and said she wanted to work things out. Phew! my first breath in hours.

"Did you tell him it's over?"

"How about if he lives in the main house?" It was like getting hit by a tsunami. And that was the end of that. I walked out the door and spent the rest of the night in my trailer at the studio. I never spent another night in that house.

Before we completed *FM*, we had to fly to Houston, Texas, to film a Linda Ronstadt concert. I was unpacking in my room when John Alonzo knocked. John was one of the best cinematographers in the business. He had been nominated for Chinatown, Black Sunday, Norma Rae, and Scarface. The list goes on and on. John was a legend, and FM was his first directing gig. He asked me if I wanted to take a little trip with him to see Linda Ronstadt perform that night. "She's performing in Nacogdoches".

"God Bless you."

John laughed, "I was born in Texas, y'know, Nacogdoches is about a two-and-a-half-hour drive south of here. I'd get a peek at what I'm filming tomorrow night, and you would get a chance to ask Linda about saying a line connecting you to the FM broadcast."

"That's five hours in a car; I thought this was a rock and roll movie?"

He said, "Fuckin A, let's get a jet!"

We jetted into Nacogdoches airport. As we walked into the backstage area, a voice called, "Hey Michael!"

I turned to the open arms of my friend Kenny Rankin. "Kenny, what are you doing in Nacogdoches?"

"I'm the opening act for Linda. What are *you* doing in Nacogdoches?"

"We're filming the Houston Concert tomorrow, and I just wanted to say Hi and clear some words for her to say but I don't really know her".

Kenny said, "Well, let's sort that out right now."

He did a special knock on a door. Waddy Wachtel, one of the best guitar players in the business, opened it. Kenny warmly introduced me, and I was sitting with Linda and her band. Kenny nodded to me and left to do his set.

When it was showtime, Linda said, "Come back after the show and we can talk about the film."

After a truly great concert I went back to the dressing room.

"So, Linda, about tomorrow's concert in Houston?" I asked. "The director, John Alonzo, is one of the best cinematographers in the business. There'll be cameras moving all around you, but you're hip to all that."

Linda absorbed this. "Do I have to say anything?" (Hmm, very savvy.)

"Yes, if you would say one line, it can be on the floor by your microphone. You'll say, 'I want to thank Jeff Dugan,' that's me in the movie, 'and Q-SKY Radio for broadcasting this concert live.' And if you point to me that would be dynamite."

Linda nodded. "How will I know where you are?"

"Wherever you point, the editor will put me – the magic of movies,"

She pondered and nodded okay.

"Can I give you a lift to Houston? I got a jet."

She said, "So do we. Want to race?"

Okay, the band was now hollering, "Jet race to Houston!" We took off, one after the other, flying next to each other in the air. OMG! Close enough to see her laughing and wave at each other. John said, "Wish I had a camera with me now, this would make great footage. Their plane may be bigger, but this is the latest Learjet. She can't win."

"She will definitely win"

John laughed and put his arm around my shoulder, "Y'know, Brandon. You're not just a pretty face."

Linda gave a great concert; the filming went brilliantly, and Linda was extraordinary. She said the line and pointed at me. We partied afterward, as you did then. Kenny Rankin and I got to catch up and I thanked him for his help with Lindsay as well as me. Then we flew back to Los Angeles.

Back at Universal Studios, Jimmy Buffet put the final chord to his *Margaritaville* set. We stepped outside the stage door for a smoke and were about to light up when a limousine came squealing around the corner.

Lindsay's head was poking up out of the sunroof, her hair blowing like the wild snakes of Medusa. She threw the script pages into the air and screamed, "Doomed!"

Jimmy, still holding his lighter, was frozen in total shock. I sat on the curb as the pages of *Starman* fell around me like giant snowflakes.

Jimmy exhaled the cigarette. "Man, that's going to give me nightmares. What the hell was that?"

"That was my Bionic wife," I said. "Looks like my script and my marriage just got canceled."

CHAPTER 17

Ooooeeee!!!

O utside the Universal stage door, where the pages of
Starman floated down like giant snowflakes, I felt numb
all over. My marriage was over. My *Starman* creation was over,
and so was the filming of the movie *FM*, so when Jimmy said,
"That's heavy, man. You need to come back to Aspen with me."

I took up Jimmy Buffet's invitation and left for Aspen.

Jimmy threw me a lifeline and I grabbed on gratefully. My
dear friend Richard Baskin ("31 flavors" Baskin, who I met
sleeping with my girlfriend Susie) was joining me on a spur-of-
the-moment decision. Richard was a musician and composer of
the soundtrack to Robert Altman's film *Welcome to LA*, singing
the title song, "Welcome to the City of the One Night Stands".
Jimmy arranged everything for us.

We arrived in Aspen, Colorado, and it started snowing but
I felt separated from the beauty. I had never skied before but it
would sure beat lying in a lonely bed in LA, hoping the ceiling
would fall on me. We had barely put our bags inside the door
when Jimmy called.

He said, "Listen, I'm doing a little concert tonight at the Jerome Bar and there's a table for you guys." Jimmy Buffet was a great man.

Richard and I drove the car to the Jerome, which was the local hot spot in Aspen. The place was packed with incredibly beautiful people. I saw one girl and my jaw dropped open and my eyes did the cartoon bulge. If you looked up "perfect ten" in the dictionary, there would be a picture of her. This was my mind, what was left of it, and the year 1977.

I turned to Richard just as he turned to me. We had been staring at the same girl. We bumped bulging eyes as we nodded at each other.

I said, "Richard, if I could be with that girl, I wouldn't look at another girl, ever." OOOOEEEE!

We finally found our table. It was the size of an ashtray. We just about squeezed ourselves into the chairs when these two young girls came up and coyly said, "Can we sit with you?" Richard and I looked at each other stupefied, as there wasn't a hair's width of room left. Reluctantly he sighed, "There isn't any room," and one of them replied, "You have laps, don't you?" Our eyes flicked, and that might have been our second OOOOEEEE!

After a great concert and Jimmy's blessing, we left with the girls but couldn't find our rental car. All the cars were under a foot of snow and looked like marshmallow puffs. The girls were locals, so they knew where we were staying. As we walked in the snow with them, I might even have been laughing a little. Well, maybe a small smile, imagining life only hours ago. The party was on.

I can only say we skied all day and partied all night, every night. On the mountain, I was crashing around with Steven Spielberg and Dan Melnick and his girlfriend Tina, although I never really saw her as she was smothered in an orange ski hat, orange goggles, orange scarf, and orange ski suit. She looked like a mascot at a football game.

I was the only one who couldn't ski. Steven and Dan were good skiers taking on the whole mountain. I had no idea what black slope meant. I would go flailing down the mountain, like the opening credits of Wide World of Sports, body in the air and equipment going in all directions. Then I would stagger about gathering up my skis and poles. It was the orange girl, Tina, who showed me patience and compassion. She helped gather me up after each disaster. The guys would just shake their heads laughing, *there he goes again*. But after each crash, I somehow got back up in one piece, sometimes a very sore piece, but the good news was, I wasn't thinking about Lindsay. Seems rocketing through the air out of control can do that! My rescue remedy.

I remember buying this sketch that reminded me of me. The guy was airborne, holding his poles outstretched, his legs out wide, his beard frozen with ice, his hat and jeans covered in iced snow. His eyes filled with panic and screaming, "Out of Control!" That was me in Aspen.

A week or two into this blitz, over ski-chalet lunch, Richard decreed, "I'm going back to the apartment, I'm going into my bedroom and I'm not coming out. I don't want to be disturbed for any reason. I don't care who's in the living room, just don't bother me! I'll die if I don't sleep."

I said, "Okay, sure, I understand, have a good rest."

I was fueled by enormous pain and had much more adrenalin to burn than Richard. Make no mistake, Richard was a party animal of the first order, but I was clearly out of my mind trying to lose myself by unabashedly throwing my body down mountains.

"One thing, Richard," he turned, "I heard there's a really good party tonight."

Richard stomped his ski boots out the door.

I was at the party in one of the biggest houses on Aspen Mountain which belonged to Ron Popeil, the inventor of the Veg-O-Matic chopping device (the biggest device till the iPhone). The house and the party were outstanding.

I didn't know which way to look when this sparkling blonde beauty with a postcard smile wrapped her arm in mine and said, "Should we go?" She made up for all of life's rejections with that smile.

I nodded and we headed for the door.

As we got our coats, this guy walked up to us and said, "Lisa?" He had on the exact white turtleneck sweater as me, and his hair and beard were the same length and color. I could even see the mirror image. I didn't know if Lisa had come with him or just met him, but her eyes said something to me about leaving with him. She whispered her last name to me as he tugged her fading smile to the door. Does an *OOOOEEEE* count if Richard isn't there to hear it?

(I did see Lisa when I was back in LA and took her and her equally gorgeous sister as my dates to the premiere of *FM*. Lisa

Sepe-Wiesenfeld is now a judge on the Superior Court of Los Angeles, California, and we're still close friends.)

That gorgeous smile was enough for me. This weary snow warrior was about to leave the party a satisfied customer, when this pretty-eyed girl started chatting with me. She was very funny, and it turned out in passing, she knew Richard Baskin and, in fact, told me she was Richard's first kiss – they had a mad crush on each other back in camp. This was too good to pass up. I had to take her back.

I banged on Richard's door. He grunted like a hibernating bear: *Go away!*

I said, "Richard, you would *not* believe who's out here."

"Go away, Brandon!"

"What if I said the first girl you ever kissed was here?"

"That would be Joanie Glick and there is no way—"

"Hi Richard!" Joanie called out.

The door flung open. "Joanie, is it you?" Richard stared his mouth agape. "Joanie? Oh my God!"

I could feel the old magic was still there, as Joanie floated into Richard's open arms. Only took him thirty years to get to second base. I went to my bedroom and collapsed.

I finally got a little rest, and in the morning, I met Richard coming out of his room. We nodded at each other and grunted a weary, much subdued *ooooeeee*. Then our heads turned like synchronized swimmers toward the aroma of brewing coffee. Wow, coffee was brewing! We found two clean mugs waiting at the machine. We poured, sipped, and looked around the place in silent amazement. The apartment was totally immaculate.

Richard said, "I must have been damn good last night!" We clinked mugs, To Joanie! OOOOEEEE!

It was New Year's Eve in Aspen. I said to Richard, "Maybe I should just stay home. It's so depressing."

"Yeah," Richard sighed, "stay home on New Year's Eve in Aspen."

We both laughed till it hurt. Then we were at the Jerome Bar. I was hanging out with Timothy Schmit from the Eagles.

We were just chilling on the staircase with a couple of beers when I saw her. The ONE from the first-night concert. In a grey miniskirt outlined by silver frosted glass behind her, she was Living Art! I was up and walking in a zombie-like state, and I couldn't stop till I was in front of her.

"Hi," I said.

"My boyfriend broke his leg today."

"I'm sorry about that. Is he in the hospital?"

She said sadly, "Yeah, but it's New Year's Eve and I'm not spending it sitting in a hospital."

I nodded, just as Timothy and the rest of the Eagles walked by.

Timothy said, "Going over to party at Jack Nicholson's house. You want a ride?"

"I'll follow you," I said. (When do you ever get fed a lead line like that and from one of the Eagles?) I turned to the lady in grey, "Would you care to join us?"

"Sure," she said. And as Richard and I squeezed her in the front bench seat between us, it was OOOOEEEE and pedal to the metal time.

I feel I ought to write a **disclaimer** here.

I deeply and most sincerely apologize for the misogynistic behavior and sexist comments, and in my sorry defense, I would like to say, the times they were a-changin'. I was fueled and tormented by emotional pain that I was denying, and I refused to stop and acknowledge the condition that my condition was in. You must come from somewhere, and I admit at this time in my life, I was only a foot from the cave door. You gotta crawl before you can walk. I beg your understanding please.

Once we got to Jack's house, it was Chicago, Boz Scaggs, Jimmy Buffett, Joe Walsh, Art Garfunkel, and on and on it went. The only one not there was Jack himself.

When suddenly this wave of inner pain swept over me. I wanted to talk to Lindsay. I snuck into a room and tried to call her, then hung up. How pathetic. I was consumed with feelings. It was like I fell in a black hole. Thoughts. Thoughts like, she is in love with somebody else! After that echoed a couple of times, I forced myself outside into the cold maybe I could freeze myself. I was standing in the snow looking at the trees when I heard this sound. At first, I didn't realize it was coming from me, like a baby's moan. It became an escaping sob... It led to more, one after the other. My body shook with each one, then it was over.

Richard came from inside the house. "Are you okay?" he asked.

"It hurts, Richard. I loved her so much." He hugged me.

Richard nodded in his most understanding way, saying, "So are you not interested in scoring with the most beautiful girl in Aspen, maybe the world?"

I nodded. "I see where you're going with this Richard, and I need this girl to quell the overwhelming New Year's Eve broken marriage pain."

Richard nodded, giving me his most charming smile. "Not if I get her first." Richard was perfect in his deflecting me from indulging my pain.

The evening's jousting was progressing well for both of us until she mentioned getting back to her poor boyfriend in the hospital. We weren't barbarians. Moments later, we three were bumping through the deep snow, homeward bound, when Richard in his most sincere tone, "Would you like to come back to our place for a hot tub?"

I looked at him with a *how could you say that* look, and he had that apologetic *I know* nod. But when she replied, "How long would it take?" Richard and I jointly responded, "Not long." We caught each other's eyes and nodded a silent *OOOOEEEE.*

Sitting in the hot tub, Richard and I clinked glasses of champagne. We watched the steam rise off this perfect ten body as she laid in the fresh-fallen powder making snow angels with her legs. Jesus wept. Not a thought about the cold as she walked back with handfuls of fresh snow for us to melt in our mouths.

It was hours later when I woke to a banging on our apartment door. I opened it and there was this young elf-like girl dressed like Santa's helper (Aspen style).

She confided softly, "I saw the paper." She held up a copy of the Enquirer with Lindsay and me on the cover. It said "Bionic Splitsville". Her big green eyes were comforting like a little Christmas cherub. "I was thinking you must be hurting something awful as its New Year's Eve and all." *Thank you, Santa!*

That was New Year's 1978, and over forty-five years later whenever Richard and I speak to each other, we start with an OOOOOOEEEEEE!!! Well, maybe these days it's more of an *oooeee*. Crawl before you walk and walk before you run. Richard and I are developed egalitarians now.

My agent tracked me down. I felt like I was in a space station and Earth was calling. He said, "Universal is reshooting the end of *FM*. They want you on set tomorrow."

I said, "Not gonna happen. There are no flights out of here; there was a blizzard last night."

"They're sending a private jet. Private jets fly under different regulations."

I felt kind of privileged having a jet sent for me, until I was in the air. Holy shit, what a ride! I wanted in when the pilots started kissing their crosses. *Lucky to be alive* – that is what Paul Newman said to me. I clung to that thought.

The car took me to Universal Studios. There were a thousand extras dancing on the set of *FM*, which was made to look like a street in Venice, California, the home of QSKY Radio. I pushed through the crowd till I found an assistant who took me to my trailer. Inside the trailer were the new pages to shoot.

I read it and thought, *I just risked my life flying back here for this pile of shit.* I ran to find John Alonzo, the director. I held up the pages and said, "John, what is this?"

He was totally deflated and shrugged. "Michael, at this point I shoot what they tell me." The writer pretty much admitted the same feelings.

I walked straight to Tom Mount's office – he was the new Universal head of production, just unpacking his boxes. I gave him a brief heads up about the goings on. I pleaded, "My character did what he did in this film because he had integrity. If we shoot *this…what's the story?*"

Tom read the pages and shook his head. "Verna Fields is your executive producer?"

I nodded yes, and he told his secretary to get her on the phone.

Tom spoke to her briefly and hung up. "Verna just got back from China. Give her a couple of hours and we will all meet up at her house: the director, producer, writer, and you."

"Okay, thank you Tom."

All I can say is the meeting at Verna's went better than expected (no static at all). Verna cut to the chase.

John Alonzo was first to say, "I'm happy to shoot these changes."

Verna said, "Okay, go finish this fucking film."

The story was mostly cut from the film. Universal's strategy was shipping a double-platinum soundtrack album, putting MCA Universal Music in profits. This movie made a great album.

John Alonzo and I had become close friends, we were already neighbors. I had been to his house in Brentwood for dinner many times, including one with Peggy Lee, enjoying the jazz and his wine collection.

Just after the release of *FM*, I was enjoying a quiet night at home alone when I heard music coming from my front garden. I opened the door to find a tall, thin man with long hair and a long face singing on my doorstep.

I said, "Can I help you?" Big mistake!

He gave me this rap about being an out-of-work musician and he saw the movie *FM* and was hoping I could help his career. Then he started singing again.

I waved him to stop. "I like your song. Do you have a tape?" *Whop bam*, there was a tape in my hand. I told him, "No promises, man. I'll just listen to your music."

I listened to this song dozens of times and I had a vision. I called John Toll, the camera operator and told him I had an idea for a film. John was the operator on *FM* who did the backflip after an amazing shot through five reflecting windows. It was late but he was intrigued and came over. I played the song for him and how I envisioned it.

John looked at me, a serious man with intense green eyes, and asked, "How long is this film?"

"As long as the song."

He said, "Who's going to make a five-minute movie?"

At the time, there were no rock videos; it was two years before MTV and there was only one cable channel in LA called Theta Cable. In between movies they had a card displaying the number of minutes before the next film began. One might say the Dark Ages.

John loved the idea in theory but asked, "Who would pay for this movie?"

I said, "I'll pay for the first one."

"The first one?"

"This is the beginning, John; this one will start our business."

"What business?"

I brain-rushed out with, "FilmSong! We'll make films of songs, and they'll run on Theta Cable between films. It's far more interesting than looking at a clock countdown and it holds your audience!"

John nodded but didn't see how it would generate money because Theta Cable wouldn't pay much, if anything, for shorts.

"The artists will be promoting their new songs," I said.

"Rockers won't pay!"

I said, "No, but the record companies will pay for our service to promote albums and singles sales of their artists."

FilmSong! I demonstrated a strip of wavy celluloid film with notes on it like a musical staff. Our FilmSong logo!

That was worth John doing another backflip. We shook and danced around the living room. John was off to find a crew. I had to sign my first act, the guy on my porch, and on the morrow, I would go to Theta Cable and then meet record company producers.

Well, two weeks later we had shot and edited our first five-minute film on 35-millimeter film, and it was about to run on

Theta Cable. Everyone who helped came to watch our first premiere. There were lots of big favors put in here. This same crew John put together shot ET.

I got a call from Loggins and Messina and another from Rick Springfield, who saw our video on the cable channel and wanted one. John and I met with his record company.

They said, "How much?"

We had budgeted the film song at $35,000.

The record executive had a heart attack! "Are you crazy? What the fuck do you think you're making – *Gone with The Wind*?"

Those were the old days. Three years later, they were paying almost a million for Michael Jackson's *Thriller*. We were hardly earning anything; we just wanted to get business going. So, on we went. We were in the film and music business! FilmSong!

But it was the early days of cable TV and music videos. It was also rock and roll. Acts just didn't show up. Crews sitting around with camera and lighting equipment was just too expensive. John and I sadly gave it a thumb-down. He went on to win the Academy Award as director of cinematography for *Legends of the Fall* and *Braveheart*.

Two years later, MTV launched, and it should have been us. I didn't have the overview. Oh well. You win some, you lose some. That's rock and roll, baby.

CHAPTER 18

One Slice Isn't Going to Kill Him

The *FM* movie was over, I was back to my life. It really was over; it all had changed. I felt like the character Brando played in *Last Tango in Paris*. The opening of that film found this man in a trench coat walking under the train trestle in tormenting pain. There is so much to Brando just walking, it tallied up my entire being. Reality came crashing down.

When I left the marriage house in Coldwater Canyon, after that last conversation with Lindsay, I never returned. I called a friend in real estate, Steve Shapiro, who lent me his own house till I finished the film and then found me a house to rent in Brentwood. An old funky ranch house on a couple of acres set back from the street. It had red carpet and red embossed floral wallpaper in the bathroom. I know it sounds like Vegas, but oddly, with the exposed wood beams, it wasn't loud and perfect for me. I tried to board Sinbad and Nubbin at the house as there were two acres of land, but the city wasn't allowing it. Residential zoning only. Jay was taking still caring for Sinbad and Nubbin, but he had decided to buy an island off Fiji. I had to find space at a stable to board them. It worked out okay, because the boarding stable was much closer to Brentwood, and I could ride and visit them more often now,

My close friends, Andy Rubin and Debra Winger were spending more time in town these days, and Me casa es tu casa…

So much was always going on in this house. I put a ping-pong table in the large dining room area. Games could go on all night. The parties were amazing. I loved living in Brentwood Barrington House.

Debra, who played the little sister on *Wonder Woman*, met an agent at the house during a party. She said, "I could use a new agent."

He replied, "Sure, the next time you're doing something, call me."

"How about I audition for you now?" Debra offered to get down on all fours, saying, "Okay, this is my dog Pete, throwing up." Mr. Sand jumped up, saying I will handle you! And y'know what, he became her agent and got her the film, *TGIF*.

I called the literary agent I met while mountain bouncing in Aspen. She was the one covered in the orange ski suit and hat, Tina Santos. She was so kind to me when I skied with Spielberg and Melnick, I owed this girl a drink.

I called, and she said, "I'm working from home, Come by."

Her house, which was extremely modern and chic, had lots of photographs of her with famous people. Particularly Frank Sinatra.

I asked if she represented him.

She said, "Why would I do that?"

"Well, there are so many pictures of you two together."

She walked straight up into my face, "Who do you think I am? What's my name?"

"Tina Santos?"

"Sinatra!"

Big Oops! I told her that it didn't change how appreciative I was for the kindness and generosity she showed me on the mountain. I guess my ears were still full of snow when we were introduced. I apologized. This book could be titled Still an Asshole!

That's how I started dating Tina Sinatra. We went to see her dad at the Universal Amphitheatre and hung out backstage. We had dinner at La Scala, and I was even invited to an Easter egg hunt at the house. We enjoyed each other's company. Tina was so knowledgable about the business and the people running it. I had a business meeting at the famous Italian restaurant on Sunset Strip, she asked which table I was sitting at. I'd never met anyone so clued in, wiseass and funny.

One night, cuddled in at my place, it was late, but the phone kept ringing. I finally answered, and it was Lindsay, who jumped on me about getting my belongings out of the garage but before I could say a word, Tina, overhearing, snatched the phone from my hand.

Tina firmly said, "Lindsay, it's past the acceptable phoning zone. It's too late to call anyone in this town. In future, please don't call here at all." She leaned across me and hung up the phone.

It took a few minutes for my pulse to return. Tina was a sophisticated woman and a Sinatra. She didn't take shit in her life or in mine it seemed.

On the other hand, Tina, who had such warm brown eyes (I called her Sparkle), was the one who made my re-entry into my feelings possible. Tina was silk and suede, nylon and edgy. She was earthy real and Audrey Hepburn magic, a sparkle of life's very essence.

Tina took me to Rod Stewart's house for his birthday and Elton John was there. This evening was one of those amazingly relaxed moments with these musical geniuses hanging around the piano and singing songs all night long. During which time, Tina casually invited me to move in with her. My mind brewed on that thought for days. We might have had a genuinely deep lasting relationship, but it was on the too-soon side for me. I was a love casualty. My heart had rusted over. I sadly had to decline, and so that was the end for Tina and me.

There was a bit of ski season left, and I thought it would be good to get away from feelings at home. I went up to Lake Tahoe, Nevada, with friends: Andy Rubin, Dr Richard Miller, and Richard Cox. Richard Cox is a lovely and gullible man. At the top of the mountain, we said we wanted to test Cox's sense of direction so he should close his eyes and turn around three times. It takes time while on skis, and when he opened his eyes, we had all skied off.

The next day there was a snowstorm. A white-out blizzard and I wasn't keen to go with the others out in that weather. The phone rang.

My agent, Ron Meyer, said, "A director is going to call you in fifteen minutes. His name is David Greene. He asked if you would make a pot of tea. What can I say – he's English."

David Greene called and asked if I had made a pot, but I was sure he couldn't see me, so I said, "Yes, it's steaming on the table." I hate tea.

"Excellent," he said. "Let us begin, shall we? *Vacation in Hell*, fade in, scene one…" He read the entire script to me over the phone. This was a first, but I have to say, in his lovely English accent, it was like a BBC radio program.

A little over an hour later, David asked, "What do you think?"

I sighed, saying, "The lead guy is an asshole; he needs a sense of humor, or you're happy when he dies."

"Exactly, my thoughts" David exclaimed. "What else?"

We talked and talked, then abruptly he said, "I agree with everything you are saying. Come make these changes with me straight away?"

"Where are you?"

"Hawaii, and you need to get on a plane today. Our agent has made all the arrangements."

"Hold on, I'm in a snowstorm in the mountains of Nevada and I will *not* get on a private jet to fly through a snowstorm."

"No, no, no," he said, "a Jeep thingy will pick you up shortly and take you to Reno Airport where you'll catch a safe commercial flight to San Francisco connecting to a flight for the Hawaiian Islands."

"I have no clothes with me except a ski suit and long underwear."

"Michael, it's Hawaii. Paradise, my dear boy. You don't need clothes here. Flip-flops and shorts are all you require; the wardrobe dept. will supply you with whatever else you need.

There's a three-hour time difference, so I'll be seeing you for dinner. Get packing!"

I left a note on my skis in the doorway: *Gone to Hawaii*.

I was on my way to Hawaii – and a good thing, too. The media was making a meal of the divorce filing. It would be good for me to be as far away as possible.

When I arrived, I was shown to David Greene's suite, a hut on the beach. He had platters of local sushi waiting, and pencils for changes we would make on the script. He was English, very tall, with a long white beard, and he was a grand chap indeed.

A couple of hours into the work, he got a call from production and said, "Michael, I need to have this chat. Why don't you step out on the balcony and view our spectacular sunset?"

David took out a vintage silver cigarette case, opening it to reveal hand-rolled joints, each one marked from X to XXXX. I chose the X. He smiled, lit it, took a long inhale, passed it to me and took his call.

I stepped out onto the balcony and drew a puff as the sun hovered, about to dip into the turquoise ocean, but just before it did, a woman erupted from the sea, her wild hair sending water spraying in the air. She turned and walked toward the beach. I was thinking this doobie David shared with me was making me hallucinate. I had never seen a girl come out of the sea in front of a setting sun ball. Not looking like her! Maybe I chose the strongest joint instead of the weakest?

Then a man came along the beach with silver hair and a beard. He was so striking; it seemed to me these were not people but frolicking gods. She was shaking the water from her blonde cornrows, and her T-shirt was stuck against a perfectly naked body beneath. He handed her a champagne glass and poured backed by the red sky.

I walked up to them. They both smiled at me, glowing in the sunset – the tans, the four bluest eyes, and the whitest teeth. You don't see people like this in Brooklyn.

It was Bo and John Derek. She was the star of the film *Ten* and was filming in Hawaii with Dudley Moore. She would become a star from this film, and John was a hero of mine way back to the *Ten Commandments* movie in the 50s with Charlton Heston. He was Joshua, the rebellious slave.

I just realized *Ten* and *Ten Commandments*. hmmm…

Vacation in Hell was a TV ratings-grabber, a mish-mosh of four women at a singles holiday hotel. I was the male predator who, because of his stupendous sexual greed, got them all marooned on an island and died for it. I gravitated toward Maureen McCormick (Marcia in *The Brady Bunch*), or perhaps she pulled me into her gravitational field. If you read her biography, *Here's the Story*, you'll see I had no choice in the matter. According to her, all the women wanted me, and vice versa, but she was the gal who pulled it off.

All the actresses in the film were fantastic, funny, and a pleasure to work with. It was a holiday job. When we weren't filming, it was piña coladas on the beach. Maureen was delightful and reminded me of all the gorgeous cheerleaders in high school who wouldn't give me the time of day. To be honest, I wasn't a *Brady Bunch* watcher, but learned Maureen was a huge international TV star.

Maureen was very involved in charities like the Special Olympics and had me all signed up for many events on our return.

From Maureen's book, *Here's The Story*:

It was through Michael that I was introduced to the Playboy Mansion. He knew people there, and we were invited to parties. On one occasion, I saw Steven Spielberg with his then-girlfriend, actress Amy Irving. Another time Michael pointed out legendary producer Robert Evans lounging poolside with a bevy of topless bunnies. One night we met Sammy Davis Jr. After the party wound down at the mansion, we followed him up to his house off Benedict Canyon.

Maureen tells of her drug dependency, the reason we couldn't continue as a couple. As she says, I told her it was an either/or situation but Maureen wasn't ready to give it up yet. Writing her story, the process she went through recovering her life, was a monumental achievement. With great respect to Maureen.

That year I made another television film called *Perfect Match*. It was one of those true-to-life dramas about saving a woman's life by finding bone marrow that's a perfect match. The woman I loved would die unless I tracked down her given-up-at-birth daughter and got her to donate her bone marrow. (I know).

The ironic twist in this story was the parents who adopted the daughter never told her she was adopted. It led to a dramatic scene: "Do we tell her she's adopted or not? We don't even know if she's a perfect match." The actor playing the father of the now-teenage girl was my friend and brilliant actor Charlie Durning. It was a heavy scene, and I never laughed more in my life.

Charlie knew thousands of lyrics. He was in rare rhyming form that day and I couldn't stop laughing. We started to do the scene and we both started crying. We looked at each other and burst out laughing.

When we tried to calm down, Charlie said, "Two guys crying is just not going to work. We burst out laughing again. "Nobody wants to watch two grown men cry." Charlie could barely say and cried, "*You* cry."

I said, "It's okay, *you* cry."

We did the scene again, and nobody cried, but we laughed anyway. We laughed all day long. Next, we had to film the scene informing his wife that we decided to tell the daughter she was adopted. It was a truly heartbreaking and unfunny scene, but I was hiding behind Charlie's back because he kept making me laugh. I couldn't keep a straight face. The whole crew was infected now.

The director said, "Action!" and Charlie came out with another limerick: "There was a man from St Glass, whose balls were made of brass, when they clanged together, they played 'Stormy Weather', and lightning shot out of his ass."

We were both crying with laughter when Colleen Dewhurst, the legendary actress and wife of George C. Scott, opened the door to us two out-of-control idiots who fell on the doorstep laughing. It was more than she could cope with. She tried to keep the scene going but it was useless and eventually fell on top of us, howling with laughter.

I miss Charlie. *RIP – and keep on laughing.*

I spoke with the lawyer about my divorce. Sounds so weird to even say the word divorce. I cannot associate it with myself, that's me being divorced from my feelings. The Lawyer informed me Lindsay and somewhere between six to nine lawyers were coming to his office for a meeting shortly. He said I could attend if I wanted to, he didn't need me there, but he instructed me not to say anything. Who did he think he was? The Gutter Confucius? The Lawyer said, "I don't want a settlement. I want to get her in the courtroom, I want to pull out her uterus on the stand." Whoa! I gathered myself and said, "Thank you, but I won't be needing representation. I don't want anything except the sauna that was a wedding gift from my parents. Thank you for your services." I think he called me a shmuck as he hung up.

One morning at Santa Monica Civil Court, a hammer came down and I was divorced. It took less than a minute and that was that. I thought my marriage would last a lifetime. It's how I grew up, with one set of parents and grandparents till they died. I was with Lindsay for three years, two years great and one married. Hammer down, bang, and over! Stop, stop, stop went my heartstrings, - the Judy Garland, trolley song.

I went to my folks for dinner. My mother made me a huge chicken and placed it in front of me. "Eat it!" she nasally ordered, "It will make you feel better." I told her I remember reading somewhere, that you should never eat anything bigger than your head.

"Schmuck," my father said, biting into a pizza slice, "you walked with nothing? You didn't listen to your lawyer, you never listen, God wasted ears on you. You could have been a millionaire; you should have been a millionaire. You were there from the beginning of the Bionic bullshit. You had your head rebuilt. Aah, What's the point, I'm talking to a wall."

My mother insisted, "Sol enough, let him eat. Eat it Michael, you'll feel better."

This was the advice from a woman who ordered pizza when my father came home from the hospital after his fourth heart attack.

"You're giving him pizza, Mom, really?" I took the slice away. My mom grabbed it back.

"One slice isn't going to kill him."

A couple days later, after digesting my mother's chicken, I was at home in Brentwood, when I got a timely intervention from my friend, Dr. Richard Miller calling from SF and inquiring, "How's divorce going?" I sighed, "Richard, I watch a stupid commercial on TV and if two people hug I start sobbing". Richard's response was, "Let's go skiing!" I said, "I wish, but as you may have noticed, it's summer!" Richard sang back, "Not in Argentina!"

So, we joined a ski racing class that was going to train ski racers in Argentina, summer here, winter there. The instructor was the Norwegian Olympic downhill champion, Otto Tschudi. I love skiing, but I was a novice. This was a ski camp in Bariloche, Argentina, (more known for its chocolate) training for downhill racing? We flew to Argentina. It was Richard, another buddy David Hayward (also an actor) and me, all crazy for the trip, landing in Buenos Aires for a night.

We had Chinese food for dinner as you do in Buenos Aires. David was into a long jag about how as a kid he used to walk out on restaurant bills. Richard and I exchanged a look and got up and walked out. David was so astonished that he got caught with the bill, he tried to do a runner, but there were guys with machine guns on every corner. He didn't get far. Richard went back and said he wasn't doing a runner; he was just trying to exchange some local currency.

The skiing was awful. I couldn't ski in Argentina. I tried for two days but it was impossible. Otto, our super skier, said, "It's like cement. The altitude is too low, the temperature is too warm. For you, Michael, it's impossible to ski here. If I were you," the Norwegian whispered, "I would take a bus to Portillo, Chile. He pointed to the distant mountains, that is where the real racers, go to train." Later, I told David and Richard the plan. Richard was in and David was wavering. He had started a love affair with the other instructor, a big, lusty blonde girl we nicknamed Foghorn because she reminded us of the huge rooster, Foghorn Leghorn, in the Henry Hawk cartoons. This Foghorn was a whole lot prettier than the rooster in the cartoon, and massively endowed. David hemmed and hawed in the entryway, should he go, should he stay, then Foghorn bellowed, and he shrugged a big surrendering smile. Big mistake.

Richard and I walked out at first light to catch our bus and there was Otto, sitting on his ski bags. We were shocked. He saw it on our faces and laughed. "I know, I am the racing instructor, but no one can ski in this cement. So, I thought it would be more fun to go with the two worst skiers in the group to the best skiing in South America. Portillo, Chile!"

The retro bus with white wall tires and pom poms everywhere was an adventure. Squirreling up the icy roads into the Andes Mountains accompanied by the sound of South American trumpets, the driver shouted on the curves as the passengers screamed and we skidded across the road toward the edge. Once we were so close everyone jumped to the other side screaming. The bus seemed to freeze with one set of double rear wheels hanging over. The driver calmly waved, *please get off the bus, one at a time.* Then the driver took our suitcases out and dumped them on the road. Otto seemed to have fifty pairs of skis with him. He tested them for Rossignol. The driver refused to go any further. He managed to turn the bus around, that was a spine-tingling show and left us there. I'm sure this was the same place where those people ate each other after a plane crash. Otto said, "We are not too far from the hotel. Michael, you stay here with the equipment, and we will come back for you with a sled." They laughed and marched off.

I was sitting on Otto's massive bag of skis, when it started snowing. I had about an inch of snow on me. I wondered how long they would be, when I heard the Gutter Confucious's voice: "Hey Smuck, soon you'll be buried under the snow, and they'll never find you. You'll starve to death because you can't eat anything without ketchup."

Then Otto and a small crowd of Chileans arrived and loaded the skis onto a big sled and pulled our stuff to the hotel.

They treated Otto like Royalty, he was skiing royalty, the Norwegian Olympic Downhill Champion. We got nice rooms, and the hotel was like the Queen Mary Ocean Liner, situated on a mountaintop in the Andes. We ate in the huge, elegant, old world dining room with tufted leather booths, glistening chandeliers and elegant service from another time. You came in from skiing and they waxed your skis and wiped your boots down while you dined. All with that South American warmth.

One night we snowshoed over to eat across the road in a place completely buried by the snow. They had dug stairs down to get to the front door. During dinner, a woman stood up and dumped her food over the head of a man sitting with her. He shouted back and threw his food in her face. Then the guy next to him threw his food at the guy. I was shocked when another man threw his food at Otto. The whole restaurant got up and threw their plates of food at everyone else including Richard and me. It was a fantastic experience and custom here. I wish there was one of these food fight restaurants in London.

The next morning, still snowing, of course, I sat on an old wooden two-seat chair lift with Richard. We held on as we climbed straight up. "Odd," I said to Richard, "usually it's gradual climb up the mountain. I don't remember a chair lift that went straight up a mountain cliff." I was having serious vertigo issues. You could almost touch the mountain with your ski. Once we got off on the top, Otto told me to look up at the ski cable barely visible in the cloud and snow. He said "Keep that above your head all the time. Ski under the cable, okay?" That gave you twenty feet to go this way or that, if the cable was in view. When the sky cleared, I understood why he was so emphatic. I was on the slim ridge of the mountaintop, and it would be like falling out of heaven if you went over the side. I fell to the ground with vertigo. Otto talked me up on my feet. He said, "Think of it this way, you can only ski one foot at a time. Don't look down there." But I looked! Jesus! Otto made me turn around backwards, bend over and look through my legs downhill. "Now turn around and see how much easier it looks?" Goddamn Norwegian, but after a couple of days, I did become a better skier. Then one morning, Otto was packing. I said, "What's up?" He said, "My wife is having the baby, and I have to be there." I said, "Otto, the snowstorm closed the pass. We can't get out." Otto nodded. "We will have to ski out." Richard and I looked at each other like we had just volunteered to do mine clearing in Afghanistan. "You know I can't ski this, right?" Otto turned, "Look guys, the army is coming to open the pass for us so we can get out of the hotel. Then we'll ski down the mountain to Santiago. I will ski down the sled with the luggage and equipment and you guys have only to look out for each other. I need to get to the airport in Santiago." Soon, tank trucks of soldiers arrived with skis and shovels. We skied down the mountain, coming to a road at last. We skied the road till we could hitch a ride. Somebody should have filmed this!

It wasn't easy… in fact, it was frightening and impossible at times, and painful, but we did it. Otto got home in time for his baby, and we had an adventure never to be forgotten. Otto is now a stockbroker in San Francisco but before he quit racing, he was the resident pro at Winter Park, Colorado. I spent time with him there and one day he said, "I have a treat for you today. You get to ski with the man who taught me to ski." That man turned out to be the man who brought skiing to America, Stein Erickson and he stood there in front of me. How could I ski with this man? This was like doing a math class with Albert Einstein. Stein and I rode up the lift. At the top we did a few stretches. I imitated everything he did. He nodded. "Okay, good! Now only one thing, one thing, that's all you must do. Follow my tracks." And he skied off. I jumped after him and that's all I focused on. The thing is, Stein Ericksen doesn't leave tracks. His skis seem to hover just above the snow. I followed them and I cannot tell you how I did it, but I never skied so perfectly in my life. I didn't fall or crash, and I arrived at the bottom with him. I was breathless and beaming. Stein smiled knowingly at me like Obi-Wan Kenobi to the young Skywalker.

From that time on, I skied in all the celebrity ski events and went across America for charity skiing: Park City, Utah; Taos, New Mexico; Lake Tahoe, Nevada; Vermont, New York; Idaho, Colorado, California and then France, Switzerland, Austria and South America. At my first celebrity event I skied across Clint Eastwood's skis while he was wearing them - he was not pleased. Skiing is a phenomenal sport; I enjoyed it so much that I directed a film for Rossignol in Austria. One of my greatest skiing moments was to ski with the Mahre brothers, who won the US Olympic Gold Medals.

I won a silver Aspen leaf belt buckle in the celebrity race in Aspen beating my friend George Hamilton. It was like winning an Emmy Award. Well, for a guy who never won anything…hold on, that's not true. I won a DC Comics jingle contest when I was a kid. I wrote, "Always read in good light,

Read DC Comics, they shine out bright!" I won a football for that.

The Aspen silver buckle win means so much more.

Skiing literally took me from down in the valley of pain up to a mountaintop triumph. When it's going right, it feels like you're dancing with God.

CHAPTER 19

Rich And Famous

I got a call. That's life in Los Angeles. My agent Ron Meyer (CAA) called to say, "You have a meeting with George Cukor at MGM this afternoon. The producers want you, but George must see you in person. The film is called *Rich and Famous,* starring Candice Bergen and Jacqueline Bisset, enjoy".

It was a nervous drive to the studio. I mean George Cukor was an Academy Award winning director of pictures like *The Philadelphia Story, Gaslight, My Fair Lady* and *A Star is Born.* I met him on the set, and he reminded me of Grandpa. If Grandpa were slim, elegant, refined and gay. He stared at me incubating my presence, then nodded and smiled and said, "Yes, you'll make a right cad." George shook my hand and went back to work.

On a flight from LA to New York, my character sits next to Jackie, and we chat and eventually make love in the bathroom of the airplane. Two days filming in LA and one day in NY at Kennedy Airport. I was so buzzed to be working with one of the greatest film directors of all time and Jacqueline Bisset, one of the most beautiful and talented actresses in the business.

The first day's filming would be onstage inside a mockup of a 747 jet, so real it did everything but fly. I was sitting in the first-class section next to Jackie. I offer her a glass of wine as the stewardess is standing at my aisle side. Then during our scene, I reveal to her my wife has died, but I have never been able to take off my wedding ring. One thing leads to another. She excuses herself and goes upstairs to the bathroom and a moment later I decide to follow her. When she opens the door to leave, I block her way. She looks at me and backs up, letting me in. The actual love scene would be the whole next day's filming.

Just before we started filming that day's scene, Jackie asked me if I minded if she flipped two words around as it sounded better to her. I said, sure. George called Action. We did the scene. Cut, yelled George. He walked to us from the camera. He looked at Jackie and said, "The line is dot da dada not dot dada da. Don't improve the script". Then he said to me, "When she stops talking, you talk," then to Jackie, "when he stops talking, you talk. The script doesn't say pause, it doesn't say beat". He turned to me and said, "After your line, cry". I looked at him, "What? I ask her if she wants another glass of wine?" George said, "After your line, cry. If you're an actor worth your salt, you'll cry!"

I looked at Jackie for an explanation and she nodded, yup, that's what it's like. "Action" called George, and we did the scene and when I asked her if she wanted another glass of wine I tried to cry. I used every acting technique I knew, bringing back painful moments in my life, including my present failure to produce a single tear. "Cut", said George, "Print!" He was happy and ready to move on. My hand went up and I heard myself say "hold it". It was like a freeze frame photo. The entire crew froze, nobody moved. The film loader held the reel in his hands above the camera frozen. George walked to me, and whispered, "Did you say something?" I could feel Jackie hiding in her seat. I said, "Yes I did". "And what was it you said?" "I said hold it". "That's right you said hold it. Why did you say that?" "Because that was bullshit". George leaned over me, beamed at me and nodded, "Yes, but it was good bullshit."

George didn't really want me to cry, he wanted me to be a lying cad. By asking me to cry in that situation he made into the dishonorable rouge he envisioned. This was a big lesson about how some of the great directors' work. George was known for getting great performances from actresses like Hepburn and Taylor. He did it by asking them to do things that rewarded their performing with unexpected results. Now I understood more about George Cukor.

Next morning I was in my trailer at MGM and there was a knock. Jackie smiled, "Good morning, Michael these love scenes can be awkward, maybe if we rehearse it ourselves it might go smoother". I said, "There aren't any lines". Jackie replied, "Well, it says I moan but I don't moan. What do you think happens first" she said looking into my eyes. "I think, I would kiss you". She nods and we kissed and then she said, "and I would probably kiss you back". All seemed to be flowing very naturally until we were interrupted by a knock on the trailer door, the assistant said, "We're ready". We nodded at each other; we were ready as well. Jacki was a professional and it set the tone for a scene that Rolling Stone Magazine reviewed as one the sexiest scenes in cinema. Oh, and she moaned. Sometimes, and rarely in life, reality exceeds fantasy.

The screening of *Rich and Famous* was a red-carpet, black-tie event that brought out the biggest stars to honor its famous director, George Cukor. This would be his last picture.

I went to the huge bar in the after-party marquis to get a drink. I was trying to get the bartenders attention when I realized I was standing next to Elizabeth Taylor. She was exceptionally beautiful, and she was smiling, at me. I was very curious to look into those eyes I had seen in movies and read about in stories and now, here they were, looking right at me.

Elizabeth tipped her head back and said, "I could not do that". I replied, "Do what? She said, "Make love in an airplane". I said, "Really'?" She said, "Have you?" I said, "You just saw me". She laughed, "Yes, very good, but I am much too afraid of flying. I suffer high anxiety in airplanes, and I could never relax enough to make love in one". I leaned into her and conspiratorially revealed, "I knew a lady once who was very afraid of flying, terrified I believe, but it took away her fear in the end". Elizabeth was intrigued and said, "Just how does that work?" I said, "Imagine you are on an airplane right now". She closed her eyes and really focused so intensely I could feel her anxiety building. Then I whispered, "Kiss me". To my wonder she kissed me right there in the middle of the party, the 'Real Thing' too, a lovely lingering kiss. Then She opened her eyes and smiled. I said, "You forgot about your fear of flying didn't you?" She nodded, "It worked, but some flights are terribly long." "Yes, they are." A moment and we both burst out laughing right there on the sound stage. Elizabeth winked at me and walked off. I just kissed Elizabeth Taylor.

CHAPTER 20

The Mansion

I'd been invited to the Playboy Mansion since working on the 1973 Playboy Films production of *Third Girl from the Left*, but I just hadn't felt it was my kind of scene.

After my divorce, my old friend Mickey Callan called to invite me to the Playboy Mansion. Mickey said, "Listen, think of Sunday afternoon at the mansion as a kind of family day, I'm not kidding, it's just friends of Hefner come up, hang out and have a surf and turf BBQ, lobster and steak and watch the latest film."

It was very relaxed with gorgeous grounds and waterfalls, with lots of my contemporaries and sports stars hanging about as well. I had met Hugh Hefner once before, but this time we talked and connected over the film industry, *The Third Girl from the Left*, writing and Playboy. What boy didn't look at Playboy back in the sixties? But I was reading Playboy, the girls were hot, but they were not my focus, believe it or not; I find clothes make a woman more desirable.

There was plenty of everything inside the mansion. All I can say is it wasn't what I thought it would be; it was a way lot more! Hef and I got on great. The mansion was the best private club there ever was. Great people, terrific food, and first-run films!

The grotto was for relaxed soaking under the waterfalls. The game room was a short walk from the main house and had all the latest video games, pinball machines, popcorn and candy trolleys, and a few discreet, *very* cushy rooms for privacy, sort of like bouncy castles for adults. (I think that was a secret).

On Friday nights, there was dinner and movies with some of the regulars who were part of an easy, relaxed, small unwritten membership. Well, it was written, or the gates wouldn't open when you said your name to the hidden speaker in the boulder outside the gate. I saw some big jazz names from time to time, and many movie stars, TV stars and directors. At some of the parties, the political biggies were present, and the pajama parties were spectacular with ice sculptures, live music, dancing, and the Hollywood glitterati, all in some form of PJs. There wasn't – and never will be – anything quite like it. It was a thing in its time. Looking at it through a 2025 lens, people may consider it a terrible place, but I can categorically say, I never saw anything untoward, or any woman abused during my time there.

I was welcome to be there any day and any time. I just spoke my name to the boulder and the huge gate spread its arms.

One night, John Belushi and I were having a very late meal up to the mansion. It was after Richard Pryor's, I'm alive after catching fire, show at the Roxy on Sunset Blvd. Everything was closed but the Mansion. I took John there because he was starving, and it was private or so I thought.

A month later, I got a late call from Bob Woodward (of Watergate fame). I had only heard of him. He wanted to interview me about the death of John Belushi two weeks earlier, for his book *Wired*. He had somehow found out I had brought John Belushi to the mansion. Sounded like a book I didn't want to be in, and I declined. It was a shame as I really wanted to meet Woodward, he was one of my journalistic heroes, but in this industry, you have to know the stories that can and should be told.

As I hung up the phone, I heard the news on the TV. A Japanese airline flight was quarantined in San Francisco because it flew too near the mushrooming cloud of a Chinese nuclear bomb test. The plane was being held at the end of a runway awaiting HazMat teams to check out nuclear radiation levels. The JAL airline quarantine was only on the ABC 11 p.m. newscast; none of the others broadcast it.

I called MacLaine, and she was rushing out the door to the airport. She said, Michael, call the EPA (Environmental Protection Agency). I did and they said yes - they acknowledged a nuclear cloud would pass over the western United States in the early hours of the morning, and at this time they didn't anticipate any significant harm.

Was that why Shirley was rushing to the airport?

What did that even mean: significant harm? What is significant harm, a head growing out of your nostrils? I called the EPA back, but never got another human, from then on it was a recording saying, we don't anticipate significant harm. By now it was after midnight, if I started driving, I wondered, could I outdrive a nuclear cloud? How fast was it going and in what direction? I should have dated a weather girl!

I called every airline, but it was too late for the red-eye flights. All the private jet companies were closed. I called Tina Sinatra, and she thought vitamin C and calcium would help bring me down. I went to see Hef. I told him we needed to fly out of LA immediately as the nuclear cloud would pass over the western US in the early morning hours. What about the Playboy jet? He laughed and called me "Chicken Little" (a children's story about a chicken who walked around saying the sky was falling). Was I the only one watching the news at 11 p.m.? A nuclear cloud was coming! It does sound a bit like the sky is falling!

I went to the Westward Ho all-night market (now Whole Foods) and bought twenty boxes of foil wrap and cases of bottled water, and I sealed myself in my house. Yes, I felt like Dr Brown, the scientist from *Back to The Future*, but two days later the Hong Kong flu hit America. The worst flu of its time! Reading this now, I do sound crazy but there was a cover-up. While I was sealed in my house, I watched the presidential debate (1980 Reagan/Carter), which mainly focused on 'improving relations with China'. Let's face it, the Chinese knew the perfect time to test a nuclear device without hassle from the US.

Once things settled back down, one evening, at the mansion, I was sitting on the wide staircase reading a script in the grand entrance hall, (why go home to be alone when I could order a burger and enjoy the mansion and excellent random company?) Hef came down the stairs from his private quarters and plunked down next to me. His chest was heaving; he was sweating and out of breath.

I said, "Are you alright?" and offered him my Coke which he chugged down. He wheezed and said me, "She was sitting on my face, and a steel Ben Wa ball went down my throat. I was choking to death as I was trying to get out from under and she thought I was giving her the best head she ever had!"

I nodded. "But what a way to go, Hef!"

Hef smiled, "I died in the saddle", he had a little chuckle, patted my shoulder, and climbed back up the stairs.

CHAPTER 21

Old Friends and New

A sunny day in Brentwood, CA. I was sitting on the balcony of the Grill Restaurant with my dear (and oldest) friend Neil Koenigsberg. I was lifting a hefty fork of my favorite Chinese chicken salad to my lips when Neil informed me, he had decided to end his long-term marriage to Alice. He had decided to be gay.

My fork remained hovering at chin height for several moments. "You might want to try a second girl as Alice was very possibly your first and only."

No, he was firmly decided on this.

(With love and great respect: Neil is totally okay with me revealing this in the book.)

Neil and I shared a unique history; we went to the same high school in Valley Stream, Long Island, New York. Neil was older, two years ahead of me in school. He was a scholarly academic type. I was a chameleon, hanging out with hoods to survive. (If you can't beat them...) I met Neil through the kid across the street, Zublatt, who taught me to masturbate, I am forever indebted to Zubi for revealing the holy grail.

One day, as I got to school, I saw Neil being picked on by the hoodie guys I hung out with. I was able to intercede, and the bond was made between nerd and greaseball. I went to my first foreign film with Neil. It opened a door in my mind. We became friends, and that has lasted sixty years now.

Neil is the most informed guy I know on movies, theater, art, and literature. At Central High, I was a hoodlum during the week and on the weekends, Neil's academic protégé.

After high school, Neil married Alice, a girl in my homeroom class. She was one of those girls with a flip in her hair and a chip on her shoulder who wouldn't deign to speak to greaser scum like me. She was an uptown girl. But years later after my first couple of movies, I was able to give her an exclusive interview, helping her get into magazine writing. The flip and chip were long gone, and we were all friends living in LA for decades.

Neil has always been there for me in his own unique way; a quiet intelligence, a supportive source who riffs with the times. He would have been a great spy. He can move through a crowd unnoticed if he wants to. He enjoys being behind the scenes but is quietly influential. I call Neil "Underground Management". He's always there to lend his knowledge and support. He is a man who feels as good in a bookstore as I feel in a Ferrari showroom.

Neil had become a publicity associate for GQ Magazine in the 60s. He was a major theatergoer and came to see me on Broadway in *Does a Tiger Wear a Necktie?* with Al Pacino. That was my first real job after acting school, and Neil has seen almost every play I have ever done in my career since then.

Neil became one of the biggest PR men in the world. He was the "K" in PMK, the biggest PR firm in America.

After Neil left PMK, he went into actor management, representing Jeff Bridges, Ed Harris, Mark Harmon, John Lithgow, etc. Then years later, Neil got the writing bug, decided he was going to be a playwright and quit his own management company. He never really needed to tell his clients he wanted to write plays, but that's Neil.

His clients said, "Try it and we'll wait for you."

And they all did, at least a year or more, but Neil focused on getting his play made in New York City, and it ran in the Theater for the New City and then in LA in a slightly bigger production with Amy Madigan directing (Ed Harris's wife, a well-known actress and Neil's former client).

After the LA production, I had an idea and talked to an English friend of mine whose son was a budding thespian. We produced the play with me and his son in the London production *Off the King's Road*. We asked Jeff Bridges to play the doctor.

Jeff said, "I've never done theater."

"Well, technically," stated Alan Cohen, our director, "you still won't have done theater; we'll Skype your performance."

Jeff, being an old friend and client of Neil's, said, "Let's do it!"

All of this is an amazing story of friendship that's still going on. Neil and I remain remarkably close friends and speak weekly.

So, back to the story. The year was 1979, and Neil called me and said he was doing the publicity (he was still at PMK) for a movie that Jerry Hellman was directing. Jerry produced classics like *Midnight Cowboy*, *Coming Home* and *The Day of the Locust*. This was his directing debut.

Neil said, "I told him about you, and he wants to meet you."

The film was *Promises in the Dark* starring Marsha Mason. We met, and Jerry gave me the part. I enjoyed working with him very much.

I was in New York City to promote the release of *Promises in the Dark*. I was running around the city from radio studios to TV studios to newspaper interviews, on an intense promotion for the film, all set up by Neil.

I got into the elevator of my hotel in New York and this lovely lady with a familiar classic blonde hairdo jumped in as the doors were closing. We were standing face to face.

She smiled and said to me, "I know who you are!"

I smiled back. "I know who you are."

She was Dinah Shore, the ultra-famous television personality of the 50s and 60s. My father had a huge crush on her. Burt Reynolds had a long and serious love affair with her, and the Dinah Shore Golf Tournament is world-renowned. I remember watching her show as a teenager, and I still remember her theme song. She was sponsored by General Motors and the theme song went "See the USA, in your Chevrolet, America is asking you to call", I still know the tune. My whole generation does.

She smiled again. "How come you're not on my show?"

"I was just thinking, how come I'm not on your show?"

She said, "You're on tomorrow. We're taping this show in Central Park at Tavern on the Green. Be there by eight-thirty and we'll give you breakfast."

The door opened, and her exit was like the sun setting as the door closed.

At 8 a.m. the next morning, I was taking a brisk walk-through Central Park, one of my favorite places on the planet. I arrived at Tavern on The Green and found Dinah, who said, "Glad you could make it. I'll put you on last. We'll make them wait." Dinah had a comforting style and confidence that put you at ease.

I was led to makeup. Makeup said, "You want anything?"

"I'm cool", I never really liked the stuff.

The studio people were on the ball, and I think they even got a clip from my film with Marsha and me to run during my interview. Working with pros!

As I waited, having coffee and reading the morning paper, I got a tap on the shoulder.

This huge man said, "Hi, my name is Larry Holmes. Mr Brandon, can I ask your advice?"

"Seeing as you just won the heavyweight boxing championship of the world, I imagine you can ask me anything you want, Mr Holmes."

We shook. *Wow, what a hand.*

"Larry," he offered.

"Michael," I replied.

Larry said he was nervous. Never did a live TV interview show before. What should he do? What did he talk about? What if she asked him stuff he didn't know? The usual nerves before a talk show appearance, but then Larry Holmes was not an actor or singer, he was a boxer, and not just a boxer, he was *the champ*!

I told him to relax. This was literally a walk in Central Park. "Dinah is very warm and a non-combatant. She will ask you about the fight and only stuff you know, and if you don't know what she means or don't want to answer that question, just talk about what you do know."

He was surprised. "I can do that?"

"What's your favorite thing?"

Larry said, "Helping kids. I got a program going in Pennsylvania."

"That's great," I told him. "Make sure you talk about it."

Larry thanked me for my help, "It was my pleasure, Champ."

A few months later, my friend Andy answered my house phone and said, "Some guy says to tell you 'It's *the champ*'." Larry had called to invite me to Vegas for his next title fight!

My talk-show interview with Dinah went smoothly, and afterward Dinah said, "What are you doing tonight?" She had two tickets to the opening of *Sweeney Todd,* and did I want to go with her?

I said, "Great, let's do it!"

"Meet me in the lobby, and the limo will take us to the theater and Orso for dinner after the show."

On the steps of the theater, we bumped into Andy Warhol. *Oh my God*! Turned out he was a huge fan of Dinah's and wanted her autograph. Well, she's an American icon just like Campbell soup. He handed us signed copies of his new magazine, *Interview*. He signed one for Dinah and one for me. I wish I knew where it was.

I got through the show. I'm not much for musicals where a barber bursts into song after slashing the throats of his customers and makes pies out of them. It's an English theme.

At Orso, Dinah and I were having a wonderful dinner. She was quite a woman. Very smart and, yes, she was older than me but extremely smart and attractive. Looking at her face was like eating apple pie with your eyes. She had that quality! She excused herself and went to the ladies' room, and then from behind me I heard the dulcet tones of Al Pacino.

"Michael," said Al with his eyes wide. "Dinah Shore, Dinah Shore?"

I turned to Al. "Dinah was my father's dream girl; he had a big crush; he would go crazy to know I was having dinner with Dinah Shore". Al nodded, "She's a special lady, I get it. My father too,". Al slowly pointed a finger reaching out from behind him, like Dinah did on her 50s TV show, and I pointed one back, we broke into the theme song together. "See the USA in your Chevrolet." Al and I shared a laugh. He winked at me and turned back to his dinner.

I was walking Dinah down the hallway to her room. She invited me in for a drink. I was excusing myself as I had previous plans and suddenly, we were kissing!

Dad, I'm kissing Dinah Shore! Dad, Dinah Shore is kissing me! See the USA! Americaaaaaaaaaaaaaaaaaa...

Back in LA, I got a call from Noel Black, the director of my second film, *Jennifer on My Mind*, the one filmed in New York and Venice, Italy. He was directing a feature film with Shirley

MacLaine, Anthony Hopkins, and the goddess from the sea, Bo Derek. Noel wanted me to play a French lumberjack. Yes! I always wanted to play a French lumberjack. To secure the role, I had to meet Shirley MacLaine personally. Was I free to have dinner with her? *Mon Ami*, but of course.

I told Andy and Debra Winger about having dinner with Shirley MacLaine in my Inspector Jacques Clouseau accent. "Zis eez way better zan an audiccion! I am how you say, exxcciiited."

Debra said, "I heard she wants all her leading men to be at least two inches taller than her or she won't work with them."

"How tall is she?" I asked.

Debra said, "Five foot ten, I think."

"But I'm only five eleven."

Andy said, "We can stuff something into your shoes to give you another inch."

I was walking like John Wayne when I left the house, but now I was six-foot-one.

I went to dinner and my feet were killing me. Shirley was fantastic and we got on great.

Shirley was saying, "I really don't see why you need to be French, play him as you are."

She seemed a genuinely good person, so I asked her straight out why she insisted her leading men had to be two inches taller than her.

She looked at me blankly and said, "Anthony Hopkins is shorter than me, and I never heard anything so ridiculous."

In my head, I could see Andy and Debra laughing their asses off; they set me up.

Shirley asked me if I would care to join her after dinner to a screening of *Being There* at MGM. We shot over to MGM and snuck in and sat in the aisle as there wasn't a seat left in the theater. It was a fabulous movie. The lights suddenly came up before we could sneak out and everyone applauded her performance.

I drove her home, she said, "Well, guess I'll see you on the set. Oh, don't cut your hair. I love it. Bye."

How nice was she! Wow, I was looking forward to this picture.

I flew to Vermont sitting next to Anthony Hopkins. We got on wonderfully. He told me how he was enjoying making films now because he got so nervous on stage he threw up before every performance.

I said, "Then why do it?"

"Why do what?"

"Theater, if it makes you throw up?"

"You know, I never really thought about it, but you make a good point there. Why do I do it? Quite right." He was lost in thought after that.

Oh no, I could have been the guy who stopped Anthony Hopkins from doing theater! Well, he just performed a stage play that was converted to a movie, winning an Oscar, and no nausea. So that's okay.

One day during the shoot, John Derek went to the director and was telling him off. "Why should Bo have to say this line? It's a terrible line."

The line contained the word *Oedipal*. Bo didn't want to say it because she thought it had dirty implications. The filming stopped while John Derek and Noel Black phoned Marty Ransohoff, the producer, in LA to discuss the line's importance in the film. Shirley suggested it would be less expensive to buy a dictionary. But Anthony took a more serious approach and felt that if the director couldn't explain to his actor the meaning of what he was filming, then perhaps the issue was far more significant. A cluster-fuck of a situation, folks. Ransohoff ruled, it stays!

In the end, Bo did say the line, but Anthony had become so disgruntled over the whole delay that when we got to our scene he was still agitated.

In the movie, *Change of Seasons*, Shirley's character is sleeping with me in revenge for Anthony sleeping with his student, Bo. She challenges his open misogyny, and we all go on a skiing trip together.

In the scene we were shooting that day, I was standing by my truck/cabin as Bo angrily drives off in Anthony's car.

Anthony came up and said, "Where did she go?" I pointed the direction, and he stood befuddled. Anthony grunted toward my truck, "Give me the keys!"

It wasn't in the script to demand the keys to my truck. I more or less offered him a way to go get her. It was more of my assisting gesture, one guy to another, but Tony didn't let me offer.

I said, "No."

Tony looked startled at me. "You have to give me the keys!"

"No, I don't." We stayed in character the whole time.

He said, "If you don't give them to me, I'll take them from you."

I said, "Good luck with that." (In the previous scene, he got into a fracas in the bar, and I not only saved him but kicked everybody's ass in the bar as well. My character had anger issues.)

He looked at me, his anger replaced with surprise. "How can I get the keys?"

"With a little respect."

He smiled broadly. "Quite right, shall we go again?"

Respect was restored.

Anthony and I bonded over that scene. He praised me for not giving in to his intimidation and then Anthony taught me a special sound, something between a whistle and a hum.

He said, "If you see me get like that again, just make this sound and it will restore me."

I loved working with him, and we'll always have our sound. I don't think Anthony loved working on this film though, not really his cup of tea. I had a ball working with him and Shirley MacLaine, both incredible actors.

Shirley and I got on so well, in one of our first scenes, the director asked us to face each other. It took a while to get the lighting right, and the artificial snowfall was a factor. Shirley and I just stood looking at each other. When they were ready to shoot, Shirley gently tilted me toward her. I said, "I think, the director said this is a fifty-fifty shot". Shirley said, "Michael, with me a fifty-fifty is sixty-forty". I burst out laughing. There were moments, particularly during the kissing scenes, that it could have happened. I don't mean sex; I mean a full-blown relationship. When we returned to film in LA, she asked me to lunch with Barbra Streisand and Bella Abzug, a US

303

representative and leading feminist. On the drive after lunch, I exclaimed, "That wasn't lunch that was a screen test". She smiled at me with knowing appreciation.

Working together was a joy, and, after the last shot, she grabbed my hair and said, "You're such a jewel, but you do remind me of my brother Warren a bit." We left as friends. Shirley was something wonderful.

CHAPTER 22

Biz Buzz

Westwood Village in Los Angeles was about ten minutes from my house in Brentwood. Home to UCLA College, it had a hamlet feeling with lots of bookstores, several movie theaters, cafés and restaurants all within walking distance. For this reason, it was very popular with studios for premiering movies to get young audience reactions as well as film screenings.

I was on my own but in the Village there's always a buzz of people. This screening was one of those high-expectation pictures: great director, great writer, great actors, and a great disappointment. That's the biz.

I was standing outside the theater feeling totally underwhelmed by the film when this woman came out behind me, physically shaking off the movie like she walked into a spiderweb. I may have said that out loud, and she burst out with a deep, throaty laugh. Obviously, we both felt the same about the movie, and I joined her in the spider web dance. She lit a cigarette, and we started ragging on the film and wound up having an enjoyable drink together.

305

This was how I met Julia Philips, the first woman producer to win an Oscar. She won it for producing *The Sting*, with Robert Redford and Paul Newman. This happenstance meeting led to a follow-up lunch where Julia asked what I was working on. I told her about my script idea, and I must have pitched it pretty good because Julia offered me a development deal on the spot for *Blood Relative*.

What do you call an unemployed person in Hollywood? A producer in development. That's an inside joke.

I developed the script for Julia's production company at 20th Century Fox, where she had a multi-picture deal; if they greenlit my picture, then it was hers to produce. I would then get paid nicely plus a percentage of the picture. In the meantime, that's right, no money, but Julia provided me with office space in her townhouse complex on the studio lot. Her offices were beautiful, spacious, and decorated in Georgia O'Keefe artwork, with thick carpeting and modern furniture. And if I may say, there is something special about driving into the studio to my private parking space. My *Blood Relative* thriller had been well-received after our pitch to the studio, and Julia was optimistic.

Julia was an attractive lady with a kinetic personality, short-cut graying hair and intense blue eyes. She had a small frame but therein was a powerhouse of focused energy that had produced great films: *Close Encounters of the Third Kind* and *Taxi Driver*, among others. She was one of the most intelligent people I had ever met, which made her sexy too, and men in the business were intimidated by her.

A few months later, I brought my good friend Ken Sylk, who had written a gangster script called *Mink*, to meet Julia. She liked it and gave Ken a similar deal and the empty office on the other side of me. We faced Julia's office, and in the center hub we all shared the secretary, Kiki. Kiki was one of those super-people who booked lunches, screening rooms, made calls, booked meetings and copied our scripts, and messengered them around town. She was also immune to any advances, no matter how clever or heartfelt, but had the phenomenal sense of humor to appreciate them, and she was worshipped by us.

Nothing is for nothing, the Gutter Confucius would say.

Julia was our boss, and she could be quite a force to reckon with. When the entry door slammed downstairs and Julia's dragon-roar bellowed through the building, grown men hid in the closet while Kiki ran for the loo. Once there was a knock on the closet door, it was Harlen, Julia's assistant, wanting in. Nobody wanted to be the first one she would see as she entered the office. We wondered what could be causing her such distress.

In the dark tenseness of the closet, Ken whispered, "She probably broke a nail."

I cracked up, and we all fell out of the closet in front of Julia. Upon seeing us, she guffawed hysterically, falling to the floor. We made her laugh. What else matters but the pursuit of humor.

Kiki handed Julia her coffee and cigarette, and Julia said, "My car is in the shop. Can one of you give me a lift home?"

Ken was quick to volunteer saying, "Mikey's going right by there."

Julia was happy and twirled off to her office.

I stared at Ken. "You fuck!" Then we laughed our asses off some more. Ken and I remember it as 'The Laughing Year'.

Few people get a film made, and it could take years. The process is ongoing. (Ken Sylk is still working on *Mink* forty-eight years later!)

"Writing is rewriting," says award winning writer and friend, Larry Gelbart (*Tootsie, Mash, City of Angels*). Larry told me he recently pitched a script, which in earlier years he didn't have to do. Larry Gelbart had weight. After the pitch, the young producers said, "Could you put a ride in it?" Larry was confused; he thought they meant something about the pace of the story. The producers clarified, "If you can put a ride in the story for the amusement park, it would help sell the script." Larry walked out.

For most writers, it was pitching the idea, get notes, write a film treatment, get more notes, write the script, get lots more notes, resubmit the script, and get even more notes. Re-pitch it and maybe get a movie deal. Studio memo arrives saying, they are thinking of a particular actor for the film so: *Change the script to suit; enclosed are the actor's notes.* Rewrite and resubmit the script and then you get a note: *They lost that actor; disregard previous note.* Wild card: the studio boss changes, and everybody starts over, all deals on hold, which is exactly where Julia was at this moment in time.

Julia was upset about how long it was taking to confirm any of her deals. Screaming into her office phone, "Why can't you pricks even remember what lies you told me yesterday?" Phone slammed down and then scream: "Lunch!"

We all happily went to the executive dining room, filled with agents pitching studio package deals, (a star and director) producers pitching stars, and directors getting pitched by producers, agents, and stars. The Gutter Confucius says, *if bullshit was white, you could ski in Hollywood.* However, it was a great time to exchange ideas and eat the best Chinese chicken salad in the city.

In the executive commissary, from behind her copy of Variety, Julia muttered, "Sherry Lansing has just been made the studio's head of production. Gives a whole new meaning to production head."

Mel Brooks stood up on his chair and said, "Attention, attention, I have a news flash, everyone please, in the event of a nuclear attack, the safest place to be, is right here. This studio hasn't had a hit in years."

The dining room double doors swung open and two burly bodyguards carried in a throne-like chair. It was Marvin Davis's custom-chair that went everywhere Marvin went. Marvin was an excessively big man and needed to sit on an extraordinarily strong chair. Marvin had recently bought the studio, which included all the picture deals Fox had under option. All were waiting for news on their deals to greenlight pictures.

When Julia saw Marvin, her eyes started to circle in opposite directions. Just as Marvin was settling into his chair, Julia climbed on top of him. Literally on top and said into his face, "Where's my deal, Marvin?"

He took it as best one can when a person, even one as small as Julia is perched on your stomach. He cajoled her by promising to address it right after lunch. That was ominous and sure enough, within a month, Julia's offices were moved from the designer townhouse to a trailer nearer the gate. The studio was deeply invested in Julia and didn't want to kill her deal and let another studio get her pictures. They didn't want to pay her off either. What they could do is tie her up in bullshit for years. (If you want details, get Julia's book *You'll Never Eat Lunch in This Town Again*. RIP Julia.)

With Julia's offices moving toward the gate, my scriptwriting was literally on the way out. That's when I met with my agents at CAA, Michael Ovitz and Ron Meyer, the two most powerful agents in the business.

Mike said, "Do you know how much money you didn't make this year?"

I looked at him. "How could I know that?"

Ron said, "I do. You didn't do *Trapper John, MD*, *St Elsewhere* or *Family Ties* with Michael J. Fox."

Mike listed a few more cop and lawyer shows, and I said, "They're all TV series and I don't want to do a TV series."

"Look, Michael, the business has changed," Mike said. "TV isn't taboo anymore. You do dozens of TV movies, but they'll dry up because the networks are offering the TV movies to the casts of their hit series to extend their series contracts. They'll get the first shot at TV movies for remaining under contract to the show."

Ron added, "Casting isn't done by the directors anymore. Networks decide. It's the winds of change in Hollywood."

I surrendered. "Okay, I'll read some pilots."

That was good agenting.

I went back to my office at Fox with a stack of TV pilots under my arm (pilots are the filmed one-off scripts used to sell a series to the network). I sat with my feet up on my desk, reading one after the other and chucking them over my shoulder into the bin.

Ken came in with a bowl of grapes. He sat down, "There was something I wanted to tell you, I just can't remember what." Ken started picking up scripts and skimming and chucking them as well. Richard Baskin (OOOOEEEE), stopped by to have lunch. But Ken and I were on a grape fast.

Richard said, "Nothing but grapes?" "Green grapes for breakfast." I said, Ken offered Richard a grape, "Red grapes for lunch and frozen grapes for dinner," "maybe mixed." We said together. Baskin asked about the party Julia was hosting at her house, he wanted to get invited.

I said the party was for NOW, the National Organization for Women.

Ken Sylk catching a tossed grape in his teeth, "Two reasons you can't go, Richard. (swallow) One, you're not a woman and eating only grapes makes me forget everything else."

Richard said, "I want to meet Barbra Streisand." "Oh yeah, I remembered" exclaimed Ken, "I just auditioned for a part in a series called *Emerald Point*," Ken acted as well. He worked and became friends with Pacino on *Author, Author*. "They're looking for a Michael Brandon type."

It was happening! *Who is Michael Brandon? Get me Michael Brandon, get me a Michael Brandon type … Get me a young Michael Brandon*, and then *Who is Michael Brandon?*

"Where was this?" I exclaimed.

He said, "Just up the hall. Esther Shapiro's office." The Shapiros' co-produced *The Colbys* with Aaron Spelling, the *Dynasty* spinoff starring Charlton Heston, Stephanie Beacham, and Emma Samms." Spelling/Shapiro were mega TV producers.

I jumped up and ran down the hall to Esther's office. I opened the door and said, "Esther, did I die? A Michael Brandon *type?*"

Esther said, "We would love to have you, but we see you in production next door, and frankly didn't know if you were acting anymore."

"Where does it shoot?"

"Here on the lot," she said.

"So, I could be in my office when you don't need me?"

"I don't see why not," she replied.

"How many days would you need me?"

She shrugged at a schedule on her desk. "Three days a week."

"Call Ron Meyer."

Shit, my agents were right. It was time to do a series before it was W*ho is Michael Brandon?*

Back in my office, I had one more pilot left to read. The script was written on funny-looking paper (English weird paper size, A4). It was longer and thinner than the usual scripts and why it was on the bottom. It was a script called *Dempsey and Makepeace.*

I called Ron at CAA. Ron said with surprise, "Esther Shapiro just called me to offer you seven episodes of *Emerald Point*, and she seemed to think you would do it."

"Yeah, it was an easy walk down the hall and it shoots here on the lot. Get whatever you can, but I called about one of the pilots you gave me: *Dempsey and Makepeace*."

Ron cut me short. "Sorry, Michael, that was a mistake. You're not right for that one. Besides, it's in England." He said *England* like it was a syphilitic boil.

"I know it's in England, but I like the part, and I want to meet."

"I already spoke to the producers, and they don't want to see you. They're looking for a California millionaire type."

"And that's precisely what's wrong with the script, Ron. C'mon, You're CAA; get me a meeting."

Ron did, and I went to the St James Hotel on the Sunset Strip to meet these two English producers, Tony Wharmby and Nick Elliot, who were packing while I spoke from the door. There was no doubt this was a courtesy meeting.

I gave them my pitch. I had learned from Julia, the master pitcher! The Californian millionaire James Dempsey III and Lady Harriet Makepeace, in their proposed script, were about wealth and class.

"Make Dempsey a homicide detective out of the gutters of New York and he will lesson-up this cultured lady, teach her the true meaning of the Bard's words and then you'll have dynamics. If that's of interest, then I'm your man. Thank you for your time," and I walked out. It felt good!

Back in my office, I got a call from Ron. "The Englishmen are taking the later plane; they want you to put whatever you told them on tape."

While the lengthy negotiations were going on between the US and the UK, the filming for *Emerald Point* had begun. My character was a very romantic hero. Aaron Spelling and I discussed the part in detail.

Aaron said, "Your character is a novelist who lives on his sailboat with his white shepherd dog. He meets Maud Adams' character in the marina, and they fall instantly in love. It's sex and sailing and as you're a novelist and adventurer, you can keep your beard. Sound, okay?"

That's how Aaron pitched it to me and in TV, he was better than Julia. However, after the network got done rewriting the scripts, the boat had sunk, the dog had died, and the beard was shaved. The romantic novelist became a stalker obsessed with killing Maud. It got even crazier than that. The network wanted to air all the episodes during the same *sweep's* week (a week when they record viewers for ratings). There were three directors and three different crews, shooting three separate episodes simultaneously. In fact, I worked on three different episodes in one day, going from location to location.

I got a call from Jake Bloom, my lawyer, The UK deal was done! I was very excited about this series, but I couldn't celebrate just yet, I had agreed to take an audition that day, even though I didn't like the part. Bobby Deniro was the star of the movie, and he was going to read with me for the director. I just couldn't find any traction with this part and the fact that I would be in England when they made this movie, sort of dampened my enthusiasm. The Gutter Confucius says, "What the mouth promises the body must submit to".

After the reading Bobby walked me aside. He looked at me shook his head. "That was a shitty reading, Michael." I nodded, "You're right. I couldn't get into this character and to tell you the truth, I signed a series deal today, and I'm off to England. I wouldn't be available for the film". "That's bullshit Michael, and you know it. When you go in, you do your best. You never know what this director is going to doing next and that shit comes around. You always put out your best". He was so right. I was humbled. I nodded, "Thanks Bobby, I appreciate what you're saying to me and you're exactly right". He nodded, cool and wished me a good shoot in England.

There was no pilot; the UK committed to a full season of shows. I'd be filming for six months. A show called *Dempsey and Makepeace.*

Before I'd get to meet the Queen, I flew from LA to Florida for a quick visit with my family. It's on the way to the UK anyway. So, I flew to Miami to stay with Sol and Miriam. Mom was thrilled and Pop was happy as well. A few heart attacks had mellowed him a great deal. Now it was early bird sittings for dinner at five pm and unsurprising visits from the neighbors. The folks showed me off, they were proud of me. That didn't stop the questions - ever hear from your ex-wife, she never liked us anyway, are you seeing anybody? Did you unplug the car battery before you left, so it doesn't go dead while you're in where you said, England? My mother asked what language they spoke there. The daily visits to the interrogation pool where nobody swam. They just asked questions as they walked across the pool's width.

My father led me into the garage for an aside talk, whispering to me, "Your mother is trying to kill me." "Pop, what are you talking about?" "I'm diabetic, right? Look in the fridge and find something without sugar." Standing in the garage I could see my dad's tennis ball invention hanging from the ceiling. Since the fifties, Pop had hung a punctured tennis ball from a string so my mother would stop the Lincoln Town Car when the tennis ball touched the windshield instead of when the car hit the garage wall. Pop still had the red toolbox. I look up at the garage shelves filled with toilet paper. There must have been two hundred toilet rolls. "Why so much toilet paper, Pop?" The Gutter Confucius responded, "One thing you can be sure of in life is having to wipe your ass, son. Nobody likes making the walk of shame."

While there, my agent phoned and said that there was a delay in London. He told me about my co-star, Glynis Barber's filming going over, and the English producers didn't want me to show up for another week.

Whoa! I could not spend another week with my family!

I asked my agent what to do. He said, "Cozumel". I thought he sneezed. "It's in Mexico on the Gulf." What would I do in Cozumel? Hel told me there was 'Great diving'. In water? I can barely swim, I'm from Brooklyn. I wear sneakers when I go into the ocean. I do not want to step on things.

The diving instructor was a blond American hippy. He said, "You want diving certification?". "Sure." I said. He told me it took eight days to get that. I said I had five. He nodded, "Cool man. Put the tank on and let's dive." I think I missed a lot of important bits cramming this course. Instead of a swimming pool, my first lesson was thirty-five feet below the surface hovering above an old boat wreck. I have to say I was trying not to panic and breathe slowly but there were lots of things swimming around down there. When an eel reached out of some coral and bit my flipper, I freaked and headed up as fast as I could go. The instructor grabbed and held me, making motions with his hands to calm me down. Later he told me "If you go up that fast your blood vessels explode." What was I doing here? My advice, if you are that afraid of diving, don't do it.

That night I had aside talk without Pop, just myself. Embrace your fear and it goes away. I decided to give myself one more day. The next dive I met a grouper fish the size of a New York sewer cover. I didn't embrace it, but I did feed it from my hand. Three days later, I got diver certification, hopped back to Miami for an early-bird farewell dinner with the folks and flew that night to London. Now cue Britania…

CHAPTER 23

God! Save The Queen!

I arrived early morning in London, it was raining! I checked into the Brown's Hotel in Mayfair. I was sitting on the bed in my hotel room, feeling that fuzzy zone after a long-haul flight. The room was okay; the heavy drapes were open, and it was still dark. All I wanted to do was just lie back and go to sleep. If I gave in though, I'd have been up all night. I could have gone for a walk, but it was pouring outside. In LA the only time you walk in the rain is to your parked car.

The producer of *Dempsey and Makepeace*, Tony Wharmby, was setting up a meeting with my co-star, Glynis Barber, as soon as she was available. They delayed filming for a week on our show because she was working on a BBC series, *Jane*, and they were behind schedule.

Jane was a BBC series about a World War II cartoon heroine who always wound up saving the day while losing her dress in the process. It was big during wartime – anything with stockings was! I hadn't met Glynis, but I was looking forward to it.

The producer had paired Glynis and me to be the leads of this new series without us having met. A bold move. In America, they would have screen-tested hundreds of actors and actresses, pairing up dozens of couples for screen tests. What a relief not to go through that process.

It was March 1984 and there were only three stations on TV, which all signed off at 11 p.m., and there were no cable stations. On the BBC, there was a show, *how to build a window box*; on BBC 2 there was a special on AIDS and how it was transmitted through green monkeys; and on the third and last channel, LWT, *The Ottawa Ice Skating Championships*.

I was so jet-lagged, I watched my first ice-skating tournament. Torvill and Dean skate to "*Bolero*" and I was sobbing. Really? Was I crying over ice skating or because there was nothing else to watch?

Isn't the sun supposed to come out after the rain? No one told me how much it rained in England. I said yes to this job, and now I lived in a country with three TV stations and one weather condition.

I went to the theater alone, ate alone, and exercised alone at a place called Pineapple. The doorman said, "Mr. Brandon," and I was all ears, but it was just a guest greeting. How desperate was I? The English were being polite, not disturbing me, but in the States, there would be a PR person like my oldest school friend Neil Koenigsberg, the biggest in the business, seeing to my needs. He would have met me at the airport and taken me to a hotel, then set out my itinerary for the week.

After an entire week of non-stop rain, there was no invitation to dinner with the Queen, not even a movie premiere or even theater tickets. Did they still draw and quarter people in Piccadilly Circus? A hanging? I'd go to hanging. I'd have gone to the opening of a door by then.

I'd rented out my house, stored my car in a friend's garage, given out my dogs and cats to friends for safekeeping, boarded the horses and said goodbye to America. Still jet lagged, I watched that documentary on AIDS just to see the green monkeys but begging for sleep. I woke up at three in the morning in a sweat. I went to the loo (bathroom), and there I noticed a small red rash on my knee. I knew immediately it was AIDS. I fell to the tile and wept. God brought me across the sea to die quietly. No one would ever know what happened to me. "He went to England and disappeared".

I pulled myself together to face my fate.

I spent the rest of the dark hours till dawn writing goodbye letters to friends and warning lovers. But I kept thinking I wasn't around any green monkeys, so how did I get it? Maybe it was up at the Playboy Mansion in the Grotto? OMG, I think I remembered this short hairy guy climbing into the hot pools! In 1984, they said that when you make love to someone, you're making love to everyone they've ever been with. Could one of them have been with a monkey?

First thing, I called the production office and said, "I'd like to see a doctor."

This wonderful girl in the office, Jenny, was so nice. "Are you ill?"

"No," I stuttered, "I just thought since I'm about to start a very long and time-consuming job, I'd like to be assured I'm in top health."

She arranged it all straight away.

I walked into the Doctor's office and this white-haired gentleman said, "How can I help you?"

I whispered, "I have AIDS." He was quite calm. He looked at me as I pointed. "It's on my knee." He indicated I should roll up my pants leg and I did so very carefully, and he went right for it. I pulled back, saying, "Whoa, do you think you should touch it with your bare hands?"

He didn't reply but just examined my skin. Then he harrumphed and said, "Are you homosexual?"

I replied, "No."

Then he asked, "Where were you before you came here?"

"I watched the green monkey special on television last night in my hotel, I think it's called Mayfair."

"No. Before you came to England?"

"I was in America. I did take a quick trip to Florida to say goodbye to my folks because I was going to be here for six months. But my co-star Glynis Barber, who stars in a show called *Jane*, was delayed."

The doctor smiled, and I think his eyebrows jumped when I said Glynis Barber in *Jane*.

"My agent suggested I go to Cozumel." I added.

The patient doctor was a good detective. "Ah, what were you doing in Mexico?"

"I went to learn scuba diving." Then I rambled on to the doctor, "I was terrified of bumping into anything under the water. Why spend all this time looking for things you don't want to see, right?"

The doctor held up his hands, quieting me down, and nodded. "Yes, you got this in Mexico. What you have is a rash from touching fire coral. Roger Moore was in with the same thing very recently; he did *007* in the same waters. Here's a cream." He handed me the tiniest tube. "Apply it tonight and it should be gone by morning. But perhaps you want to talk about stress."

Was I lucky to find him!

I rushed back to the hotel, lucky to find that my *Farewell Friends, I'm dying* letters hadn't been posted yet. Phew! I tore them to bits in my room with the thankful Paul Newman contemplation, *lucky to be alive*. I decided to screw the hotel phone costs and called my friends in LA to tell them what happened. It's worthy of a laugh now! While I was getting their phone numbers from my Filofax, three pieces of paper fell onto the bed.

The first telephone number came from Michael Douglas, who said, "If you're going to London, you gotta call this guy."

The second one was from actor Robert Culp, who starred in the 70s hit series *I Spy* and *Columbo*.

The third was from Alana and Rod Stewart, together on her birthday.

As I looked at the three, I realized they were all the same person Johnny Gold. *Nee-noo nee-noo*, how weird was that? *There are no accidents*, says Dr. Richard Miller.

Johnny Gold became my best friend in the UK, in fact, he was the best man at my wedding, signing the wedding book at the Camden Council on that remarkable day. He was the man I would speak to when the sun came up over the Duke of York

Square and he'd call to say, "Morning, kid, how's the writing coming?" I fondly referred to him as "The Rabbi", my dearest friend and mentor for thirty-seven years. So sadly missed, and June 11, 2022, just seven months later, his magnificent wife Jan followed him on. Deep hollow sigh from my soul.

Johnny Gold was welcoming from my very first call to him. "You will meet me for dinner this evening at Tramp."

"Great, what time?"

"Eleven."

"At night?" In LA, we went to bed at eleven.

He said, "We only open at eleven. Come at 10:45 and we'll have a drink first. You can walk from your hotel. Ask your doorman – everybody knows Tramp."

Johnny and his wife, Jan thought I was Michael Landon from *Little House on The Prairie* and *Bonanza*. Alana had called and totally mucked it up in her good-natured way. We had a good laugh over that, and we were well on our way to becoming fast friends. I often went home after working late on *Dempsey and Makepeace,* took a quick shower and on to Tramp for the evening with Johnny. Another great thing about having a driver; what's not great about having a driver?

At Tramp, I never knew who would be joining Johnny's table. Many nights it was just us having dinner, but over the years nearly my entire social network evolved from this one man. Zero degrees of separation. It became a table of friends like the round table of King Arthur: Jackie Collins and her wonderful husband Oscar; Joan Collins and various husbands; Michael and Shakira Caine; Errol and Ginette Brown; George and Angie Best; Leslie and Evie Bricusse; Roger and Louisa

Moore; Mickie and Chris Most; Bill Wyman; Rod Stewart; Freddie Mercury; Imran Khan (cricket player who became prime minister of Pakistan); Paul Young; and Tom Jones. Then add the Americans who came to town: Mel Brooks, Sly Stallone, Michael Douglas, Dyan Cannon, Linda Grey, Robert De Niro, John Travolta, and Kathleen Turner.

Johnny Gold should have been the mayor of London. Everyone I knew in England, except Glynis, I knew through Johnny Gold.

BACK TO BUSINESS

I arrived at the Ritz Hotel for my first meeting with my co-star. I was getting well into my character of Dempsey and strutted into the Ritz like Davy Crockett without the raccoon cap. I was brash, loud, irreverent; an American. I was also Glynis's worst nightmare. Tony had told me, she had seen only one piece of my work, *Rich and Famous*, and I was a complete cad in that film. She had never met a creature quite like me before and was probably thinking, *why do I have to meet one now?*

I thought she was attractive, sweet, maybe a bit reserved. Who am I kidding? She was knockout gorgeous! I could hear the Gutter Confucius' wisdom in my head: *Son, don't shit where you eat!* Of course, he was right, but I asked her out anyway. It turned out she had a boyfriend. I described my first meeting with Glynis in my journal and I did warn myself to keep it professional, but who listens to themself?

The day after my meeting with Glynis at the Ritz, I found my way over to the *Dempsey and Makepeace* production offices in Peckham. It was an actual warehouse off Old Kent Road in a much less attractive part of London. A concrete warehouse with fluorescent lighting and space divided up into production offices, and one corner was set aside for the SI10 police headquarters set we used in the show. Our only set.

My mother actually asked me what language they spoke over here.

I told her, "It's England, Mom – they speak English."

She made a nasal sound. "Like us?"

"Not like you, Ma."

The crew spoke Cockney and Northern or Geordie versions, never mind the Irish and Scottish dialects. The prop guy asked if I'd be needing a kettle? I looked at him. He said, "Your watch, mate, the kettle, you watch the kettle, right?"

Cockney rhyming slang was a language unto itself and often took more words to say the same thing, which didn't rhyme. Dog and bone meant *phone*. Her trouble and strife referred to *the wife*, and apple and pears – *stairs*. I guess my mother was right to ask what language they spoke here! I did an episode where I was undercover as the local gas man. The crew was hooting with laughter at my Cockney imitation when I said, "Gas Board, ma'am!"

I found Tony Wharmby's office, and I asked him to introduce me to the writing staff. He showed me to a room with a chair and a table. Ten scripts and a pen sitting on top. No writing staff. I was gobsmacked, whatever that means! In the States, there was always writing staff, and the head writer laid out the season's stories with the arc of each character (what happens to each character over the entire series). This was called the show bible.

Tony said, "I only bought the scripts, not the writers. It was your idea to change the concept of the Dempsey character into a hard cop from New York. Now you must do it on paper." Me and my big mouth.

True, I got myself into this, so I sat down and got to work in earnest.

Turned out most of these scripts felt like rehashes of old detective programs written for two guys. Sometimes just switching the dialogue between the two characters made it smoother. I didn't have to wait long to see how my co-star Glynis felt about all the changes. Glynis was feisty and a feminist before it became fashionable. She tried hard to maintain her dignity and that of her character in this macho, misogynistic detective concept.

I wrote a line for Dempsey and Makepeace driving to Makepeace's ancestral home. Dempsey didn't know it was Makepeace's stately family mansion and remarked, "Hey, Makepeace, if I lived in those days, I woulda been a knight in shining armor." Makepeace retorted, "Dempsey, if you lived in those days, you would have been shining the armor at night."

I immediately knew it was a funny line, and it worked for audiences on both sides of the pond, as they say. Glynis agreed it was a good line, but it needed more setting up. I can't remember what I said back, but it really got up her nose, as they say. We were getting on well, most of the time, but that day she had enough of this brash American bully and got angry. She let me have it with both her reserved British barrels. "Up yours with a lavatory brush."

"That's it? I laughed; that's your worst - a lavatory brush?" It ended up with her getting so mad she chased me out of the office.

I moved out of the hotel to a house I rented on Glebe Place in Chelsea. I found it through Richard Gere, who had just wrapped on a picture and was about to return to LA. Glynis kindly agreed to go with me to look at the place. I think she went along because she had a thing for Gere. He told me, "It's a great location. You get more than a place to live, you get a whole social life." I'd known Richard from LA. We had dinner a couple of times, attended the same parties, and were both into meditation.

The day I moved into Glebe Place, I met Willy Feilding, the owner of the flat. He was the Earl of Denbigh and a true English character.

I had only placed my bags inside the entry door when Willie said, "Come along and I'll show you your local."

I informed Willie I had a full-time driver and didn't need the subway. (Your *local* in New York City is your nearest subway.)

Willie laughed and said, "No, dear boy, it's your local watering hole."

The English way of life: lunching and drinking, then recovering in time for a late dinner party. What could I do?

Willy took me on a short walk to the Foxtrot Oscar on Royal Hospital Road; a block from Mick Jagger's home, he secretly told me. This was the watering hole of what was called the Sloane Rangers, of which Princess Diana and Fergie were members, like the Hamptons' *Hoo-hah Henrys*. The rest of the clientele was made up of posh Etonians (Eton graduates) and legendary English eccentrics, including the famous Daily Mail columnist Nigel Dempster.

Willie gave the secret knock, and the door was opened by the proprietor and local hero, Michael Proudlock. (I'm godfather to his son, Oliver Proudlock of *Made in Chelsea*, a TV reality show of upper-class kids fame, and I'm very proud of him, indeed.)

Proudlock kept refilling my glass. There's a way restaurateurs have of keeping everyone's glass full without ever noticing it's refilled. I was never much of a drinker, and I suddenly noticed Willy, my landlord, had gone. It was dark outside. How could it be dark? It wasn't even 4 p.m. *They have the same sun here, don't they?*

I got up and promised Proudlock I'd be in touch. The liquid lunch we just had was in the next day's Daily Mail in Nigel Dempster's column, "My Foxtrot Oscar interview with Yank detective Michael Brandon". I didn't remember giving an interview but now I had a bigger problem; I couldn't remember where I lived. Well, I hadn't lived there yet. It took an hour to find my five-minute-walk home two streets away.

I was holding onto the vines around the door (which Willy told me Virginia Woolf had planted) while I figured out the keys. I staggered inside, tripped over the suitcases that I'd left in the entryway, and spent my first night on the Glebe Place floor where, Willy also told me, Nijinsky once danced.

When I woke up, I was staring at the most peculiar vision of Snow White. It wasn't the usual Disney Snow White. This Snow White was in various sexual positions with all seven dwarfs. I thought it was the drink, but it turned out Willy Feilding had painted these naughty artworks of Disney characters. Good morning, London!

CHAPTER 24

Dempsey "Life Is Hard and Then You Die"

It was daybreak as I returned home from finishing my three-mile run along Battersea Park. I crossed back over the Albert Bridge to Glebe Place and a nice hot shower (well, a warm UK trickle) while the coffee beans were brewing. I brought the beans over with me from America. I heard you couldn't get a decent cup in England. It was true so far. What was here in March 84 was not coffee.

Bill, my driver, was a very affable fellow and asked if I wanted to stop for a cuppa. I knew this meant tea, and I don't drink tea. I told Bill I brewed my own coffee every morning. He asked if I wanted a newspaper.

I said, "I don't know the newspapers here."

"I'll get you a selection and then you can decide."

I wanted to see the city, so I jumped in front with Bill. I sensed he was uncomfortable about it.

He said, "To be honest, Gov, you should be in the back."

I asked about his car.

Bill was a very honest man and, with an embarrassed laugh, said, "She's an old Ford Granada that squeaks in the back. Needs shocks."

I told him not only did it squeak but there wasn't much headroom either.

"I wish I had the dosh to get a new motor," Bill said.

I learned *dosh* is money. "Bill, you seem to be a good man to me, so tell your boss this show will take approximately six months to film and I'm happy for you to be my driver for the whole of that time. But I would prefer a more comfortable ride."

"I'll talk to the office. What kind of motor would you like, Gov?"

"Bring me a selection. Hey, Bill, what's Gov mean?"

Bill showed up with a blue Jaguar. There was even less room in the back. The following day, a Rolls Royce. He said it was his boss's personal motor, and he was impressed I offered Bill, the length of the show. When the crew got down on their knees and bowed on our arrival, I gathered that a Roller was over the top. See, I've picked up the lingo!

The next day, Bill pulled up with a simple dark blue stretch Mercedes. I say "simple" as it was unfortunately not one of those old Mercedes 600 limos I love. It was a straightforward stretch without the bells and whistles, far less ostentatious and more useful because we could fit makeup and wardrobe inside for rides to and from the set.

Bill smiled. "It works a treat."

Works a treat? I liked that one.

The one thing that really made Bill nervous was me forcing him to get in the back of the limo in the morning, with me driving.

"They'll fire me. Please, Mike?"

"They can't fire you, Bill, you're my driver. Get in."

Then I would drive him to the location. I told Bill it was the only way I could learn the city, so "sit back and enjoy". Bill screamed when I sped into my first roundabout (okay, every roundabout). These circles without traffic signals that are fed by four lanes of traffic were insane. *Hello, they invented the traffic signal!*

"Hey, Bill, is my driving gonna give you nightmares?"

Bill screamed back as he held on, "If I live long enough to have one!"

The first week of filming, I met Ray Smith, the Welsh actor playing Chief Spikings, our governor (The Gov). He sounded just like Richard Burton. I guessed all the people from Wales spoke like that. After an early morning start and a lucky bit of sunshine, I was in Dempsey's Merc (they made a toy of me in this Mercedes). The hood was down (not the *boot, bonnet,* or *top,* but the hood!) and I had my Ray-Bans on. Dempsey lived!

There was so much film equipment in the car, I could hardly get in it. I had to turn on the cameras, the lights, and sound, then do the clapboard, number the scene, say *Action!* and drive off doing my dialogue on the walkie-talkie police radio to Charlie Five, which would be Makepeace's call name. It was a little like guerrilla-type filmmaking.

Lunch was called. I was the only one at the catering truck. In America, the queue would be so long an assistant would cheat you in line with the crew or bring it to your trailer.

I thought I'd gotten it wrong, and said to the cook, "They called lunch, right?"

"Yes, they're all in the pub, Mate. Ten minutes before the end of lunch, they come running for grub. New potatoes, Mike?"

"What?"

He repeated in his strong Northern accent, "*Nyew potahtoes?*"

I tried to read his lips 'cause I didn't know what he was talking about. New as opposed to old potatoes? I just held out my plate and he gave me some little round potatoes.

"Puddin', Mike?"

"Sure, I'll have puddin'." Looked like a brownie – yeah!

I was spitting out what turned out not to be a brownie, but something called blood pudding. Congealed blood cakes are illegal in the US. I squeezed out of the trailer bathroom wiping my face when this tall, thin man bounded into the trailer and dropped to his knees in front of me, undoing my belt.

"Whoa fella!" I yelped.

"I'm Nigel, your new wardrobe dresser, and I was just replacing your belt." Nigel held up the new belt.

"Nice to meet you, Nigel, but could you do that standing up?"

In the States, the wardrobe department puts your costumes in your dressing room or your trailer. They don't dress you; well, maybe if you're a woman and there are straps for microphones etc. Here, it's an English tradition. I didn't want to offend so I submitted.

Nigel was putting on my socks, which was extremely strange. I felt like I was four years old. I have to say he did it very well and didn't shout "Stay still!" like my mother.

There was a boom of thunder, the skies opened, and the rain came down in buckets. Then the assistant came in holding one hand over his head like it was keeping him dry. It wasn't. "They're ready for you."

I said, "Ready for what?"

"To continue the shot from before lunch."

"You realize it's pouring now, and it was sunny earlier when I had the top down, so it won't match."

He looked genuinely puzzled.

The director was hurrying by us under an umbrella (*brolly*) and said, "Everything okay?"

I said, "Well, it's about continuity. I can't drive the car with the top, sorry, hood – down. It's raining and won't match."

The director laughed. "Michael, this is England. People know it's sunny one minute and raining the next. See you on the green."

Here, people would just assume the weather changed! Wow, this was a revelation. They couldn't do that in America. They wrote "mismatch" complaints to the network all the time: *She was wearing gloves in the elevator but when she came out, she wasn't wearing them.* They love bloopers! That's why the film industry is centered in LA. The same weather every day, and if you do get a rainy day, you shoot in the studio. It's called wet weather cover.

One morning, about a week later, my driver Bill growled and handed me a newspaper while I got into the stretch. I saw myself on the cover pictured with several famous actresses reporting that I had sex with all of them. The entire inside center section was a two-page spread featuring a picture of me surrounded by a wheel of well-known film and TV actresses, saying I had slept with all of them. I nearly croaked. For one, it mostly wasn't true, and secondly, what if these women thought I really did tell the papers this stuff?

I called my agent, who said, "Call your lawyer."

Jake, my lawyer said, "If you sue them, they'll only get to reprint it. If you beat them, they'll put a postage-stamp-size apology lost somewhere in the paper and frankly, Michael, it's just not worth it."

I called the paper and asked for the journalist who wrote the article. I didn't hope for much, but I said I was so impressed by the article I wanted to thank him personally, maybe find out what he liked to drink, and he came on the phone. I said it was a great interview, but he missed out on a few juicy bits about some famous actresses and their kinky habits. He jumped on the bait and said he would come to lunch with me the next day in my trailer.

I called the prop department guys, who were always up for mischief, and went over my plan. They loved it.

The next day when the journalist arrived, I invited him into my motor home and offered him a cigarette. He basically admitted without much denial that he took most of his interview from old articles he read and made up the rest of it and was quite proud of it.

While he was gloating, I picked up the set can of petrol and poured it over his pants. It smelled like petrol and looked like petrol, but it was just water with some smelly coloring added by the prop boys. I held up my lit cigarette. He was squirming all over the booth and making piggy noises and jumped up, running for the trailer door. It didn't open because two burly prop boys were holding it shut.

I asked him to not write anymore lies about me. He swore he would never write another word about me ever! I knocked twice on the trailer wall, the door magically opened. He leaped from the trailer. Today, that act would put me in a shitstorm of trouble, but that was forty years ago.

I bumped into Jackie Bisset in London not long after that incident. She was in town visiting her mother. I told her I wanted to apologize for this article in the paper because I had never given the interview or said those things, but she was way ahead of me.

"I know all about the press here. Let me give you a tip, Michael. You can break their noses." She demonstrated with a right hook. "That's right, it won't cost more than a couple of hundred quid. It's not like America where they sue you for millions. Just break his bloody nose."

So tough, we laughed.

Glynis and I were working stupid hours, late nights and through the weekends. The production was trying to shoot an American type of schedule, which is impossible when the days here lose the light at three-thirty or four in the afternoon. Not to mention the inclement weather.

I remember how Tony, our producer, would use his unique way of asking the crew, out loud, if there was anyone who didn't want to work late that night or on the weekend. Of course, no one fully raised a hand; they might be out of a job. He was a sly one but a very likable man.

I met one of the original writers once. He came by the set while shooting the episode he wrote, and said, "I gave you the key to the character, but you're not using it."

"Really?" I said, "What was the key?"

"I reckon."

I waited, but that was all he had to say. "I don't get it."

He said, "'I reckon' – that is what they say in New York City, and that is the key to this character, and you are just missing it."

"Well, I was born in New York City, and we don't say 'I reckon'. People from Texas say I reckon, but in New York we say, 'I figure'. I figure this, I figure that, but we don't reckon. So, I figure this conversation is over, you reckon?"

Every actor will tell you that most of a filming day is spent waiting. I was flirting with Glynis daily, and she had a boyfriend who was getting very jealous. But it was just my way of kidding. It was Dempsey coming on to Makepeace. Believe me, I understand it's a different world today but back then it was innocent banter. It keeps up the energy as well as sparking up the characters on a long, cold day at the Docklands.

I apologized to Glynis when I saw our chit-chat banter was getting on her nerves, but eventually things did get strained between us. We got up each other's noses (very English) and Glynis started really disliking me due to the pressure from home and the enormous amount of time we spent together. That was getting in the way of our work, and I asked the producers to find another actress. (I know, can you believe it?).

Tony (the producer) said he totally understood and was looking for a replacement. He lied, of course, because the UK and the American networks were loving what was happening on screen. Whether it was love or hate, the chemistry on screen was sizzling.

I finally had a day off. I found the list Richard Gere had left and called the gym around the corner.

A girl answered. "Bodies."

The way she said it was so sexy; I hung up and called back. "Bodies."

I hung up and kept doing it just to hear her say "Bodies".

I walked over to the gym and asked, "Who answers the phone?"

I was told that it was Louise in the office. I walked back and knocked. I opened the door and the prettiest girl with black hair and blue eyes said, "Can I help you?"

I said, "Do you answer the phone here?"

"Yes," she replied.

"How do you answer? What do you say?"

She said, "Bodies, and I know it's you who keeps hanging up on me."

"I just love the way you say 'Bodies'."

Bodies was a great gym, and I met lots of people I still know today, like Daley Thompson, the Olympic champion.

Louise was my first English date. She seemed very unimpressed with the business. In fact, she was unimpressed with just about everything about me. I had another day off and I wanted to just stay home and watch TV and chill, but Louise said she had something special planned. What could this unimpressionable girl contemplate to be special? Lo and behold, I found myself at a football game, an English football game, on my day off!

I had no idea what was going on or who was even playing. I gathered this was an important game – some final or cup thing – but I was just exhausted. Here we were sitting in very special box seats right on the pitch, I believe it was called, and after the game, I was in the locker room to meet the winning team.

It seemed her father, Ted Croker, was the general secretary of the Football Association. He was a genuinely nice man. I liked him straight away. Then, Ted introduced me to his *arsehole* doctor.

I was a bit surprised and said, "Y'know, Ted, in America, we call them proctologists."

Ted exploded with laughter. "Not *arsehole*. Arsenal."

They pronounce arsenal with two syllables: *arse-nal*. Word went round the locker room and the whole Arsenal team fell into hysterics. *Welcome to England, Yank.*

I spent at least three nights a week at Tramp with Johnny Gold. It was easy and comfortable and there really wasn't time for a regular social life. I worked from the crack of dawn till well after dinnertime. Most nights, Bill would wait while I picked up my Chinese takeout order. I wish I had invented Deliveroo back then. There was no food delivery in London. Just try convincing a London cab driver to lay out cash for dinner and deliver it!

One night, eating my takeaway, as they call it here, I got a call from Linda Gray while she was filming *Dallas* in Texas. Linda was a dear friend and my aunt-in-law from my marriage to Lindsay Wagner. Linda's husband Ed was Lindsay's mother's brother, if that makes sense.

When my marriage to Lindsay was over, Aunty Linda stuck by me. She knew the whole scene and offered me her support. It was a tough time for me, and now it was the other way around. Her twenty-three-year marriage with Ed Thrasher (a Warner Brothers Records exec), who had been her very first boyfriend, was over.

She needed some TLC after her separation from him. She didn't know how to date but was getting deluged by men with offers, all kinds of offers. I told her to come over to London and take a break. She was filming in Texas and told me there was a week before *Dallas* began filming back in LA.

"I'll come," she said.

The prop boys dressed up the props truck with curtains, a chandelier, and silver servings for a unique dinner for two. Linda laughed a lot, which is just what the doctor ordered. We went to Nick Rhodes' (Duran Duran) wedding at the Savoy Hotel, complete with fifty flamingos. A week later, Linda enthusiastically returned to LA, to Sue Ellen in *Dallas* and felt a lot better about her new single life. Linda is always helping people or serving some charity. She's a very good human being and a very good friend.

Back to filming on the D&M set, Tony was explaining that Glynis and I would be in this Mini when the car crusher comes down. "When it touches the roof, we cut."

Okay, we were in the car and the crusher came down, touched the roof, and didn't stop. It crushed the roof and sent the windshield exploding in all directions and then continued coming down. Glynis and I were huddled together on the floor as the roof of the Mini came closer and closer. It wasn't supposed to be this crushed!

She and I barely survived getting crushed to death. It was the same on many of the stunts on the show. We didn't have dedicated stunt doubles. When I stated that in American TV, we have union laws concerning this, a minion confided, "You're not in America."

After Glynis and I suffered small injuries that postponed filming, it was resolved. Time is money, and money makes a difference. It's the American way.

I met Valentino Mucetti, my stunt double. Val was the best! There were times I looked at the film and I couldn't tell whether it was him or me doing the stunt. But there were two things about Val: one, Valentino had vertigo. I had vertigo! We were usually way up on some girder on a construction site, and Val was saying, "You can do this one if you like, Mike." I would say, "Get your ass out on that girder, Val." The second thing was that Val's mother owned an Italian restaurant. Need I say more?

On a swinging chandelier stunt, Val pulled it out of the ceiling. Lying on the floor and brushing off the dust, he said, "Sorry, Mike, I'm going on a diet, I swear mate."

"Val, you're supposed to make me look like Errol Flynn, not Homer Simpson!"

When Barbra Streisand and my buddy Richard Baskin, now a couple, came to visit me on the set, it was like the Queen came to visit. Impressive, to say the least! Later over dinner, I bitched about Glynis the whole time. Barbra brings that one back to me every time we see each other. In fact, years later, Glynis and I, as a couple, were over at her house for dinner, and Barbra, in her most affable way, told Glynis verbatim what I had said at that first dinner in London. It was hysterical, well for everyone but me.

Glynis laughed. "I know all the nasty little things he used to say about me."

Barbra laughed too. "Oh, he was bitchin' about you, girl. I think, somewhere inside, he knew he met his match!"

We completed filming on the first five episodes, (the first episode was a two-parter) so more than half the season, in an intensely grueling three and a half months. Now, with a three week break before filming the remaining five episodes, I decided to fly back to LA and chill out with an American shower, a good cup of java enjoying the sunshine.

On the long flight home all I could think about was Nubbin and Sindbad. I missed them so much

Jay had sold his ranch and moved to Fiji and Andy rented a house in the Pacific Palisades and Debra was gone on locations filming movie after movie. I boarded Sinbad and Nubbin at a horse stable closer to Brentwood. This worked well for years, until I got the job in London.

I picked up my car that I left with a friend with an extra garage. I drove out to the stable and went looking for Sinbad. The owner told me Sinbad had gone lame and being an older horse it wasn't feasible for him to suffer. I looked at him. He nodded like it was a common thing, "We put him down". He said it in that American flat western tone that it didn't hit me at first. Then, told me he had given Nubbin to another boarding stable, as he kept racehorses, polo, riding and jumping horses, not wild mules. The Gutter Confucious saved this man's life, "*Son, you know the math, your fist will not fit in this man's mouth, walk away*".

I drove out to where nubbin was being kept. It seemed like a decent horse boarding facility but when I found nubbin I went numb. She was in a small damp stall, and she had foundered. A very serious issue with hoof tissue. Her hooves were deformed growing like curved up elf shoes. The inflammation is painful, she couldn't walk. I called the horse vet and after seeing Nubbin, he called a special farrier who hoisted her up in a harness to take her weight off as he cut her hooves in such a way as to relieve the pain and help her get back to normality. Left unchecked this could cause lifetime lameness.

I had gone off to England and trusted people to look after Sinbad and Nubbin and look what happened. Ok, Sinbad was an older horse when I bought him, and he did have a bum joint. I knew all that and I used to massage in creams and not ride when it bothered him. But most of the time Sinbad was in good form. It was eight years later now. Oh, Sinbad.

Nubbin was pure neglect, mine, and I took full responsibility for not being a better dad. I visited her every day until she was able to walk steadily and without pain. Nubbin's hooves grew normal, and she was once again, prancing around the pasture. I certainly wasn't going to leave her there when I returned to London. I had to find her a home.

Kim had become a llama breeder now and her barn and corals were full. I just wanted Nubbin to have a good free life like she had known. It came in the form of a petting farm. I had heard about a reverend who had set up a huge petting farm with large pastures. Nubbin could run free when she felt like it, come down to the fence and get carrots from kids who adored her. They scratched her shaggy coat and fawned all over her. I planned for regular farrier visits to keep her hooves improving and communication between me and the reverend. Nubbin loved it and I felt it was the best place. I felt a lump in my throat when I hugged her goodbye. She had her head over my shoulder with my face against her neck.

I went back some months later to visit her. She was standing out in the field grazing. I called Nubbin and her ears went forward, and she turned to me. She kicked her rear legs in the air and trotted down to me and put her head on my shoulder, and I started crying. She brayed like she was too. We were happy to see each other. It's how I remember her. I feel a great loss not having her in my life. But I had decided to live in England, and she was settled. It will never be right for me. That last hug and having to walk away breaks my heart still.

When Richard and Barbra visited me in London, Barbra insisted I call and come to dinner on my return to LA. I'd been to Barbra's before – the Beverly Hills house for Thanksgiving, and the Malibu house for films, dinner, and a couple of special concerts Barbra gave for charity.

A slight detour, if I may, at one of Barbra's concerts, 1981, I believe, I met Dyan Cannon. It was an amazing night under the stars complemented by Barbra's perfect voice. After Dyan and I had been dating a few months, she asked if I would come with her to Cary Grant's house for Christmas dinner. Dyan said it was for Jennifer's sake, her daughter with Cary, and I would be doing her a big favor. She wouldn't go without me.

"Okay then! If it makes you happy, let's go to Cary's for Christmas!"

Cary had Christmas carol singers come inside to sing just before dinner. He was very funny, telling wonderful stories and Joanne, his lovely wife served up and elegant Christmas dinner. Jennifer was happy to have both her parents together for Christmas. Jennifer gave Cary sock garters along with a pair of socks. Cary took off his pants straight away and put the garters on, making Jennifer and the rest of us laugh. Cary suddenly asked about the time. Grabbing my arm, he led me to the bedroom, climbed on the bed, pulled out a joint and the remote, and patted the bed to join him. We smoked and watched Cary receive his special award from the President of the United States.

I can't describe the expression on Dyan's face when she came out of the loo, adjusting her blouse. She looked up and saw Cary and me sitting on the bed, sharing a doobie, Cary in his shorts and sock garters. Her face and the slow-motion walk across the bedroom were equal to the *Pink Panther* comedy classic and had Cary and me crying with laughter.

Back to the story,

I called Richard and Barbara to say I was back, and dinner was on! Before dinner at Barbra's house in Malibu, I was playing paddle tennis at the deserted, closed-down Malibu Sand and Sea Club with Al Pacino, my best friend Ken Sylk and Larry Grobel, a freelance writer for *Rolling Stone* magazine. Ken called saying they needed a fourth player.

The beach club was originally built by William Randolph Hearst (Orson Welles based the film *Citizen Kane* on him). Hearst built the beach house for his silent film star mistress, Marion Davies. It had one hundred and ten rooms.

Al had permission to use the closed club's courts. Paddle tennis is a less prissy version of tennis and gets quite heated at times for New York kids like us. We grunted, yelled, and jumped around like street monkeys (not to be confused with green monkeys).

During the game, Al asked what I was doing later. I told him Barbra was having a BBQ for me.

Al paused. "Oh, Barbra Streisand, eh?" Then he asked Ken what he was doing, and Ken said he was invited to the BBQ at Barbra's as well.

Al looked at us and said, "Can I come?"

I was surprised. "You want to come to Barbra's?"

He said, "Yeah, sounds like fun."

"Well, I have to call," I said, "because it's about the about numbers, y'know, seating."

There were no mobile phones then, but there was a pay phone in the parking lot. We decided to take five, and I walked out to the phone box. I called and asked Richard about Al coming, and he said he'd ask Barbra and call me back on the pay phone.

It rang and he roared, "Ooooeeee, it's cool!"

I told Al, "It's okay for dinner."

We were into another fast-slamming game when Al won a point and held his hands in the air, asking, "Can I bring Diane?" Al was dating Diane Keaton at the time.

I said, "Why didn't you say that before?"

"Please call," pleaded Al. "Please?" He held up his hands together.

"Numbers, Al! I'll have to call Richard again".

"Okay, let's take five."

Back at the pay phone, I called Richard (*ooooeeee*) who called Barbra and called me back (0000eeee) and told me, "Barbra said it's too many people."

"Should I tell Al he can come but Diane can't?"

"No," said Richard. "It's too many for the house so Barbra is calling the Sea Lion Restaurant to book us a table." (Turned out she was setting me up with a blind date that night, but I didn't know this at the time.)

I told Al, "Dinner's on," and from that moment on he started singing Barbra's "Guilty" for the rest of the day. He was doing Barbra, "We got nothing to be guilty of", singing and slamming for a hysterical afternoon.

Later that night, we arrived at dinner and realized the restaurant had closed off half of the dining area into a private room. Why not? The group consisted of Barbra, Richard Baskin, Ken Sylk, his fiancée Ava Lazar, Al Pacino, Diane Keaton and me, oh yes, sitting next to me, my surprise blind date, Sherry Rivera, the ex-wife of the TV news presenter Geraldo Rivera. Sherry was a very pretty lady and a good friend of Barbra's. Was it me or could I hear … "Matchmaker, matchmaker, make me a match"?

(C'mon, Glynis has a boyfriend, remember?)

We were having drinks and ordering soup, when Ken said, "Hey, Al, why don't you do your imitation of Barbra?"

Diane Keaton spat her wine across the table, and Al chuckled guiltily. "What are you talking about?" he said.

Ken chimed in, "Go on, do it, it's great!"

Al was caught in the headlights.

Barbra said, "You do an imitation of me, Al?"

Al, all serious, said, "Ken's joking, Barbra."

"No, I'm not," said Ken, "he's been doing it all afternoon."

Diane began to slowly sink down into her seat. She was very shy, and in a couple of minutes it looked like seven adults and a small child were sitting at the table.

Barbra laughed. "Do it, Al, c'mon. I'd love to see it!"

Al laughed. "He's joking, he's pulling your leg, Barbra. There was no imitation."

Barbra stared at Al. A face-off. She looked at Ken. "Ken, honestly, did he do an imitation of me?"

Ken looked from Barbra to Al and back. "Yeah, and it was really good, Barbra!"

She looked at Al who was looking at Ken with that Michael Corleone face.

Al smiled weakly at Barbra. "I don't sing, Barbra."

Luckily, the waiter arrived with the soup. All was quiet during the soup-serving.

Barbra stood. "The salad buffet is in the other room."

All the girls but Diane went for salad. Al, Diane, Ken, Richard, and I had ordered the soup, so we stayed.

As the salad group left, Al leaned toward Ken. "What is the matter with you?"

"I thought it would be funny!" Ken said.

Diane said, "Shhh, please! I can't stand it!"

Al leaped onto the chair and began singing, "We got nothing to be guilty of, my love."

Diane was covering her eyes, pleading, "Please don't do this."

Al jumped down at the same moment Barbra, Sherry and Ava returned with their salads. Barbra looked at us. We were all seriously slurping soup. It was like when the teacher walked back into the classroom after chaos.

"What happened?" asked Barbra suspiciously, "Something happened."

Ken, slurping, said, "Al did his imitation of you."

Diane was now totally under the table. Al was staring at Ken with an open mouth dripping with soup, Sherry was cuddling my shoulder and smiling at me.

Barbra said, "Al, come on, I want you to do it."

"No," said Al.

"Really," said Barbra. "I would love to see your imitation of me. Do it, Al!"

Al seemed to waver, but he held the line, shaking his head. "Really Barbra, I don't sing, Ken is pulling your leg."

Stand-off! The dinner moved on and up, and a lovely time was had by all, even Diane.

After dinner, in the Sea Lion Restaurant parking lot, I was pulling Al off Ken. We were laughing but Ken had put Al in an uncomfortable situation. We were laughing in between the cars when Barbra's lilting voice drifted over us: "…and we got nothing to be sorry for…"

Al responded, singing the Barry Gibbs part, "Our love is one in a million…" and she sang and then Al sang, and then we all burst into song (yes, including Diane), "and we got nothing to be guilty of," and we danced around the parking lot.

An end to a great night and the finale of my two-week break, just in time to return to London for the next five episodes of *Dempsey and Makepeace*.

Top Left: With Marsha Mason in *Promises In The Dark 1979*, Middle: *FM* Movie Poster 1978, Bottom: With Jacqueline Bissett, *Change Of Seasons* – Rolling Stone Magazine called it "One of the sexiest scenes in cinema".

Top: Visiting Michael Douglas & Andy Rubin on the set of *The Streets of San Francisco;* Middle: With Longest Friend, Neil Koenigsberg; Bottom Left: with Debra Winger and Andy Rubin, Bottom Right, The Italia *"Lucky To Be Alive!*

Top Left: With George Hamilton at a John Denver Celebrity Skiing Event, Top
Right: In Aspen with Otto Tschudi; Middle Left: Skiing with Richard Baskin,
Middle Right: Running a Madcap Marathon with Hugh Hefner;
Bottom: Directing My Rock Video;

Top Left: With Johnny Gold at Tramp: Top Right: On Set With Christopher Lee in *The Care of Time;* Bottom Left: With Michael Proudlock, Bottom Right: With Ken Sylk.

Top Left: David Cassidy at Peel Cottage, Top Right: Pablo serving dinner; Middle
Left: Pop fixing the wiring in Peel Cottage, Middle Right: With The Folks, Glynis,
Lena & Michael Proudlock at Peel Cottage; Bottom: The Folks in London.

Top Left: *The Big Squeeze,* Top Right: With Bill Darvil my driver;
Middle Left: With Tony Wharmby, producer/director – *Dempsey & Makepeace,*
Middle Right: with Glynis and Ray Smith; Bottom: Glynis & I, press tour Santa
Monica Beach

Top: Glynis, Hazel & Bill Collins, Me, Chris Most, Shakira Caine, Jan Gold & Michael Caine; Middle: Jan Gold, Me, Ginette & Errol Brown, Deborah, and Bill Wyman at a charity cricket match; Bottom left: Cannes Billboard *Believed Violent* Premier, Bottom Right: With Richard Baskin & Glynis at the Rock Azure

Dempsey & Makepeace - The Cast & Crew

CHAPTER 25

Out With a Bang

The deserted dockyards where tall idle cranes, stood dinosaur like monuments overlooking the empty warehouses that housed our film company. *Dempsey & Makepeace* was always filming on the docks, in parking garages, or on deserted construction sites. It was cheap to film there, and we could control explosions, gun shootings and car crashes.

The return to the second half of the season had begun. Five more episodes would add to the six we'd already completed for the first season, counting our two-part opener.

Our set department dressed the front of this building to look like a betting shop. Dempsey and Makepeace were perched on either side of the betting shop door about to break in. Guns were drawn and held at the ready.

It was absolutely freezing on the docks; our breath was visible as our words froze in the air. This scene entailed blowing the front door off the betting shop. It was rigged with little charges to pop and smoke, and when the door fell in, Dempsey and Makepeace charged the villains, guns blazing.

"Any questions?" asked the director from deep inside his double-insulated Patagonia parka, as he rubbed his gloved hands together and headed off to the camera.

"Yes." (Clickity, click – Glynis' teeth.) "Actually," chattered Glynis, "you s–s–say the door b–bl–blows open bu–bu–but exactly what does that entail?"

Reggie, the sound engineer was informing the director he could hear Glynis's teeth chattering like Morse code.

The director was already annoyed, since setting up for this shot took most of the morning (not our fault), and he was already behind schedule. Perturbed, he explained to children, "There will be a pop, some smoke, and the door will fall in. Then you both charge inside the shop." He exhaled. "You understand? Okay, let's shoot!"

"Excuse me," I said.

The director stopped and turned to us, pulling back his hood. "What now?"

"You said a pop," I continued. "Was that a small pop or a big pop?"

He angrily waved the special effects man forward to explain. (Let me explain: There is a big discrepancy between special effects people working in the business. The expensive good ones, and the cheap, *you better watch your ass* ones, which was what we had on occasion due to our budget).

I asked the effects man, "You say it's a small pop and some smoke?"

"Yes, a tiny charge." He pointed to the two hinges. "Pop, pop, same time, and a little smoke."

Glynis and I nodded *okay* at each other. That told us more.

362

The director nodded (the obnoxious prick hated us) and strode back to the camera. He yanked his hood back over his head, growling impatiently, "Can we shoot this, please!"

I quickly put up my hand and walked toward the director. He yelled, "What is it now?"

"If this is such a small pop, how come you and the entire crew are all the way across the street behind thick Lucite shields?"

Glynis walked next to me and said, "I think we would like a pop test."

A we agree nod, between Glynis and me.

The director ripped off his hood, and maybe his hair toupee as well. He was shouting sarcastically, "Okay, a rehearsal pop for the 'actors', please. Roll camera one on the pop rehearsal; this is without the artists, no actors."

Glynis and I stepped behind the Lucite shield wall near the camera. The camera crew were our friends. The crew was our family. We were a tight-fighting unit, like a frontline battle unit facing the daily challenges of production logistics, budget, and nature. It was the hired episode director who would come in with preconceived ideas of us, having heard rumors we were difficult (which we aren't – we just cared) but it was easy to see how that stuff got spread about.

"Okay, ready for test pop."

"Ready!"

The special effects guy counted down – one ... two ... three –BLAM!!

Nobody could hear anything for two minutes. The blast was so loud, we were temporarily deaf. The door did blow in, but so did the entire set. In fact, the entire building was leveled. There was nothing but rubble on the empty lot where a whole building had been moments ago. The fire blast was seen miles away.

The bomb squad arrived, followed by police helicopters circling above the suspected terrorist bomb explosion. You could see a quick cut from the rehearsal blast used in the *Dempsey and Makepeace* titles. It could have been used on the ten o'clock news describing the deaths of two actors if we had stayed in the shot.

Gutter Confucius says, *Better to be a pain in the ass than buried in the grass.*

We completed the first season, a two-hour opening show, and nine further episodes with all body parts intact. It was like the end of a tornado, from whirlwind to quiet stillness.

I was lying awake before dawn, but I didn't have to get up and Bill wouldn't be waiting in the blue Mercedes in front of the house. There were no lines to learn. It was over! It was an understanding that just washed gently over me. This job had consumed my entire life for so many months. One focus: rewriting and creating a new show. I felt good, I was totally wiped out, but I felt good.

The American producers wanted me and Glynis to go on a press tour to launch the show in the States. They would fly us via the Concorde to New York, then onto Chicago (home of the *Herald Tribune*, our American producers), San Francisco, and finally, Los Angeles.

One problem. By the end of filming, after giving Glynis acting tips, calling her "Tinkerbell with a gun," and trying to get her fired, she thought I was a total asshole! Okay, maybe I was a little; maybe slightly more than a little. Okay, I was an asshole! Okay a big asshole.

Glynis detested me at this point and refused to fly on the same plane as me. The production tried to buy her boyfriend, an actor in *West Side Story*, out of his contract for a week, but theater management wouldn't go for it. So instead, they flew Glynis's eighteen-year-old sister Janine, who happened to be in London visiting from South Africa, on the tour.

We Concorded to New York, separately, of course. Glynis and I did all the press interviews and TV interviews and even went to see *Hurly-burly* on Broadway directed by Mike Nichols (Mike, remember me, I got Maureen Stapleton to do your movie?). Glynis didn't speak a word to me the entire time in New York.

In Chicago, after hours of hotel press conferences, we managed to escape and took a <u>silent</u> stroll along the famous Lake Shore Drive.

In San Francisco, we had a meal together. She did speak to me. I think she said, "Pass the salt, please." It was something!

In Los Angeles, we were in the same hotel and all my friends came by to say hi. I introduced them to Glynis, who happened to be at the pool, and they all loved her. Even after what I told them about her. They buzzed around her.

Maybe I needed to take another look. Glynis liked all my friends, and they all liked her. I saw her from my friends' fresh perspective. She was very relaxed with them and funny and glowing. I already knew she was beautiful, but now she was uniquely charming.

I asked Glynis if she would like to see my dream. I took her up to the rocky land that I owned in Malibu. A twelve-acre mountaintop with huge boulders and Native American caves on it overlooking the sea. My dream was to build a hacienda up there with the huge rocks coming right into the house surrounded by glass. I had searched for an amazing retired Mexican architect who had built the Villa Vera Hotel. He only agreed to build my house after I sent him photos of the land. I told Glynis that was why I was doing the series, so I could afford to build this dream.

It was the end of a beautiful day with an amazing sunset over the ocean. Before we returned to the hotel, I took Glynis for a long walk along the ocean. She had never touched the Pacific Ocean before. We walked barefoot along the Malibu shoreline. She was telling me about South Africa, where on rare occasions you could see a visual line where the Indian Ocean meets the Atlantic Ocean.

It was Glynis and Michael, just being ourselves, without our characters. I left Dempsey in England, and right here, right now, we were relaxed and laughing. My friends were right; she was – and still is – lovely and funny and a very special lady.

Later that evening, Glynis knocked on my door to say goodbye as she was flying to London first thing in the morning. The thought suddenly occurred that if they didn't pick up the series, this could be it for us. For the first time, she had a smile in her eyes for me. I moved closer, slowly, and we had our first tiny, tender kiss.

We were standing in the doorway of my room. I was hoping she might come right inside with me, but suddenly we could hear the phone ringing in her room just across the hall. We looked at each other … I held her hand, but the moment was broken. She tipped her head toward her room, smiling, and slid into her room. In the morning, she was gone.

But that look in her eyes was amazing. I couldn't get it out of my mind.

The *Dempsey and Makepeace* promotional tour was over. I moved back into my California Brentwood house and resumed my normal life. I felt like the maintenance man, taking care of all the crap I didn't bother with for so many months. The boring bits called real life.

Thankfully, I went to work on a television film called *Deadly Messages*. I couldn't stop thinking about Glynis and what I had tried to do and how badly I had behaved. I was an asshole – she was right! I sent her a birthday card with a positive, hopeful message. I couldn't hope to undo all the hard feelings that had passed between us, but I felt that in LA we had moved on.

Then my agent called with the news: *Dempsey and Makepeace* premiered to fantastic ratings. It was a huge hit in England. They were calling it "The *Moonlighting* of England" (the Bruce Willis/Cybill Shepherd hit). What made it such a hit? The unique chemistry between Glynis and me, of course, I'd always known that.

CHAPTER 26

D&M, The Second Series
London, January 1985

I checked into the Blakes Hotel in Knightsbridge. I let a couple of friends know I was back, like Johnny Gold, owner of Tramp, the London nightclub (who said, Dinner tonight, kid?" "Say no more!") and Michael Proudlock, owner of the Foxtrot Oscar, who insisted that I stay at his house.

"Check out of the hotel immediately, Brandon."

I explained, "I prefer to stay in a hotel when I am looking for a house to rent. Besides, it's too late to check out now." But Michael was very insistent! "Okay Michael, tomorrow!"

The next afternoon, I arrived at Michael's large house in Kensington. I met Lena, his Swedish wife, and Laura, their gorgeous baby daughter. After a bite to eat and too many sips of Michael's knowledgeable wine pouring, the jet lag hit, and I went to my room.

I awoke in bed; so cold, I thought I was outside. I searched the room for a thermostat but couldn't find one. There was a thin layer of ice in the toilet. I put on almost all the clothing in my suitcase and I could still feel the cold from the mattress sucking my body heat. I imagined I was a monk in a monastery drying cold wet sheets with only my body heat. Shirley MacLaine told me about this Buddhist monk's initiation. I took off all my clothes to use my body heat for warmth. I think that monk froze to death. The days may be short but cold nights last forever...

At breakfast, I huddled around this oven thing in the kitchen called an AGA (like the sound you make when a doctor puts a wooden stick on your tongue). Michael's Swedish wife, Lena (no wonder she wasn't cold), explained Michael was in his morning bath. Defrosting, I imagined. Forty-five minutes passed. If anyone were in the bath that long in America, we would have called an ambulance.

Michael arrived with the wet financial section he had been reading and placed it near the AGA to dry, intoning a musical "Morning, Brandon."

"Proudlock, look – I can make rings with my breath."

Michael said, "Brandon, in England, we don't turn on the heat till mid-October."

"In America, we turn it on when we're cold."

I knew I had to find a place to live. *To live* being the key words. I particularly hate the cold and had lived in LA for over a decade. I couldn't spend another night on the Proudlock tundra. The estate lady said, "I'm afraid I only have one house to show you, and it's very nearby where you are staying."

Peel Cottage was on Peel Street and had a blue plaque on the front that said Sir William Russell Flint lived and died there, and that it was the house of Robert Peel, the police commissioner who started the bobbies. Why not "the peelers"?

From the street, it seemed smallish, but inside it was huge. There was even a guest wing. But it didn't matter; I was basically hugging the radiators. These were nice and hot. Huzzah! The living room was the biggest room I had seen in London. Big enough for a football game with a raised gallery to watch from. What a place to have a party, like my fortieth.

"I'll take it, but I have to move in today."

The estate lady was taken aback. "The owner is in Italy, and we have to draw up a contract…" I crossed my arms "…but I could call…" she muttered.

"Today," I said. "I need to have it immediately." She nodded, "Shall I show you around the rest of the house?"

I followed her on the house tour, and in the kitchen, there was a man peeling vegetables (Peel Cottage). I looked at him and he smiled warmly. I nodded and smiled back. I lost the estate lady.

When I caught up with her, she was speaking on the phone to the owner. It was okay to move in that day.

"Great, who is that man in the kitchen?"

"Oh, that's Pablo. He comes with the house."

I think my jaw dropped, "I'm paying a fortune in rent, and I have a roommate?"

"No, no, he's not your roommate; he's your houseman."

"My what?"

"He comes with the house, a condition of the owner."

"Whoa, I'm from Brooklyn, and I don't know about housemen, I like living on my own."

She replied firmly, "I'm sorry, but the owner insists Pablo remains." She pointed at the phone she was still holding.

I asked her to give me the phone, which she did, and Brian Clarke was a truly nice person, but he insisted Pablo would have to stay on, looking after the artwork, keeping the place clean, running errands.

"Michael, he will improve the quality of your life. I promise you, try him for one week, and if you still don't want him, I will fly him to Italy to stay with me."

One week? It was that or spend another night hugging the AGA. One week? Sorted as they say!

I needed to get my suitcase and run some errands. I didn't know if I should tell Pablo I was going out or not. My no-class American upbringing.

I said, "I'm going out for a while."

"Will you be wanting dinner?" Pablo asked.

I just stood there. "Yeah, I guess so?"

"Just yourself?"

"Yeah."

"Okay," he said, "sevenish?"

I nodded and left. *I have a houseman*!

When I got back, I was in for a bit of a shock. I was so busy feeling radiators that I didn't really look in the dining room. It was unique, to say the least. There was a life-sized woman's half-body coming out of the ceiling, holding a candelabra. How did I miss that?

At the end of the long, gray, polished metal inlaid table, designed by the owner, sat a plate. The table was lined by three or four huge high-back gray chairs on each side and one at each end. I sat down at the head of the table behind the plate. I studied the woman's body coming out of the ceiling, the wine chilling, and the table candles burning. There was even some music in the background.

I felt like a right English gentleman. Astonishing how my life had changed. Nobody back home would've believed this. *Hey diddle-e-dee, an actor's life for me.*

Pablo entered with a napkin over one of his arms, like the butler in the movies.

I said, "Pablo, what is this?"

He said (in a soft, friendly Columbian accent), "Eez an abocado, stuff with smoked haddock and coppered with cabiar."

I stared at the caviar-covered thing, never having eaten any of what he just said. "Pablo, do you do a BLT?"

"What is BLT?"

"A bacon, lettuce, and tomato sandwich." I held out my finger's rigid for crisp bacon, twiddled my fingers upside down for lettuce, and made a round tomato with one hand and sliced it with my other hand and then two flat hands forming the bread of a sandwich. (I do this in restaurants, my friend Ken Sylk always speaks menu talk in this manner, i.e., a hooked finger for a cup of coffee.)

Pablo pondered, and said, "Pro–pab–ly for lunch?"

I nodded but Pablo stood waiting, so I took a spoon of the offered *starter*, as they call the first dish in this country. Wow was it good! Pablo smiled as I made appropriate (or inappropriate) noises of enjoyment. It was like discovering classical music. There was a concert in my mouth. The rest of dinner was equally tantalizing.

My first house guest for dinner was, of course, Glynis. We were getting on better, and feelings were being stirred – on my part, anyway.

Well, Brian Clarke, the owner/artist, was right; Pablo did improve the quality of my life, and many other lives subsequently. I began to throw dinner parties. A couple each week, with Pablo's agreement and a bonus.

Dinner parties depended on my work schedule, of course. Then whoever was in town from the states. Michael Douglas, Al Pacino, Bob Hoskins, Mel Brooks, Stephanie Powers, David Cassidy, and John Travolta dined on Pablo's cooking.

Mel Brooks used to call on landing at Heathrow Airport. "What's he making?"

On the UK side, Pablo outdid himself with a five-star dinner on Johnny Gold's fifty-first birthday, which included Joan Collins, Jackie Collins, and Errol Brown. Dodi Fayed used to bring boxes of lobsters from Harrods, and Pablo made lobster curry using Coca-Cola in the rice that still makes my mouth water. The director Irvin Kershner (*The Empire Strikes Back*) was a regular as he lived in the UK. I had Michael Proudlock round for his birthday dinner where every wine bottle was from his birth year, mainly to impress him but also to demonstrate how a radiator works.

Now with *Dempsey and Makepeace* airing weekly, the press was hot to get a scoop on Glynis and me. During the early days of D&M, they invented stories about us being a couple. Now, during the second season, it became an obsession with them to prove we were...

Glynis and I had a pre-dawn call on London Bridge. They were filming a stunt sequence involving a gold Rolls Royce. I asked our production manager why he called us in so early. We had been sitting around for over five hours not working. He could only say that he didn't know what order the sequences would be shooting in.

Politely, I said, "Look, it's freezing out here. We can't park the trailers on the bridge, and you have the big stunt scheduled after lunch that would involve the stunt people not Glynis and me. So how about Glynis and I go to my house for lunch? Call my driver if you need us."

Glynis and I got into the stretch Merc, and Bill took us to Peel Cottage. I was planning on a Pablo BLT *especial*.

However, it was not to be, I didn't have my keys because I was wearing Dempsey's wardrobe. I left my keys in my trailer.

Glynis said, "Let's go to my flat. I can make us a salad."

So, off we went to Primrose Hill. Things were going well between us now. Glyn had a new trailer to change in, with her own loo. (Note: I down traded my enormous motorhome for two smaller ones. It was too big for our locations and made for a happier set.) If her boyfriend was jealous, that wasn't my problem. He had no reason to be jealous because you couldn't find a more honest and loyal person than Glynis. Believe me, I tried everything to no avail, so I can vouch for that.

While Glynis was preparing a salad, I was looking around her flat. The inner sanctum of the woman I had spent most of my time with that last year. Glynis is a delightful and refreshing human being, and her apartment felt the same. She is like a bucketful of sunflowers.

Turns out that at the exact same time we were having salad, Glynis's boyfriend was standing before a judge for alleged DUI. His defense was the emotional breakup of his relationship with Glynis Barber, the actress. The relationship stress had led him to drink. Unfortunately, he gave the address of Glynis's flat.

The press lived in wait for a juicy opportunity like this one. The gang of paparazzi fled to their cars and surrounded Glynis's flat. Glyn and I were innocently munching our salads when the door buzzed.

"Bill's early," I said. "They can't have finished that stunt yet."

Glyn had a funny look on her face as she went to the door. I stood up when I heard all these voices shouting at the same time. I saw the flashing from the cameras in the entryway and heard all the clickity-clack and yelling, "Is it true what your boyfriend said?"

Glynis slammed the door. She was leaning against the door jamb in jaw dropping shock. Like she just saw Bambi's mum burned to death. She was breathing hard and holding her chest. From what she gathered at the door, her boyfriend was in court for suspected drunk driving and gave his breakup with her as the reason.

"Can you believe he gave my address in court? Now the press is outside, and here I am with you!" Glynis stared at me like I was Dracula. "Oh my God! Oh my God! My reputation will be ruined."

If you know Glynis, then you know this is quite important. She's a proper lady, a goody-goody.

"We were only having a salad."

I could see she was really upset about this. I walked to the window at the back of the flat, yanked it open, and climbed out on the ledge.

Glynis said, "What the hell are you doing?"

"I don't want to smear your reputation, good lady. I will take my leave." Then I looked down, and my bravado melted. It was three stories above cement ground, I was frozen with vertigo.

Glynis had to help me back in. "The press will say Glynis's boyfriend was distraught because his girlfriend was in their flat dilly-dallying with this American actor."

"Glynis, we had a salad!"

She was so upset. "We were already splitting up, but that's not what the papers will say, I assure you. Oh, God, I can't believe this is happening."

I picked up the phone, called Tony Wharmby, our producer, and explained the situation. He was quickly on the case, and fifteen minutes later, Glynis and I could hear sirens approaching.

Glynis's face went white. "Oh no, now the police?"

I said, "Not exactly the police, our television police, from the show. Our stunt guys will push their way to your door and escort you back to work. When the press follows you, Bill will glide around the corner and pick me up. Don't worry, I'll lock the door."

The beaming smile returned after a sigh of relief.

Knock, knock. "Miss Barber? A word, please?"

It worked a treat, as they say. Miss Barber was thrown all sorts of questions as she was escorted to the D&M police car. She played her part perfectly and all were gone a minute later. Bill cruised up to the curb, and I collapsed across the backseat.

"Saving a lady's reputation," Bill said. "Not your usual, Gov."

"You're right, there, Billy Boy, but it feels even better."

We laughed as we sped back to Tower Bridge.

The day was saved, but there were many more to come. Especially once we were secretly dating. Our first public appearance as the stars of *Dempsey and Makepeace* was when we attended the royal premiere of a Spielberg picture. I was in black tie, sitting uncomfortably for an hour in the movie theater.

I checked my watch and, seeing it was finally 8 p.m., remarked, "It's going to start."

Glynis said, "Prince Charles and Lady Diana aren't here yet."

"Then they'll miss the beginning."

That cracked Glynis up. Her laugh was contagious and spread around the theater. Of course, it was my American ignorance; they would hold the film however long until the Royals arrived.

After the film, I introduced Glynis to Steven Spielberg, whom I had known since the 70s. I watched Steven's first film, *Duel*, on TV. I was knocked out by the direction. I was so impressed I called Universal to congratulate this guy. When I finally connected with him and raved about his storytelling, he asked who I was.

I told him, and he said, "Michael Brandon, the actor?"

"Yeah."

And he said, "My girlfriend thinks we look alike."

"Well, Steven, I don't know what you look like."

"Come over Sunday and have lobsters with us. I do a *mean* Sunday lobster!" I met Steven Spielberg over his Sunday lobster feast.

After a brief chat with Steven while exiting the Leicester Square Odeon, the special protection for the royals asked us to wait while the police formed a corridor for Charles and Diana to walk out to their limo. It was fun to watch this from the other side of the velvet ropes.

Then it was our turn, and suddenly pandemonium took hold. We couldn't get out of the theater. People were plastered against the glass doors. The police formed a wedge, put Glynis and me in the middle, and marched out in force, pushing and shoving like a rugby scrum.

Bill's face as we approached his car showed fear for the first time. He puffed himself up like a bodyguard, pulling the door open for us. We fell in, and he slammed the door while he squeezed through the crowd back to his driver's seat. This was our first experience with the popularity of *Dempsey and Makepeace*. It was overwhelming! Photographers were holding cameras on the rear windows.

I said, "Bill, get us out of here!"

Photographers were running alongside the car, taking pictures. A couple of them climbed on the bonnet (hood) of the car, trying to take shots through the windshield.

Bill was yelling, "Off the bonnet, mate," while trying to drive the car through the crowd without killing anyone.

Glynis was on the floor of the car, terrified by all the banging on the glass and doors. One guy leaped onto the boot (trunk) trying to get a shot through the back window. Bill hit the gas hard and we left him well behind.

I was comforting Glynis while at the same time feeling this buzz of adrenalin. I looked up and caught Bill's eyes in the rearview mirror. He nodded. I guess this was the way it was going to be from now on.

LWT got a request from the palace: Princess Margaret would like Glynis and me to be her special guests at a luncheon at Grosvenor House. The D&M production worked the filming schedule around us so we could attend. "It's good press for the show."

Her Royal Highness Princess Margaret quite liked talking to Glynis about beating up villains. I was eating bread rolls, as paté wasn't my kind of food. After lunch with Princess Margaret, (I'm sure it was her – but she was puffing so much smoke, I could hardly see her), we excused ourselves to return to the filming.

The princess was informed of our early departure, so protocol was observed. She lifted her drink. "Well then, off you go you two. No rest for the weary or the wicked."

On the way up the stairs from the ballroom in the Grosvenor Hotel, two men jumped out from behind a curtain.

One said, "Michael, Glynis, is it true? Are you a couple?" The photographer was backing up the stairs while the reporter walked alongside me. "C'mon, are you together?"

I said, "Are *you two* together?"

"I'll tell you if you'll tell me," he said

I replied, "Frankly, I don't give a damn," and I continued to help Glynis up the round staircase toward the door.

He continued yelling in my ear, "Come on, tell us, are you together?"

He was so close to me, I put my hand out to make him step back a bit. That's when the camera flash went off. The cover of the next day's paper said, "Dempsey Snarled and Threw Me Down the Stairs." Can you believe it? Well, it cemented my Dempsey reputation for decades. That guy was Nick Ferrari, the number one LBC morning radio newsman today.

Back in the stretch, Glynis and I smiled at each other –We were becoming a real couple, although it was private.

Glynis insisted she wanted it that way. "You can't tell anyone."

I whispered, "Bill knows."

Glynis nodded, "You'll have to kill him."

CHAPTER 27

The Folks Are Coming

P ablo was putting flowers in the guest wing (love that) 'cause my folks were flying over from America. My mother once flew to visit her sister, Ethel, in California on a TWA constellation. NY to CA took half a day then. It was the iconic airplane with three big tail fins and the four-propeller engines. That was in the 1950s, and Cary Grant was onboard.

I remember this because my Aunt Betty was in line to board the airplane with my mother and I saw this liquid splashing on the floor underneath Aunt Betty, I pulled my mother's hand and pointed. My mother shook Aunt Betty's arm, but my aunt just pointed to the man in front of her and whimpered, "It's Cary Grant!" I didn't know ladies could pee standing up.

As for my dad, this was the first time my father had flown willingly since World War II, when the army marched him onto an air cargo transport with hundreds of other soldiers. My father told me they had MPs (military police) armed with machine guns all along the tarmac to make sure no one ran away. It wasn't fear of fighting; it was the fear of flying.

"I was scared shitless," Pop said, "we had no idea where they were taking us, and none of the guys had ever flown before. There were no seats on this cargo plane – just these long thick ropes running from front to back. We were trying to balance on the ropes, soldiers with full packs and rifles and we fell all over the place. Then the thing started moving and the engines were roaring. There were no windows in the plane so we couldn't see out, and everybody vomited. It smelled worse than an Orangutang's asshole."

I assured him British Airways' first class was slightly better. I could almost guarantee he wouldn't have to sit on a rope unless he requested one, and today everybody has their own personal vomit bag.

I was working, so Bill met them at the airport in the stretch-Mercedes. "First time in a limo that wasn't a funeral," said Pop.

"Look where they put the steering wheel," said my mother in her nasal voice, "no wonder they drive on the wrong side!"

Neither of them could understand a word Bill said, but somehow my father and Bill really got on. They talked about airplane bathrooms and they both had a love of cars in common.

Pablo, my *cordon bleu* chef, took the bags and led them up to the "guest-wing". He started to unpack my mother's suitcase, but she wrestled the bag away from him, saying, "Never mind, Pablo [pronounced *Pairblo*], I can unpack my own suitcase."

Bill picked me up after work. "Your folks couldn't stop talking about the flight. Your mum couldn't believe how much food there was, and the waitresses wouldn't take any money.

Your dad was amazed they had bathrooms up there. He kept asking, 'Where does it all go?'"

When I arrived at Peel Cottage, my mother was in the kitchen 'teaching' Pablo how to cook.

"Mom, he's a chef."

She said, "He does things weird. I'm just giving him a few tips." *God forbid!*

When my mother made a steak, you didn't need a knife; you just dropped it from four inches above your plate and it broke into bite-sized pieces. She was an awful cook. I never knew what a salad was till I left home. My father only ate with us on Sundays at a restaurant. He didn't eat with us because he came home late from the garage, and he preferred to eat alone rather than hear children whining, "Dad, he put a booger in my spaghetti! Dad, Michael's picking his nose again".

My mother gave our dog diabetes. She fed him ice cream sundaes with extra chocolate sauce. "He loves them."

One time, Mom was giving the dog his diabetes shot when a neighbor said, "It's got diabetes. Why don't you just put it down?"

My father walked in. "I got diabetes – you wanna put me down too?"

I left Pablo to fend for himself and found my father pulling out the electrical wiring from the den wall. "Pop, leave it alone, please. Don't fix anything, it's a rental."

Pop replied, "Thomas Edison must've wired this fuckin' house. Believe me, this shit's old! I'm fixin the lamp, hey, wait a second."

Pop got up and did what he did all my life; he put his arm over my shoulder and took me aside. We were the only ones in the room. Why was he taking me aside? It was the father–son talk.

"Hey, I want you to know, you're doin' alright for yourself. You're doin' a great job of taking care of me and your mother. You got a chauffeur, you got a cook, got a big house. How much money you got?"

With great pride, I said, "Pop … your son's a millionaire."

"That's not what I asked," he replied. "I asked how much money you *got*?"

"I don't know the number exactly, but I figure—"

"Don't *figure* me. Do you or don't you know exactly how much money you got?" The Gutter Confucius spoke. "If you don't know how much money you got, you're gettin' ripped off."

"Pop, I have the best accounting firm in Los Angeles."

Pop appraised me, "You know the difference between you and a monkey?"

"No."

"Neither do I."

It had always been difficult to talk to my father about money. My dad worked hard for everything he earned. Now, he was so tight he made the buffalo on the nickel shit before it left his fingers.

Whenever I got a job, I called my parents first to tell them.

My mother always said, "Who else is in it?"

And my father always said, "How much you gettin'?"

Why did I bother?!

My folks did love Glyn. What's not to love? Although my mother couldn't understand a word she said. She would look at Glyn when she spoke, then turn to me and in her New York nasal, "WHAT DID SHE SAY?"

After dinner, Glyn and I walked them to the guest wing.

My mother whispered to her, "I want a grandchild, and I want it legitimate."

Glyn looked at me in panic.

I shrugged. "You'll get used to it."

In the morning, we all climbed into the limo as Bill drove us to the set. Bill pulled over two streets from the location. Glynis kissed me and waved "See you later" to the folks and got into the Jaguar which had pulled alongside Bill's Mercedes.

My dad said, "What's going on, where is she going? Doesn't she work with you?"

I told him our relationship was a secret. Glyn didn't want anyone to know, so she gets in her car, and Bill and I wait a couple of minutes before we arrive.

My father burst out laughing. "Are you shitting me? If these two drivers know, everybody knows!" Pop put his hand on my shoulder (another aside). "More importantly, how are her teeth? You want to get a girl with good teeth. That can be expensive."

That evening Pop fell in the kitchen and hurt his back. I had to give up my bedroom so he wouldn't have to climb the stairs. I stayed with Glynis in her apartment ten minutes away. It worked out fine for everyone except *Pairblo*, who had to cook what my parents would eat. It worked out for him in the end; he got a huge "bad cooking" bonus.

It was an exciting trip for the folks, a once in a lifetime kind of thing. As Mom and Pop walked through airport customs, they stopped to wave and throw a last kiss. Did I see my mother touch her stomach and mouth "legitimate" to Glynis? Then Mom held up her hand, waving, but it wasn't her hand – it was her wedding finger she was waving.

Glyn and I collapsed into each other's arms, exhausted.

With our goodbyes finished, we got back to Bill, who was leaning on the car, staring up at the sky. I asked if he was looking for falling shit from the planes.

"Your father does make an interesting point, maybe they dump over the sea," Bill thoughtfully replied, "He said maybe that's why there are no windows in the bathrooms, so you can't see it when you flush".

Glyn and I got in the car. When we returned to Peel Cottage, I could sense Pablo was relieved to see we were by ourselves.

"Dinner is ready." We walked into the dining room and sat down. Pablo poured us a glass of wine, and just as Glyn and I clinked glasses, he said, "I make for you one of your mother's home-cooked specialties." Glynis and I both stared at Pablo with horror on our faces. His warm Columbian smile filled his face. "I was yoking!"

My next visitor to London was my manager, Jack Grossbart, from LA. Jack was making a solo trip to visit me. I told Bill to pick him up at Heathrow (one of the few times I needed Bill during a normal day, like when he picked up my parents or covering my ass, getting flowers for Glynis). I asked

Bill to bring Jack back to the set for lunch. It was late morning when I noticed Bill's car was still parked near my trailer.

I walked over and said, "Why aren't you on the way to Heathrow?"

"I was on my way, Gov, when Dr Death stopped me and said I was not to leave the location." Dr Death was the nickname for our production manager. It's a thankless job, can't please everybody. I nodded. "He said that?" I walked to my trailer and decided this had to be nipped in the bud. Bill was my driver. So, I lay down for a nap.

Tap, tap, I heard on the trailer door. I said, "Come in."

It was the third assistant, who said, "They're ready for you on set."

"I don't think I feel well. I'm just going to lie here."

The next tap had more authority, it was the director and then it was Dr Death himself. "The assistant said you're not feeling well. What's wrong with you?"

"Well, I'm not sure what it is yet, but I did notice Bill waiting in his car instead of picking up my manager at the airport as I requested him to do. Do you know why that is?"

Dr Death's eyes narrowed. He said, "I may need him to pick up call sheets this afternoon."

I nodded. "Well, that's fine, usually, but I specifically gave him an important job and you countered it without speaking to me."

Dr Death defended his position. "I don't need to talk it over with you. It's a company car and I can use it for whatever and whenever."

"On the contrary. Bill is my personal driver, not a company driver, and I allow you and the production staff to use him for whatever and whenever you need, as a courtesy. Look at my contract and you'll see my personal driver clause. Now, as to what's wrong with me, it depends on what happens next. What do you think, Doctor?"

Dr Death had his own ways of tormenting us daily. There was always some issue about nowhere to park the trailers where we were filming, so Glyn and I would have to stand around outside waiting, or the inconsiderate early calls day after day. Or making the schedule inconvenient when you had previously informed the office of a special event and needed an early wrap time. I spent most of my waking days working on this show, and occasionally you had to attend a charity function, and you needed cooperation from production.

I could see Dr Death's mind clicking away. Then he said, "I'll send Bill to the airport."

"Many thanks, and let the director know I'll be right on set."

That was the first time I ever did anything like that, and I didn't ever do it again. I've seen and heard all kinds of stories about famous actors and singers pulling power plays. It's not my thing. I had no idea what the exact wording was in my contract, Dr. Death was probably right, but I couldn't leave my manager standing at arrivals, could I?

We had a little break in the second season, and the press wanted photoshoots of Dempsey and Makepeace and offered a full-on ski holiday in Val d'Isère, in the French Alps. We could each bring a person, all expenses paid. Glynis brought her sister from South Africa, and I brought a guy I trusted, for whom I had directed a Rossignol ski film, to be my cover.

It was working well until one morning when all the press people joined us for a big buffet breakfast. We loaded food on the table and then, from across the table, Janine, Glynis' sister called, "I had no electricity in my room last night. Did you have any in yours?" Glynis tried some damage control, but her sister just wasn't catching on.

Glynis stared big eyed at Janine. Janine got it but out loud, "Oh yes, we're in the same room", covering her mouth, "Oops sorry Glyn."

Suddenly it felt like being in a shark cage. Like my father said to Glynis, *they know*! If they didn't before they did now.

At the end of the second series, Glynis chartered a sailboat that her cousin had bought and built in France. He was going to sail it to South Africa, but he would meet us in Rhodes, Greece, with this brand-new 110' motor sailboat and his crew of two and give us his first charter sailing along the Turkish coast. It was so beautiful because it was the mid-80s and not touristed-out yet. It was raw and unspoiled. After Turkey, we would sail to the island of Kalymnos in Greece, where my London friend Manoli Olympitas had his family home.

The first part was the lovely island of Skiathos. We rented a scooter and discovered private beaches and climbed down to little coves. We had a favorite restaurant where home-cooked baklava and homemade ice cream were to die for. Holding hands, we walked home in the total dark with fireflies blinking around us like little stars.

One day we rented a small motorboat and went around the island to the remote side where there were white pebble beaches. The water was so clear you could see the bottom, and when I dropped the anchor, I watched it descend to the bottom and grab onto a rock. It was heavenly until the sky darkened almost in minutes, and we swam to our boat from the white marble beach and headed back. But the waves became enormous, and we were being smashed all over the boat.

I was trying to remain calm while the boat went up almost ninety degrees in the front before it started descending over the next wave. I was extremely nervous about our situation now. I told Glynis to put on the life vest from under the seat. She took it out and it crumbled in her hands. She looked up at me, but there was nothing to say. We both knew we were in deep, deep, trouble. There was nothing and no one around and the rocky cliffs weren't reachable. We had to get around to the port. There was real reason for worry, and little Glynny looked so small and helpless as she was battered about from side to side. I told her to bail out water while I just kept aiming the boat into the waves because that's what they did in the movies.

Finally, we neared the port and took a deep breath as the sea got calmer. There, on the dock, was the old lady who rented us the boat, on her knees praying with lit candles for our safe return.

We stayed safe in our villa where I chased mosquitos, Glynis yelling, "There it is! No, over there! Did you get it? You didn't get it, I heard it, I just heard it, it's over there! Get it."

We found her cousin in Rhodes and sailed the Turkish coast. It was so remote with these patches of water so beautiful in color, we had to leap off the boat. One night we anchored in a small bay and her cousin told us we were out of food. There was only watermelon. Then, as if on cue, a light on the beach. The sign said *EAT*, I swear!

We took the dinghy to shore. The shack had a deli counter but only watermelon inside.

The proprietor came out and said in rough English, "Eat?"

We nodded.

He said, "You eat chicken." He grabbed up a squawking chicken.

Glynis shook her head.

The man said, "You want meat?" and nodded to a small cow out back.

Glynis and I both shook our heads.

"What you want eat?"

Glynis said, "Fish?"

I waved my hand like a fish.

"Fish?" He looked annoyed. Then he picked up a bucket and his fishing pole and walked out to sea. He came back in ten minutes and started cooking over his fire with sticks holding the fish, which tasted incredible.

The last part of the trip was to join Manoli on the Greek island of Kalymnos. The crossing from Turkey to Greece was in a force five wind. Everyone was on deck except Glynis, who insisted on packing the bags before we arrived. She looked like Shrek when she came up from below, not good being below deck in a rough sea. I watched the color return to her face as we entered the calmer waters of the walled port. Manoli was waiting with a bottle of wine.

I took a picture of a priest walking with a nun on the dockside, and he yelled at me and pointed to the skies calling down lightning to strike me for taking his picture. Manoli interceded on our behalf, and all was well to the great amusement of the entire port.

The next day, Manoli took us snorkeling over a sunken city beneath the clear still water. It was very clear to see Glynis and I were in love.

CHAPTER 28

The Old Bank House

It was looking good for a third season of D&M based on twenty million viewers loyally tuning in every week (that's *The X Factor, Strictly Come Dancing,* and *Dr Who,* together!). The British loved the show. So did the French, Polish, Dutch, German, Spanish etc. 75 countries in all.

I didn't need to ask Gutter Confucius to know I was wasting money on expensive house rentals. I was sending all my salaried money to my business manager in LA for safe keeping, to build my mountain hacienda in Malibu. I was living on expenses.

I met a real estate agent and went hunting, but the process of viewing houses was dismal on my budget, and I hate shopping for anything. Trying on more than two pairs of pants is equal to having a root canal. I know when I walk in the front door if it's for me, the light and height but sometimes the owners are there, then you must look respectfully and not ask if "Bilbo Baggins lives here!"

I just about gave up finding a place when the agent said, "I would like to show you a house, not in Chelsea or Kensington but Hampstead, because this seller is very motivated."

Hampstead – that's in the north of London.

I went to Hampstead once on location when filming D&M on Hampstead Heath. Glynis suggested to this Yank that we walk into the village for lunch. Wow! Hampstead is the kind of village an American envisions when they think of England. The unique little shops and bookstores, lots of bookstores (Neil K would wet his pants). The way the village ambles up and down the charming little side streets.

The Old Bank House had lots of charm. A little metal gate opened into a narrow, flowered entry to a recessed townhouse with a private walled garden in the rear. It was listed as historic, meaning the exterior of the building was protected and couldn't be changed. This house was older than the dollar! However, the inside was fully modernized and had an open floor plan, set back off the high street complete with a balcony and roof terrace, and, yes, a huge power shower and a sauna. And no way could I afford this.

The agent said, "This seller is motivated, so make him an offer."

"He might be motivated, but he's not stupid," I said. "I can't afford to buy this house. It's all just too much." I needed the Gutter Confucius.

The agent badgered me for weeks.

Finally, I said, "Okay, I'll make an offer, but please tell the guy it's not an insult, it's all I can afford." I wasn't playing with him; it really was all I could afford; he should never have shown me this house. It was just what I wanted, with high ceilings and beams and a fireplace splitting the living room and the TV room, but out of my league.

After I said it, the agent said, "Could you bring your offer up at all?"

If the Gutter Confucius were there, he would have chased this man down the street with a monkey wrench.

"Okay," I breathed, "but this has to include everything in the house, or I will have to sleep on a pallet on the floor like in medieval times."

He was going to call the owner. It was a long wait.

I was striding down the street singing the Rolling Stones' "You can't always get what you want". I tried to stay detached, but you know what happens whenever you really want something; those little demons of desire come out and drive you mad. *You gotta let it go.*

I walked inside my house to the *rrrring* and then the agent's words, "You bought the house!" I couldn't believe I owned my first house! This was the biggest, most expensive and the greatest thing I ever bought in my life.

The seller owned a famous pub in Maida Vale. I met him there after we agreed on the sale to personally thank him. Jonathan Crisp, the previous owner, asked a favor. I could hardly refuse after making me so happy; would I keep the gardener on? Mr. O'Toole was a lovely man but if he used his Irish magic and pulled you into one of his conversations, he could hold onto you for quite a spell.

I called Michael Proudlock to tell him I bought a house.

He said, "That's great, Brandon, you're a true Englishman now."

"I'm not sure about that, Proudlock. It has radiators that work year-round."

"Where is it?"

"Hampstead."

"Sorry, I shan't be coming there. My ball of string doesn't run that far." To Proudlock, Hampstead was as far as Delhi. But in the end, he and his father Nigel did come to see it, and after viewing they both nodded their approval. That was all I needed.

Then I had a very hard call to make, to Brian Clarke, owner of Peel Cottage. I asked him about keeping Pablo. I know, I know, it's considered very bad form in this country to nick one's help, and I totally get that. That's why I first called Brian, who was still out of the country, and I promised to relinquish Pablo on Brian's return. Brian was glad Pablo was so appreciated and felt it was the right move if Pablo agreed, which he did! Life was falling into place in England.

My grandfather, Hymie Tumen, lived in London after he deserted the Red Army and fled Russia with Sonya, his wife, and escaped to England in the early 1900s. He opened three tailoring factories in London before they took the ship in 1911 to America.

Hymie was now unhappily ensconced in an old-age home in Hollywood. The family had insisted after he survived his third mugging in New York. On every trip to LA, I would bring him the little whiskey bottles from the plane and Cuban cigars from the UK, which he'd cut into four pieces. He'd sigh, "It's such a shame, but that's as much as I can smoke before they catch me."

When I told him I bought a house in London, he laughed at the cosmic joke. He smiled, "You should look up my brother."

"You waited till you were one hundred years old [born on Christmas Day, 1887] to tell me you have a brother? What's his name?"

"Tumen, Same as mine, dummy," said Grandpa.

"Where does he live?"

He took a long draw on the short cigar and said, "Notting Hill."

That knocked me back. I'd never heard Grandpa mention England or a place that it was within walking distance.

"When was the last time you spoke to him?"

He blew out the smoke and bobbed his head remembering, "1911."

We laughed and drank.

The Old Bank House had a small walled-in garden, I made sure not to be in the garden when Mr. O'toole, the gardener arrived. It would be the entire morning. I asked Pablo to give Mr O'Toole his check. Pablo looked at me, those big, brown Columbian eyes begging like a puppy, but the check was already in his hand. I gazed out from the upstairs balcony over the garden and sure enough, there was Pablo, nodding his head, captured, as Mr. O'Toole, was spinning some endless yarn.

At the dry cleaners, two doors up from the Old Bank House, I bumped into an old friend, writer Larry Gelbart. Turned out he kept a place next door in the Brewery Mews, an old stable converted into houses right behind my garden wall. That's Hampstead!

Larry would pop round the wall to watch Wimbledon on my giant TV and munch Pablo's Guacamole. One boring match, Larry scribbled on his note pad and said, "I've drafted the epitaph for my gravestone, in the distant future, what do you think?" He'd written: *Finally, a Plot.*

Glynis told me that Pablo broke a champagne flute. First, I had to think about what that was. Oh yeah, the champagne glasses did have a fluted style to their design. They were stored in the polished black hanging bar that came with the house, with the polished black dining room table. Still living the dream.

Everything in the house came from the magnificent Heals department store. The previous owner of my house was my kind of guy. He probably walked into Heals and picked out the fourteen-piece de Sede leather sofas and marble-based arcing lamps and giant TV all in one go. I moved in and hung up my clothes, I borrowed hangers from Glyn but that was it.

I looked at Glyn, puzzled.

She sighed, "You should talk to Pablo about it."

"What about it?"

Glynis was brought up more civilized house than I was in Brooklyn. She said, "He broke a very expensive glass."

"Yeah, well, I'm sure it was an accident."

She sighed and realized it was useless talking to me.

A couple of weeks later, Glyn held up another champagne glass. "He broke another flute. You have to say something."

Okay, second offense. I went to Pablo. I had no idea what I was supposed to say, something like, "Please don't break the glasses".

Instead, I handed Pablo some money and said, "Pablo, go to Heals and get a half-dozen more champagne glasses exactly like these, okay?"

He nodded, *sure*.

I walked into the kitchen just after he returned with the new flutes.

He was washing them and whistled. "Ju know whet deez cost?"

"Yes, I do, and now you do too."

He smiled and we never had another broken champagne flute.

Glyn mentioned to me that Pablo was watering the plastic plants.

I said, "And look how well they're doing! No, I am not going to talk to him about it. He's a cook, not a gardener. Talk to Mr O'Toole."

That was the end of the subject.

Women have different needs than men. Glynis liked it hotter in the house than I did. She walked by the thermostat and turned it up to 22, and I walked by and turned it down to 19. I did my best Proudlock imitation, "We don't put on the heat in England until November," and we both cried with laughter.

One morning, Glynis asked Pablo to iron the sheets.

He looked at her. "Ju wont me to eyron de shits?" Glynis gestured with an ironing motion. "Okay."

We went out, but we forgot the gift we were taking with us and came back in to find Pablo on top of the bed ironing the sheets. I truly loved this gentleman. The three of us were like Faulty Towers.

I walked out of the Old Bank House door one morning into the little covered entryway that led to the high street, and two bobbies were standing there.

I said, "Good morning, gents, staying out of the rain?"

One of the cops said, "No, Mr. Brandon, we were posted here this morning because of the bombing in Libya."

"Honest, fellas, I had nothing to do with it."

They laughed. "Your President Reagan bombed Libya, and all high-profile Americans are on our watch right now."

That blew my mind.

I called my folks. "Guess what? I'm a high-profile American."

"How much are you getting?" said Pop, and your mother wants to know who else is in it?"

We were about to begin filming the third series of D&M. We thought it would be good for me and Glynis to have dinner with our producer, Tony Wharmby.

Just before we started eating, he said, "I just want to tell you, I'm leaving the show, and I won't be on the third series with you." Glynis and I were dumbfounded. Then Tony said, "But I'm not leaving you high and dry."

I think he did exactly that. This had to be in the works for months. He was jumping ship, using the success of D&M to step on up. Nothing wrong with that; that's what people do in this business. However, Tony kept us isolated from the network and was always the man in control. He was our producer, director, and the creator.

Tony said, "Ranald Graham will run the show from here on."

It was a very smart move on Tony's part. Ranald was the only one we wouldn't put up a stink about. There was no one else who could run the show but Ranald, being the writer we most respected and genuinely liked as a person. One problem, though. He wasn't a producer. What a ride was coming!

Most directors were unable to keep to the US film schedule, and what we didn't have time to shoot often just didn't get filmed. That certainly didn't help the story plots or our morale on the show. Ranald couldn't write all the scripts and produce the show at the same time. It was more than you could ask anyone. Ranald was trying very hard, but we were all suffering battle fatigue, the entire crew and production.

Ranald made a grand effort to help us, and brought in John Huff, a film director, to direct an episode. It was a great idea because we were demoralized after dealing with TV show directors who couldn't cut the American-type schedule. Huff was a step above.

One day he came into my trailer as I was rewriting a scene to fit the current location. I handed it to John, and he approved, saying, "I heard you guys were ball-busters. I heard lots of bullshit about you guys, but you're both terrific. Couldn't be more helpful if you tried."

We weren't aware of these machinations because we only ever dealt with Tony.

Huff got our battle-weary troop in line by seizing the helm. For example, when we were shooting a very dramatic moment, the sound engineer, Reggie, yelled, "Cut!", Johnny surprised, "What did you say?"

Reggie looked up, taking off his headphones. "I said 'Cut.' There was plane noise."

Huff said, "I don't care if a herd of elephants comes storming through here; nobody says *cut* but me. I'm the director; there's only one director on this set and only I will say *cut*!"

Reggie nodded and we went back to work.

Huff did the same thing to the camera DP, who differed about the shot Huff wanted.

Huff said, "I appreciate your expertise, but shoot it the way I want."

We needed him to get us back in shape. Huff, Glynis, and I got on great! Everybody wanted Huff to direct every episode but, alas, he wasn't available.

Huff and I were having lunch together in my trailer to talk about the next scene. He said, "Why aren't you directing?"

"John, I've been asking for three years."

Huff said, "Tell the network I'll ghost you. That way they can't refuse. I can step in if they think you're screwing up, but of course I won't, unless you want me to."

We smiled at each other, and we shook on it.

That's how we did it. A union rep came down and said they saw no reason why I couldn't direct the show and added that the crew petitioned that I should. I was directing the last episode of the series.

"Guardian Angel" was the title Ranald gave the show. At this point in production, Ranald was suffering. He was ill and stretched beyond human endurance. I kept asking him for the script and he kept saying he would send it, but it would never arrive. I was less than two weeks from shooting. I had to cast and scout locations, all the while filming the current episode. I didn't want to fall on my ass in front of network.

I went jogging with Ranald, who was a superhuman runner, but he was running on empty that day.

He looked me in the eyes and said, "Okay, I'll give you what I have."

We walked into his basement office in Fulham, and he handed me a stack of scribble.

I looked up from the pages and said, "Ranald, we're fucked!"

As I said, Ranald was the best we had. He and his wife, Caroline, were dear friends of ours. I didn't realize how much strain he was under. (Unknown to him then, Ranald was suffering the early stages of motor neurone disease.)

I spent every minute I wasn't working on the current episode working on the one I was going to direct. The nights were long, and Glynis would say, "You have to sleep," and lead me to bed. I would catch a nap after lunch in my trailer or between setups.

The worst was falling asleep during a scene. We were filming in Makepeace's Ford Escort. It was Glynis's closeup and while makeup was giving Glynis a touch-up, I started snoring. She whacked me, and we got on with it. At least it wasn't while she was acting!

Together Ranald and I put some wonderful characters into the story. I sketched and he colored it in, and the other way around. Glynis put in story ideas about what Makepeace would do if she quit her job. I wrote all night and faxed Ranald. In the morning new pages, it was coming together. We were nearly there.

Then I had to cast without a script. I called Kate O'Mara, whom I knew from *Dynasty*. I called Don Simpson, who had his own great series, and begged him to take the part Ranald inspired of a seer who lived under an overpass and perceived hidden meanings in bridge graffiti.

I called Richard Johnson, the famous British film and stage actor whom I knew from Kim Novak (he had been married to Kim before my relationship with her). I asked if he would do an episode of D&M. He said he would be happy to read the script, send it over. I told him I couldn't do that (there wasn't one yet) but I told him about his character. He would be the villain who takes it all with him in the end.

There was silence on the other end of the phone, then he said, "Who's directing?"

"I am."

He replied, "Tell me when you want me and where?" What a Gent!

The first day of shooting. I dressed up as Cecil B. DeMille, complete with jodhpurs. This first scene was at a country club, but the budget afforded us a small public tennis court with a strip of green grass. I had the crew line up their cars blocking all the tatty, un-country club shops in the background and I'd shoot across the car grilles as Richard Johnson pulled the Jaguar right up to camera lens. He stepped out and walked to an umbrellaed lawn table, joining some men. However, it was English weather and raining so nothing was happening.

Two hours later, I was waiting for a break in the weather when Richard Johnson came over and whispered, "It rains at country clubs too."

I looked up and *BONG*. I called the AD. "Tell the actors in tennis clothes that the game ends due to rain."

On *Action,* they grabbed their stuff and ran from the tennis court. Club employees would be closing the umbrellas and guests would be running to the clubhouse. Then we'd cut inside the café for the scene at the coffee bar. *Thank you, Richard.*

My next day's shooting was the five-minute opening sequence to the episode, and I planned to do it in one shot. I explained the shot to Glynis, "You're standing by the river looking out as the camera settles on you, contemplating the deadly shooting of Dempsey."

Glynis nodded. "I feel I would be sitting on a bench."

"No," I explained, "after the gunshot inside, the camera sees the stretcher carried out of the warehouse to the ambulance. Then the police car pulls in and Ray Smith gets out and walks by the covered body stretcher loaded into the ambulance and walks to you at the edge of the river. Ray calls your name, but you're staring at the water. It's one big shot with lots going on, all coming to you standing at the water's edge."

Glynis nodded again. "Remember when you said you hate directors who set up shots without rehearsing the scene first? You have become that director."

I threw my hands in the air. "Yes, I have. Yes, I have become that director for this shot, I now see that there are certain mosaics that need to be set up in a particular way—"

Glynis interrupted. "You're bullshitting me into standing."

"I am."

"I will stand if you want me to." She was smiling and I smiled back.

"No, Glynis, you're right!" I called the props department. "Get the lady a bench!

Glynis beamed, "I knew you would give me the bench."

I nodded. "Did you?"

"Yup, I'm sleeping with the director."

The morning needed a laugh.

For three years, we suffered parking lots, underground garages, construction sites, and freezing docks as our filming locations. Then there was a piece of the story that needed grandeur and a proper setting. I chose the Natural History Museum. Glynis would have been an archaeologist if not an actress, and I liked her idea for Makepeace if she wasn't a cop.

I took Mike Humphreys, our genius director of photography, to visit the museum on Sunday. I had meticulously mapped out the scenes to be shot and I walked Mike through every shot. He absorbed it all, nodding and not saying a word. He knew how important these scenes were to the story and how impressive I wanted them to look.

We exited the building before he spoke. "How many days to shoot this location?"

I laughed. "Days, Mike? We have tomorrow morning from 7 a.m. to 12 p.m. to shoot it all."

The museum insisted that all crew and equipment be removed by noon.

Mike looked at me, then pointed to the sun. "Michael, if the sun's out, we have a slim chance, and if it's not, we have none. This building is like a huge cavern. But there's lots of glass in the roof and if it's sunny I can make it work."

On Friday's call sheet for Monday, it requested *crew* to all wear their trainers. We were going to hit the beaches at daybreak.

The trucks rolled in the morning. It was as perfect as it could be. The sun did its thing, and so did we. The Entire crew jumped around afterward and felt great because they did it and they did it well!

But we weren't finished. We still had to shoot the finale. John Huff came by to visit on the museum filming day. He had tried to talk me out of the museum, but I stuck to my guns. He was impressed.

I told him I was planning the last scene, when the villain, Richard Johnson, reverses his Jaguar and drives backwards off the pier, taking all the money with him.

Huff suggested rocketing the car off the pier. He said, "If you drive it off, it looks naff like *this*," and he folded his wrist down. "But if you rocket the car, it arches over the water. Much better."

I asked special effects and talked it through. All agreed it would look better ... but how much would it cost and how long would it take? They assured me the car could be rigged in a couple of hours and we could use five cameras to make sure we had it all covered in one go (so it was one take), and it would be done. And since the effects guy owned his own personal launcher, no extra costs. Tempting.

It sounded good, but it was like launching a missile. As the master Irvin Kershner said, "Things can go wrong, especially when you let them out of your control."

Or as the Gutter Confucius said: *Shit happens.*

It took six hours to rig, not two. The day was disappearing, and I was losing all this time waiting. I made this call, and I had to live with my decision. Finally, they said, "Ready in thirty, and I got the camera crew into the boat. The special effects guys told them the best and safest position for the camera. I had divers and safety crew on in case of accidents. I had a camera mounted on the end of the pier to get the car going over, another one on the pier to see it go by, and another in the car on Johnson's stunt dummy double. (We'd already filmed Richard driving backward, looking into the rear-view mirror, laughing.) All we needed was the car going into the air.

I was standing at the main camera where I could see the whole scene. I got the word; I nodded to sound, and we were recording. I said, "Camera one, yes! Camera two!" A wave from the boat camera. Three, four, and five were switched on with walkie-talkie confirmations. I called, "Action!"

The effects guy yelled, "Fire Torpedo!"

The torpedo launched and blasted through the grill of the Jaguar, going through the car and out the boot (trunk), barely missing the camera boat by inches. The crew in the boat were all soaked, but no one was hurt, and the boat and camera were still floating. It was my heart that sank. A disaster!

Cut! All kinds of department heads came to apologize, but I had to be practical and save my film. I asked props and designers to fix the holes in the grille and boot of the Jag, which was in the exact same position. I asked the effects guys how long to rig another torpedo and was it ready to go?

They said, "No."

"NO?"

"Sorry, Gov, there was only one missile, but the divers are in the river right now trying to locate it. When they do, we can reload it for another go."

But the divers couldn't find it. It was lost, deep in the bottom of the muddy Thames River. Twenty years from now, someone will find it and call the bomb squad. Meanwhile, I stopped listening to people and walked to the end of the pier. Kersh was right; this one bit me in the ass.

Okay, forget about launching the car. As soon as the torpedo holes are repaired, we are driving it over.

The effects guy said, "The car is no longer drivable."

I asked him, "How fast can your pickup push the Jag?"

"If I lock off the steering wheel, I can get it going pretty fast, but wouldn't it spoil your shot to see my truck pushing it?"

"I want you to push the Jag as fast as you can and stop your truck two car lengths before the end of the pier."

He said, "I'll chain my rear bumper at two car lengths to stop the truck, Gov." He knew he might lose his bumper, and he'd already lost his missile, but we needed the grand finale shot.

We shook and went to our battle stations.

It worked! We were able to make the car look as dramatic as possible going over the pier. It was amazing! All the feelings that day's filming brought up. We all felt desperation out there on the pier, just like we felt exaltation at the museum. It's all about thinking on your feet with a fantastic crew supporting you. I loved it all.

Variety's review – "'*Guardian Angel*' was the best episode of the season."

THE END OF D&M

The saddest part was saying goodbye to our crew. After three years, we were family. The entire crew, production, editors, camera, lighting, wardrobe, makeup, hair, drivers, and actors… we had hundreds of people working on the show and to this day it's hard to find an English production where a member of crew doesn't walk up and say, "Hi, I worked with you on *Dempsey and Makepeace*." It was the best of times.

CHAPTER 29

On And Off Again

Glynis and I went to LA had a huge blow out and broke up! Probably about my commitment issues. Okay I'm still an asshole! She wound up staying at my friend Ken Sylk's house. Ken had just gotten engaged and was spending all his time at his fiancée's house. Glynis had signed with an LA agent and been offered a series lead, and had a place to live, so I felt better about returning to the UK.

I returned to London and got an offer from the BBC for a film written by Dennis Potter. *Visitors* was to be shot in Italy, in a quaint village called Todi. Then I found out who was playing my wife. Yup, Glynis Barber. I called her and told her that if this was a problem, I would bow out. Glynis had turned down the series and reckoned, as both the husband-and-wife characters were having affairs with the other married characters, played by John Standing and Nicola Pagett, it wasn't a happy marriage and so we wouldn't have to act lovey dovey to each other. She wasn't finding LA as enchanting as London.

Todi was sensational. You could smell the food growing in the fields. The village was situated on a hilltop located in the region of Umbria – the best food in Italy. I get hungry just thinking about Todi.

Glynis and I had arguments across our balconies. John Standing would step out on his balcony and arbitrate peace at least for the night. What a place to spend a month and not be in love!

At the end of the film, Glynis and I were on a break, as they used to say in *Friends*. She was living in her London flat, and I was back in the Old Bank House. "Hello, Glyn, I was wondering … Is it okay to take a break from our break and maybe have some dinner? … Yeah, that's Great – the usual at eight?"

Well, we weren't back together but we weren't over either. It was kind of a stalemate love truce.

I had a call from friend and director Michael Shultz in LA. I worked with him on Broadway and then on Ally McBeal and the Practice. He was directing a tv movie called *Rock and Roll Mom* for Disney with Dyan Cannon starring. How great to work with two old friends. I flew to LA and stayed with my friend Andy Rubin who had a house in Santa Monica.

My friend Andy answered his phone and said, "Yeah, he's here, but who is it really?" He laughed, holding out the phone to me. "It's for you. Andy did a tumbling bow and offered the phone, "Prince Edward."

I took the phone expecting my agent, but it was HRH Prince Edward, who apologized for intruding (how did he know I was here?) He said he was calling on behalf of the Duchess of York. The Duchess was inquiring if I would be one of her knights in a charity joust.

I always dreamed of being a knight. I was gobsmacked, (love that word) I was going to get knighted.

"Absolutely!" I responded.

Prince Edward was delighted and said he would be in touch when it got closer to the time. He then suggested drinks at Buckingham Palace where I could meet with the royal fitters for the joust. *Sounds good to me, Your Royal Highness.*

I hung up, and Andy said, "Who was that?"

"Well, my churlish knave, that was his HRH Prince Edward, Charles's youngest brother. Seems there's to be a royal joust for charity, and the Duchess of York, wife of Prince Charles' middle brother Andrew, hence the Duke of York, has requested me to be one of her royal knights."

It's entirely possible I may have done a *tatatata!* with my hand as a horn and galloped across the living room. Andy said, "I'll see if they list Jousting Tutors in the Yellow Pages."

I finished the *Rock and Roll Mom* picture and returned to London and Glynis, who was happy to see me. We were back on again. Pablo was making one of his special dinners for us, he answered the phone and said, iz dee pa lace? Prince Edward's did his follow up call to invite me to the Palace, Glynis was with me, shyly gesturing, ask *him if I can come?*

"Can I bring Glynis?" I asked.

HRH said, "We would be delighted for Glynis to come."

After I hung up, Glynis said, "You could have said Glynis Barber, so he knew who I was."

"Oh, he knew, the prince said he would be delighted for you to come." I believe Glyn blushed.

Bill took us in the freshly polished stretch to Buckingham Palace. He had to remain with the car, the bomb inspectors, and the sniffing dogs. But he loved every second of driving through the gates of Buckingham Palace.

Glynis and I were led up to the ballroom. Everybody was there. Seriously, I can't begin to say who they all were. I was so wide-eyed myself, looking around. It was like a pick-and-mix of opera stars, Formula 1 drivers, movie stars, TV stars, news hosts, rock stars, football stars, and a healthy sprinkling of royals to top it off.

A waiter came by with the hugest tray of drinks I had ever seen. I don't know how he carried the thing. It was the size of a dinner table for six. It looked like he was dislocating his shoulder every time he pivoted the tray around to present the drinks. One of every kind of drink known to the galaxy, except what Glynis asked for – a Perrier.

He pivoted the huge tray back over his shoulder and nodded. "One moment, madam," he said, then walked down a very long hall, turning out of sight.

A moment later, the same man turned back into the very long hallway with the same huge tray, but now only a single Perrier was perched upon it. He walked up to Glynis and pivoted again, presenting her drink.

"Your Perrier, madam."

I was chatting with Fergie, the Duchess of York, whom I had met a couple of times in Tramp, when an assistant came informing me that the fitters would see me now. I was escorted upstairs where several people began to measure and record my entire body sizes. I envisioned an armored suit in flat black like

Ivanhoe, the movie with Rod Taylor and Elizabeth Taylor: King Arthur arrived as the Black Knight and saved the day. I thought the fitter was taking notes.

I didn't know anything about the Royal Knockout. I really believed I was going to be a genuine knight, and I would be taking tournament-jousting lessons. The reality was that my suit of armor turned out to be a big fat duck-like costume with huge rubber feet. What a schmuck! Those fitters must have been holding their sides until I left the room.

That Knockout evening everyone was dressed in full tuxedos and gowns, hundreds of star-studded people, attending the royal hosted dinner. Prince Edward was making a speech, thanking us all for participating in the charity. I was of course sitting next to Fergie (Duchess of York), we were all with our team captains, when a bread roll bounced off the table. Fergie caught it so fast I was impressed. She winked, saying it was Andrew.

The next morning at the games, I was trying to figure out how to run down a flight of stairs in huge rubber duck feet. It was almost impossible not to fall, and I was up against Gary Lineker, a professional footballer. However, as Dempsey, I'd learned how to run down the stairs without looking down at my feet. You can't look down at your feet while chasing villains on TV; it looks naff (uncool). I figured Gary would be looking down at his giant feet, and that would give me the edge.

A TV news crew and reporter stuck a microphone in my face asking about the competition and Gary Lineker took the moment's distraction by the news crew to sneakily hook a rope to the back of my duck suit. I didn't get five feet down the stairs before I was yanked back, anchored to the door. It was very funny and well done. He of course just jumped them ten at a time. I was angry at Gary for years. I still want a rematch. Well, dinner would do.

Joan Collins and I had flown up to the event in a helicopter, during a whopping storm. She yelled, "Land this fucking thing!" the pilot put down in a field till the storm passed and she probably saved our lives.

When the event ended we were told "Thank you Ladies and Gentlemen, please find the buses in the parking lot."

On the bus ride home, that's right, no helicopter, home I was sitting next to John Travolta. We are both East Coast boys (John's from New Jersey). We had a good time on the bus, and I invited him to dinner.

"Okay, let's do it!"

I invited Nigel Mansell, Formula 1 champion, as well, but he couldn't make it.

"Surprise, Glynis! I brought someone home with me."

Pablo did his food magic, and we all had a good laugh. After dinner, John and I got into a long conversation while Glyn excused herself and went off to bed.

John and I talked for hours, and then one thought connected to another, and a memory about an actress named Diana Hyland. John had been in love with her many years ago, and she passed away from cancer in 1977. I saw her on the 1960s TV series called *The Eleventh Hour*, a one-hour black-and-white drama. She made such an impression on me that I wrote the only fan letter I've ever written. John was astonished and asked me if I had ever met her.

I was a teenager when I wrote that letter. It was ten years later, after becoming an actor, that I stopped by to visit an old friend, Renée Valente, at Columbia Studios. While I was in her office, Diana Hyland walked through the door to say hello. Renee introduced us, and it was an awkward moment for me and Diana left.

Renée said, "You were very quiet."

"Renée, I'm sorry, I couldn't speak. The only fan letter I have ever written in my life was to Diana Hyland, and she just walked in your office."

Renée jumped up. "You have to tell her!" she said, and she went after Diana.

I said, "No, Renée, please don't!" Renee called Diana back and told her about the only fan letter I ever wrote was to her. I was so embarrassed. I apologized for Renée bringing it up, but when I jabbered about *The Eleventh Hour*, Diana caught her breath.

"Michael, you wrote the letter in care of TV Guide."

I stopped and said, "Yes, I did, but how could you possibly remember...?"

"That letter arrived two days ago," she said. "It was lost for ten years, and it arrived two days ago, all wrapped up in faded yellow plastic. My husband and I made quite a thing of it because I had all but forgotten about that incredible episode, but your letter brought it all back." It was a kind of a *nee-noo nee-noo* moment and then Diana hugged me and left.

John wanted to know all about *The Eleventh Hour*, a series about psychiatrists and their patients. Diana was a painter, revealing her use of psychedelics to reach her inner creativity. Her performance had a real impact on me.

John got very emotional, remembering Diana. "She was an amazing woman, Michael." Recovering, he suggested we go to a club.

I said, "Let's go to Tramp."

"Sure."

We were putting on our coats when Glynis came down the stairs and said, "Where are you going?"

"Tramp," I said.

She looked at me like I was nuts. "You're filming in a few hours…"

"Oh, Glynis is right, John, I forgot I was working tomorrow, I mean today."

He said, "It's cool, no problem. Nice to meet you, Glynis. "We all hugged, and he left.

I looked at Glynis. "Really, did I just pass on clubbing with John Travolta?" I did the moves up the stairs (*Dancin' yeah! Dancin' yeah!*).

Glynis laughed, "Oh shut up!" But she did the moves too, dancin'.

In 1987 I did a photographic exhibition for Prince Charle's charity, the Prince's Trust. We raised a large amount of money and Glynis, and I were invited to the big Princes' Concert in thanks.

Glynis and I went to Buckingham Palace first and then followed the royal escort to Wembley. We danced behind Prince Charles and Princess Diana during the concert. I was instructed to go to the royal marquee during the intermission.

HRH and the princess would walk up the lines of people on either side to meet me and thank me personally for my donation to The Prince's Trust. I was given a royal crested tie earlier and I was wearing it that evening.

I must briefly interrupt this story to tell you that earlier in the week, Princess Diana and I had both been invited (separately, of course) to the ballet premiere of *Beauty and the Beast* directed by Wayne Eagling, who was a friend of mine. The ballet suddenly stopped, the curtain came down and the house lights went up in the auditorium. I was led by an usher to a small VIP room in the Royal Opera House to wait until the ballet could be started again.

Princess Diana came into the same room. What a surprise! I asked Her Royal Highness if she knew why the ballet had stopped. She burst out laughing and could hardly even speak but finally got out the words that the Beast got a hernia when he picked up Beauty! Not what I was expecting, I burst out laughing as well.

When Diana could talk, she said, "Wayne is squeezing into the Beast's costume to finish the ballet."

"Before or after he lifts Beauty?"

Sorry, but that brought on another round of laughter!

So, I was standing at the top of the procession inside the marquee and Princess Diana arrived first. She looked at me and we both cracked up. I'm sure we were both flashing back on the Beast's hernia. Then she saw my maroon tie with Charles' crest on it.

She said, "Take that off; it's so naff."

I was pulling it off my neck when Prince Charles arrived, proudly exclaiming, "Oh, you're wearing my tie!"

I looked at the princess, who politely brought up her hand to cover her smile. "Yes, Your Royal Highness, your wife kindly pointed out the knot was uneven, and I was just fixing it."

Prince Charles said, "Let me get that for you," and he tied my tie. Perfectly, I might add. *Thank you, Your Royal Highness.*

CHAPTER 30

After It's All Gone

I was sitting in my accountant's office in Century City, California. Lots of glass and views of Beverly Hills and Los Angeles behind his revolving leather chair. I had laid out my plans for the building of my new house on the mountain top land I owned in Malibu. I had twelve acres of raw land with huge boulders. I wanted the boulders included into the house plan, incorporated into the walls and surrounded by glass. There was a natural place below for a waterfall with a pool made from the natural rock formations. There were amazing views in every direction; almost three hundred and sixty degrees, except for the one peak that had the deserted missile silo from World War II.

I'd sent my accountant every penny I'd earned for the last three years, my entire earnings from all the *Dempsey and Makepeace* episodes. I lived on my *per diem* (living allowance) and from that paid for everything in London, including my mortgage on the Old Bank House in Hampstead.

The accountant leaned on his desk and said, "What monies are you going to use to do this building?"

I felt like he was speaking a foreign language. "What monies?" I felt the earth tremor beneath my feet even though we were twenty-three floors up. "The monies I sent you for three years; to build this house on my property."

He crossed his fingers like he was praying and looked up. "Michael, those monies are gone. You do know there was a stock market crash?"

"Yes, I heard about that, but I wasn't in the stock market. I was invested in Fenimore, and you said that was one hundred percent safe."

The business manager jumped back in his chair. "Yes, Michael, 'safe' … but nothing is safe in a market crash."

I felt the hair on my arms tingling. "Are you saying my money <u>was</u> in the stock market? But I never invested in the market; you said the funds were protected."

"I sent you reports every month."

My words came slowly. "How much … How much did it go down?"

"Michael, it's gone. All of it. We tried to save it by buying on margin. We took a hit of just over half a million."

I leaned forward. "I don't understand. Are you saying not only is every penny I made in the last three years gone, but I'm a half million in debt? Is that what you're telling me?!"

"Take it easy, Michael. If you can hold out, that margin could come back in a year or two."

"I'm broke. I gave you everything I had, everything I earned, and you say to me **we** took a hit." I stood up. "You better tell me why I shouldn't throw you out of your fucking window."

"It's unbreakable glass." He backed up toward the window, then realized maybe it wasn't a good idea and came back to his desk. "I didn't cause the stock market crash. It wasn't just you; it was everyone. Michael J. Fox lost a fortune in Fenimore!"

"I'm sorry for Michael J. Fox's loss but Michael J. Fox is a rich man. He might have lost a lot, but he has a lot more. I have nothing. According to you, a lot less than nothing!"

Maybe this is what you get when you trust an accountant who names his two dogs, Cash and Flow. I trusted him to safeguard my earnings because he would do better than I could. His expertise was expensive as well, and right then I just wanted to throw him out the window, but he'd probably just bounce back up like a rubber duck.

I felt like I woke up in a hospital and both my feet had been amputated. I wanted to scream. Everything was gone! I busted my ass for three years working to build the dream. All my earnings, my entire savings – nothing was left! In the crash of '29 everyone leapt out of windows but now you can't even throw your accountant out of one because their unbreakable!

He was talking meaningless numbers at me. A mathematical tsunami gushed over me, but my body was still standing there in his office. I was numb, my insides screaming, my mind imploding. *This must be what it's like after a bomb goes off.*

I called my lawyer.

He said, "If you signed those papers, he says he sent you, I don't think a judge is going to find for your case. He'll say you should have read them before you signed them, you gave him the power to do it."

I was told that the amount of money I might get back suing him for mismanagement wouldn't even cover my legal bills.

"It's my fault I couldn't read those sheets of numbers he sent me. I'm an actor, that's why I hired him."

The Gutter Confucius was right; there was no difference between me and a monkey. Well, most monkeys aren't in debt for half a million. It seemed there was nothing I could do to get my money back.

Glynis and I had been on and off those last months. I'd been staying in LA and trying to work on a script idea. I'd pitched it to Vestron Films, and they were interested. I was hoping to get development money, but the deal only paid after I wrote the screenplay. Luckily, Richard Baskin lent me his house in Bev Hills, while he was directing a movie in New York.

I was sitting there trying to focus and write my screenplay while dealing with the chaos. I called my old shrink I knew very well and told him how I felt.

He said, "That's great!"

"Did you say great? I'm lying on the bottom of my life."

"Yes, but the only way from here is up."

"Actually, I called to borrow a gun."

He laughed at a very high pitch and hung up.

I was living in a state of disbelief; my foundation had been rocked like Chernobyl. I still couldn't call my dad. I was a royal smuck.

I had an invitation to dinner from our friend Jackie Collins. I was picking her up at her house and we went to Wolfgang Puck's house. (Not his infamous restaurant) He was cooking dinner personally at home, for a few people. Sidney Poitier and his wife Joanna were other guests and Sidney leaned over to me and said, "Are you free to have lunch with me tomorrow, one o'clock at the Dome on Sunset?" I nodded and smiled, accepting.

I had known Sidney and Joanna for years mostly through Jackie. This was a first. I showed up early, but he was already at an outside table. I sat down and Sidney said, "I just wanted to say thank you." I said, "You're welcome." We laughed and ordered drinks. Sidney said, "I am from Nassau Bahamas. Michael, and years ago, you did a great kindness to my cousin." I was baffled. Sidney continued, "I got him into the academy of dramatic arts". I jumped up, "Cedric Scott was your cousin?" Sidney has this amazing smile. "Yes, Cedric was my dear cousin, and you befriended him". I smiled, "I remember him so well I can see him right now, the first day in the academy he stood up. He was very tall and had a thin mustache." I tried my Bahamian accent, "My name is Cedric Scott, I am from Nassau Bahamas". "Well, maybe if his accent was as bad as yours, he might have made it. Language was probably why he didn't go back. But he told me you took him to your parent's house for Thanksgiving weekend and showed him around New York City. He knew no one. He asked me if I ever had the chance to thank you. It meant a great deal to him". I nodded. "Thank you, Sidney, it means a lot to me right now."

Except for that deep breath from Sidney, I wasn't going out to parties or anywhere, but one evening I relented. Ken and Andy talked me into a Helena roller skating party. Helena was like the It Girl in LA, and Nicholson's girlfriend. I went and bumped into my UK friends, Leslie and Evie Bricusse. Leslie was one of the most successful composers in the business. You could wallpaper an entire house with his gold records: "What Kind of Fool Am I?", "Who Can I Turn To?", "Goldfinger" etc. I knew them through Johnny Gold, of course, and we'd had dinner on both sides of the pond.

Leslie asked what I was doing in town, and I told him I was writing a screenplay. He said, "Come write in Mexico. We have a villa in Acapulco. We're leaving tomorrow."

I apologized, but I couldn't write in Mexico. It was too hot; I'd only want to lie in the sun and sip margaritas.

"You can do that too," said Evie. They laughed "We have big air conditioners, and your room is next to the pool. You can write in the morning and have breakfast left at your door. We meet on the terrace for lunch and then a siesta at the pool, and then I write until dinner, said Leslie. That's my routine, if it works for you, you are most welcome."

I accepted with grace. The Gutter Confucius said, *If God seems far away – who moved?*

Well, it was almost too good to be true. After the crushing news in LA, this was heaven on earth. I had two air conditioners cranked up to the max. You could hang meat in my room. But it was great for writing. The coffee and papaya were left at my door in the morning and at lunchtime I leapt into the pool and joined my hosts on the terrace for delicious conversation and lunch.

Evie was a gorgeous woman, with Ava Gardner good looks, and Leslie was a very smart and talented man with a great head of hair. He wrote *Victor/Victoria* while we were there. At Evie and Leslie's request, I called Glynis to invite her to join me at

Leslie and Evie's. Okay, I wanted her there with me, but she wasn't having it.

Ten days later, George Hamilton turned up, and I have to say the work hours were diminishing and the party time was on the rise.

After we had the fish cooked in rock salt (the specialty at Capt. Jack's Fish Shack), we went to the club in Acapulco to dance. We were the special guests of the Mexican owners, who reminded me of the boys I worked for in New York City. The glass structure began to rotate and move out over the cliff with the sea below, and there was dancing on a see-through floor with lasers blasting across the room. This futuristic disco probably cost more than the Starship Enterprise. Maybe it was the Starship Enterprise!

The music was so loud, and this girl latched onto me with a massive grip, pulling me on the dance floor. A grip like the squid monster from Jules Verne, while smoking a ciggy, and a beer in the other hand. Beam me up, Scotty! The crowd was heaving, but I finally escaped back to my booth. The same girl leaped over the table into the booth, landing in a martial art pose. She looked at me with hungry eyes. I was really frightened when she shouted at me in Spanish, but she was ordering a bottle of Dom Perignon.

She leaned in very close and whispered in a Viva Zapata accent, "You want to arm wrestle?" Then she grabbed my hand and placed it in position on the table.

I was arm wrestling with a girl in a Mexican nightclub. She was bloody strong, and I noticed she had more hair on her arms than me. At the same time, her other hand was trying to get inside my pants under the table. I was wrestling on two fronts.

I looked at George Hamilton and mouthed the word "Help."

George was laughing and whispered back, "She's related to the owner, and she likes you! Be careful, they already sent over several bottles of Dom, which cost more than a car in Mexico."

"George, I'm in trouble here."

He gave me a nod, then said, "Senorita, we are going to dance and then I will beat you at arm wrestling like you are a tiny chihuahua."

While they danced, I slipped out the door, and I didn't see George until late the next afternoon as he came out of his room, holding his arm in a funny position.

"Thanks, George!" I yelled across the pool.

He nodded and mouthed "You owe me one" and headed back to his room.

I flew back to LA with a finished script. I did it! Thank you, Leslie and Evie. The next day I would go to Vestron, the production company, and make the deal for money. Or so I thought.

The big morning news in Los Angeles was that the Writers Guild had declared a strike. No script submissions, no deals, nobody could read a script or option a script for production. I pretended I didn't know and went to Vestron Films and got, "Sorry, we have to abide by the Guild rulings." They looked at the script in my hand like I was holding Homer Simpson's glowing plutonium.

I got an urgent call from Michael Proudlock (*Foxtrot Oscar*). He told me that Glynis was coming down to his country house in Gloucestershire over Christmas (that's where Glynis and I went every Christmas).

"She's coming down with a guy she's been dating."

(How dare she?)

"Brandon, my wife tells me that the guy is intending to pop the question while they are here."

"Pop what question?" I asked.

"Brandon, this man is going to ask Glynis to marry him. You've been well warned, dear boy. As Churchill said, 'Never, never give up.'"

I didn't know what to do, but I knew it had to be major, or I'd lose her. I took off my old leather bomber jacket (she loved this jacket and still has it). I bought this set of rings. There were five thin overlapping rings with different colored stones. The delicate kind of thing Glyn liked. I put them in the pocket of the jacket and sent the package overnight to Proudlock. I imagined him skulking like Dudley Nightshade, twisting his mustache, and humming *nya-ha-ha* as he secretly placed the package under the Christmas tree. The next morning, when the presents were being opened, one unexpected gift would bring joy to everybody except the chap who was about to propose.

Proudlock would be chuckling into his morning tea during his marathon bath. I owed him a big one! I thought I'd buy him a thermostat! Actually, I bought him a special edition Mickey Mouse watch.

LONDON

I spoke to Glynis after Christmas, and she sounded awful. She was ill with bad flu. I sent a doctor to her house, and he put her in the hospital. I flew back to London and straight to see her. We were so happy to see each other. Glyn got well and we got back together. (The other chap didn't really have a chance. She would have refused his offer). I told Glyn I was a broke monkey and that I had to put the old Bank House up for sale. I just couldn't afford it anymore.

I got a call from my lovely English agent, Jean Diamond, and she said she had something interesting to talk to me about. It was a French production making four films back-to-back over the next year. The character Lepski, was based on the lead in a series of James Hadley Chase novels set in the South of France. Lepski, a retired Miami cop who moved to France to play golf instead of chasing lowlifes in Florida, was hired by an insurance company to investigate art and jewelry thefts. This sounded so good, I couldn't believe my ears. I was to have lunch with two Frenchmen, the director and producer, the next day at Daphne's.

Turns out the director, Jeannot Szwarc (*Jaws 2*, *Supergirl*), had lived in LA since the 60s and was pretty much a charming American, even though he was born in Paris. The producer was Sergio Gobbi, who just stared at me like a French Telly Savalas from *Kojak*.

Jeannot said Sergio didn't speak any English, but his eyes flickered when certain things were said. I could hear the Gutter

Confucius in my head, "Son, there are sharks that swim upside down so you can't see their fin".

Jeannot lifted his wine glass, "You and I are going to have a great time in the South of France, Michael. I may be slightly short of drop-dead gorgeous, (Jeannot being short and overweight), but I will always have beautiful women around me, because I am a great cook and the way to a woman's heart is through her stomach. Stick with me, kid, and you'll be farting through silk shorts."

Jeannot was charming and committed to making this deal work. Mr. Gobbi hadn't said a word during the entire lunch, a cunning negotiator, fin up or fin down, Sergio made the deal.

This was an unusual meeting, I must say. It was due to the fame of *Dempsey and Makepeace* (*Mission Casse-Cou* in France). The series was even more popular in France than the UK. *Viva La France!*

ANTIBES, SOUTH OF FRANCE

Glynis and I first flew to Paris for the press release and a party of investors, politicians, and celebrities. Sergio Gobbi and his wife Nicole had set fire to Paris with the news. There were tons of press in the famous Fouquet's Restaurant on the Champs-Elysées for the launch.

Paris is the most beautiful city in the world. Very romantic too! After all the press, Glynis and I flew to the South of France, staying in the historic Majestic Hotel in Cannes, compliments of the production. Glynis and I had to find housing for a year of filmmaking. I felt like I'd done this before. Well, *déjà vu* is French, no?

I was standing at the gate of the Roc d'Azur on the Rue du Pont Bacon, around the corner of the Hotel du Cap, Antibes. The house gates opened to a view of the pool built in rock surrounded by the Mediterranean. It was heaven, and heaven didn't come cheap. We talked and talked but the estate agent was tough.

Glynis and I walked about, talking about it.

"I can just get an apartment, save the money, pay off my debt" I said sensibly.

"You only live once."

"Not according to James Bond," I replied.

But it's true, the experience is what it's all about, hence the lifelong dilemmas between me and my dad.

Gutter Confucius would say, "Automobiles are just a means of transportation, getting from point A to point B."

My argument with him was, "It's *how* you get from point A to point B – that's your life."

Pop would reply, "Talking to you is like talking to a wall."

"We'll take it," I heard myself say to the estate agent.

Glynis screamed and jumped in my arms. The cost was astronomical. We argued with the owner like hostage negotiators to get the month of June included.

I could never tell my father what it cost. The buffalo would have shit itself off the nickel and my dad would have had a sixth heart attack. It was after his fifth heart attack, when I was staying with my mom while Pop was in the hospital. My sister was unpacking takeout Chinese food in the kitchen, and I was watching TV when the house shook as if a train rushed through it. My sister screamed dropping the food and my mother opened the door to the patio room, but the room wasn't there. It was gone! The whole back of the house was taken off just like all the other houses in the path of the tornado. Furniture was hanging from the trees or floating in the decorative canals. My mother slowly took out her pack of Tareyton cigarettes, tapped out a smoke and lit it and took a deep inhale. She exhaled her smoke into the open space at the back of our house and said, "Don't tell your father."

I know Roc d'Azur was the right choice because I still relish thinking about that house. Leslie Bricusse was in his classic Riva speedboat spluttering up to my private dock with Liza Minelli aboard. We jumped in, and off we went to Club 55 in St Tropez to join our good friends, Joan Collins and Percy Gibson for lunch. Some people live like this all the time!

The villa came with two old married servants. When we had our first dinner party for our producers and friends, Leslie and Evie Bricusse, the mayor of Cannes, Bernard Chevry, Sergio Gobbi and his wife Nicole, my co-star, Guy Marchand (the French Frank Sinatra), Guy Hamilton, the director, Marisa Berenson, as well as my late friends, Mickie Most, and his wife Chris. Dinner was a monumental disaster. We were starved for food, but none came.

The mayor of Cannes went into the kitchen to find the servants drinking and staring at the washing machine. He started cooking and threatening the servants with prison. Things started to happen then. The food was prepared, and the male servant came out with a huge platter of fish. He would hit you in the arm with the platter and say "*Poisson?*" The inch long ash on the cigarette dangling from his mouth was right over the fish. Sort of a cliffhanger. Everyone's eyes were glued to that ash. Would the fish make it to them before it fell?

The replacement couple arrived two days later. They were much younger. The girl walked in wearing a French maid's costume, a tiny black dress with a white apron, high heels, and fishnet stockings, which didn't go down well with Glynis. I said nothing but that evening I noticed her husband walking around the pool with a rifle.

I said, "What are you doing?"

He pointed to the shoreline. "I am on patrol."

I told him to put the gun away or he could patrol from the other side of the gate. We decided to keep the replacements but without the gun or fishnets.

I had been working for weeks on my French lessons, but Guy Hamilton (director of four James Bond films) and the first of our four directors, wasn't keen on shooting extra takes in French.

He said, "It takes longer to say the lines in French, besides your accent is terrible". "I know, it's supposed to be, I'm American". I just didn't feel Hamilton liked actors. When I would be standing next to the camera, doing my off-camera lines for other actors' close-ups, I could hear Hamilton mouthing rude comments.

During a night shoot, I was pushing a very large garbage wheely-bin as a protective shield, while the bad guys were shooting at me. Hamilton had planned an explosion without telling me. The lid on the garbage bin blew over my head, and the force of the explosion hit me in the face and knocked me to the ground. My eyes were burning, and they took me to the hospital to have the explosive wadding removed from my eyes.

When I returned, I questioned him, "You set an explosive in the bin without telling me?"

He laughed. "Looks great on camera."

He behaved like a man who didn't care whether he was liked. My revenge came in the form of David Carradine, who was my co-star on this film called *Try This One for Size*. (David was the famous Kung Fu older brother of my friend Keith Carradine.)

David said to the director, "I need to put a kung fu kick in this scene."

Guy looked at him incredulously, "This scene, where you're having lunch? What are you going to do – attack the waiter?"

David replied, "My kung fu fans expect it from me."

But the big one came on the day we were shooting at the art museum (an expensive location) when David said, "I have to go to my father's funeral," just before the first shot of the day.

"Where is it?" I asked.

He said, "L.A." and a moment later his wife pulled up at the curb with the top down, waving, *David, let's go!*

David jumped into the car, and they drove off, as the director rushed to me yelling, "Where is he going?"

"I think he said LA."

Guy Hamilton just had his lid blown off. David's leaving was incredibly inconvenient. I had to work extra days, but it was still gratifying.

The second film was much smoother. *Have a Nice Night*, directed by Jeannot, took place almost entirely in the Majestic Hotel. Marisa Berenson was acting in that one, and Jeannot was cooking a lot (the way to a woman's heart… to be honest I don't know if he got dessert).

Glynis and I enjoyed the South of France. We had our local baguette and coffee bar and open market. There were no tourists this time of year, and we walked the streets of Cannes and Antibes and visited the wonderful villages in Provence. The weather was mild the entire winter, and we were out on our deck most of the year. We found a little pizza place that made the thinnest crust and Tatou, in Golfe-Juan, for the best bouillabaisse in the whole world. Not to mention the frequent dinner parties at the house of Benard Chevry (the mayor of Cannes).

The famous chef Roger Vergé, of the infamous Moulin de Mougins, gave Mr Chevry one of his chefs. The dinner parties had menus telling you what you were about to eat and the wine you would have with each course. The food was beyond describable. *Magnifique*! This was way above my taste grade. Jeannot's heart would be in his silk shorts.

Glynis was taking cooking lessons with Roger Vergé and would head to the market at the break of day to find the right fish and vegetables. He even made her buy knives and special cooking pans. The problem was, Glynis could only cook for parties of ten or more.

Glynis and I were having talks about commitment. Well, she was talking, and I was trying to listen. Let's face it; I was damaged goods. My only marriage had been a disaster. My parents were together for over fifty years and my grandparents for over sixty-five years. I didn't make it one year. Gutter Confucius says, *if it ain't broke, don't fix it*. What was wrong with the "way we were"? Cue Barbra Streisand.

It was a difficult time for us and getting worse. We were about to split up when our friend Lulu called from London (the singer famous for *To Sir, with Love*). Lulu wanted us to know there was an incredible meditation weekend coming up.

I asked, "Where?"

Lulu replied, "Rome."

"We're in France."

I get it. I figure once you're in Europe it's all close by – take a left at the bottom of France and drive till you smell pizza. I told her I was in the middle of a film shoot and wouldn't be free to go. Glyn just wanted to get away from me at this point, and London was her plan.

Then a strange thing happened. The producer said there would have to be a break in the shooting. There were budget issues, and he had to fly to Paris. Production asked if I could keep the Peugeot sports car at my house as it was gated. Hmmm. Suddenly I had the time off and the means to travel. Glynis and I both wanted us to work. We would go to Rome and take it from there.

Lulu was waiting for us when we arrived in Rome. This was our introduction to Siddha Yoga, a natural way of meditation that still resonates with me after all these years. The weekend was a nourishing and soul-satisfying experience that we both needed. It helped Glynis and I to deal with each other with mutual respect and gave us some life tools. All I can say is, the drive back was a lot better than the drive there. We topped it off with romantic visits to Sienna and Florence.

Presumed Dangerous (*Présumé Dangereux*) was the name of the fourth and final film of the James Hadley Chase series. My guest star in this film was Robert Mitchum (*The Night of the Hunter, Cape Fear, Farewell my Lovely,* and *Ryan's Daughter*), and the director was Georges Lautner (who made over forty films). Lautner was famous for all the iconic Belmondo movies. He was a delightful man, and it was a great honor to work with him. He invited me to his house up in Grasse, in the hills above Nice. We ate outside under a canopy of grapevines.

Mitchum was a whole different ball game. He had done it all and worked with everybody, and now he was just enjoying life. We got on like gangbusters. He knew more jokes and could tell more stories than anyone I had ever known, including Michael Caine. He drank a couple of bottles of vodka a day, but he could hold it.

The producer was confiscating his vodka, and Robert asked me to hide a bottle for him. He wasn't forgetting lines or being difficult, so I agreed. One day we had to start very early at a villa in Beaulieu to get a certain lighting. This was an extremely hot day. I was hiding Robert's vodka in my trailer's freezer.

The assistant called *dejeuner*!

Robert smiled. "Did he say lunch?"

"He did. Shall we go to my trailer?"

Robert flourished his finger. "An excellent idea."

Then the assistant director bounded up, saying, "*Excuse moi*, but would you mind staying here in your chairs a while longer?"

Robert said, "You called *dejeuner*. It's a hundred degrees, but you want us to stay here. Why?"

"Because I promised the journalists that they could interview you when you finished the scene."

"Oh," said Robert, "you *promised them*, did you? That's interesting, because when I arrived at the gate to the villa, there was this huge, hairy guard there and I *promised him* he could fuck you!" Mitchum was all tongue and cheek.

There was a welcoming dinner for Robert, and we all dined outside. The producers sat Glynis apart from me. They sat an actress, who was a friend of the producer's wife, next to her. The dinner was going wonderfully until Glynis got up and excused herself and left. This actress had asked Glynis in her smooth French accent how she could be with a man who always wanted to fuck all the women. That was the final straw.

I tried to explain as I drove Glynis to Nice airport the next morning, that I didn't understand why that girl would say those things. I had never been out of line with her. Nothing I could say would change her mind.

At the check-in counter, Glynis was crying while I was pleading with her to stay. I followed her right to the gate. I didn't want her to go. The French understand love, and the customs officers were telling her to stay. They even let me walk through customs as I continued begging. The D&M series was so popular there, they were holding the plane. They only stopped me at the stairs as she boarded. It was our *Casablanca*.

441

I stood with the teary-eyed French gendarmes' arms around me, watching her go.

Larry and Pat Gelbart checked into the Carlton Hotel in Cannes on their annual golf trips. When I told Larry that Glynis had left me, he offered to come by. I was living in St Paul de Vence now. Roger Moore helped find me a house very near his own home. Same designer as his, with the oval infinity pool – a lovely but lonely place without Glyn.

Larry Gelbart came up, and we sat by the pool all Sunday afternoon and drank Bellini's, champagne mixed with squeezed French peaches.

"Larry," I said, "I never said anything or did anything inappropriate with that girl. Why would she say those things to Glynis? None of it's true! I'm innocent."

"Sometimes the bullet that gets you has somebody else's name on it." Larry sipped his Bellini, and said, "You want my advice?"

"Larry, you're the cleverest man I know."

"Marry her."

I stared at him. "That's a lot of advice."

"Look, you've been together and apart, together and apart, and you still always come back to each other. Neither of you found anyone better, and Michael, the one thing you don't want…" Larry leaned toward me "…the one thing you don't want, is the one that got away. That ghost will haunt you for the rest of your life.

Larry and Pat have been together a very long time. When it was Pat's seventieth birthday, Larry went out and had a stick of dynamite tattooed on his bicep with Pat's name ribboned across it. How romantic is that?

I handed Larry my Bellini and walked into the villa. I picked up the phone and called Glynis in London. I said, "Okay."

"Okay, what?"

"Okay," I repeated. "What you want."

"What do I want?"

I stammered a bit. "Engagement."

"Engagement for what?"

"Mm–Maaa–Maa–rriage. Engagement to be married."

She was quiet for a while and then softly said, "When?"

I gulped loudly. "Well, after we're engaged, we can discuss that."

Glynis chuckled, "Engagement doesn't buy you an extension to your non-committal bullshit, Brandon. It must be within the year, or the answer is no!".

I gasped. "But it's already August! No, no, you're right! Engagement to be married within the year. I love you, Glynis – marry me."

The sun was beginning to set on the Mediterranean. I returned to Larry, who had that knowing twinkle in his eyes as he held out my Bellini. I nodded, "Larry, I hope you know what I'm doing."

We burst into celebratory giggling as we clinked glasses.

SOUTH OF FRANCE – PORTO NICE

The huge yacht was tied to the dock. This was the yacht used in the James Bond movie with the big round windows on the sides.

Robert Mitchum and I had finished our scene. He and the crew were off to complete the day's filming at another location. I was wrapped. I had just done my last scene in the fourth and final James Hadley Chase movie.

I hugged Georges Lautner, the lovely director. I said my goodbyes to the French crew, the dear cameraman Jean-Yves Le Mener, and the makeup folks and the French sound girl who held the microphone boom above her head, topless on warm days. English and American crews don't do that.

Sergio and I shared an embrace. We did it! He grabbed my face in his hands. He was happy – four films completed on schedule. He left me leaning on the polished wood railing, as Robert came and gave me a long hug. We had gotten close these several weeks and recently celebrated his seventieth birthday with lunch at the Colombe d'Or in St Paul de Vence. (I gave him a polished wood cane with a full flask attached.) While we had lunch, I asked him about Jean Simmons, a beautiful actress he did two films with.

Mitchum smiled. "Oh yeah, Jeanie was something."

I admitted I had a major crush on her, especially after *Spartacus*. She was so beautiful, so demure, so elegant.

Robert told me about filming *Ryan's Daughter* and said, "That damn director, David Lean, the prick could never remember my name. For weeks, he had us in costume and makeup standing around while he waited for a shitty little cloud to be in the perfect spot."

Then the man behind Robert turned and tapped him on the shoulder. "Sorry, chap, I think we worked together years ago. What was your name again?" It was David Lean, and he was lunching with Robert Bolt who wrote *Ryan's Daughter*.

A phenomenal and classic reunion.

Robert waved from the gangplank as he stepped onto the dock and into the waiting limo. I would miss Mr. Mitchum.

The captain of the yacht leaned on the railing next to me. He waved, and a steward brought a cappuccino to me.

"You know," said the captain, "I'm Dutch and this boat is from Holland. In my country, you are very big."

"Thanks for the cappuccino and the compliment."

He said, "Your producer booked the boat for the whole day, so it's yours to command."

I looked at the captain's smiling face and said, "Cast off, Captain, I'll lunch at the Hotel du Cap."

"Aye, aye, Mr. Dempsey."

The massive yacht anchored off the Eden Roc restaurant at the Hotel du Cap as a tender took me ashore. A table was ready. I guess anybody showing up for lunch in the Queen Mary deserved attention. A perfect salad Niçoise and a glass of Domaines Ott Blanc de Blanc. I was looking at the magnificent yacht anchored and waiting for me. I was living the life of a movie star. If my folks had been there, my mother would be pointing (nasal), "Is that George Clooney," and Pop would exclaim, "Miriam, look at this menu! Know what they charge for a tuna salad?"

Back aboard, we cruised toward St Tropez. I had a massage on the upper deck, and as the captain turned us back toward Nice, we shared a drink and a chat. He knowingly excused himself, allowing me the sunset. I looked off the port bow (how about that?) and we were cruising past the Roc d'Azur, the house I rented for almost a year.

What a year! I had lost everything, and grace caught me in its palm. I sipped and took it all in, not just the cognac but the whole last year in the South of France. Wow! To get four films back-to-back in this part of the world, finish my last day of filming on this private yacht, not to mention being totally free from the enormous debt, and the big one: I was engaged to marry Glynis, the woman I loved.

If that isn't a perfect ending … and a perfect beginning…

The end.

Epilogue

Okay,

There really was too much to tell and I had to cut half from the first draft to finally make this book. I didn't want a kiss and tell or an ambitious climbing the ladder of success story. It's not a confession either. More a revealing of how my life's journey found its way through good times and bad. It's a bit of everything and I hope I didn't offend either reader nor someone in or not in my stories. I may have left out someone and I am sorry. Mostly to my sister who you will get to know in the sequel.

We end here because simply put, there's too much to tell.

Hey, there's more to tell.

- The amazing wedding and the honeymoon to die for, we almost both did, but the work that followed is filled with stories.
- My picture with Christopher Lee in Austria.

- Jerry Springer, the opera at the national theatre and an Olivier nomination, another play called, Wet Weather Cover, maybe the best part I ever played. What about Captain America, The First Avenger, or Doctor Who, the final two parter with David Tennant.
- The amazing story of thirty-five years of marriage.
- The birth of our son, Alex.

It's been confrontational and intense process. It's also been fun and I have laughed out loud writing some stories that took me back to the moment they happened. The telling has its own life and the memory lives. The revisiting of past relationships and finding myself confronting old feelings with a new outlook has removed a lot of the rust around my heart.

A worthwhile experience shared with gratitude.

Thank you, thank you, thank you.
Michael

Acknowledgements

In memory of my brother Elliot – 1950- 2024, a genuinely good guy. Had mom's warm eyes. I loved him

Lynda LaPlante, my best friend, for her encouragement and loving support.

Neil Koenigsberg, my underground management friend of sixty-five years and going strong.

Joan Collins, Elspeth McPherson, Manoli Olympitas, and Ken Sylk for their notable criticism.

Alan Samson and David McCaffrey for their publishing guidance.

Simon Fielder, who produced my one man show, A Stand Up Story, at Richmond Theatre.

Alan Howard for the photograph session and cover photos.

Roddy Chisholm Batten – (www.clintons.co.uk), for his meticulous legal vetting.

Rick and Beverly Mayston, my literary agents who guided me toward my publisher.

Taryn Johnston, my publisher, Chronos, whose insightfulness has made this a better book.

Andrew Rubin 69, who remembered more about my life than I did. Andy was there for Fifty years of it. During his final days, as I sat with him, he sometimes opened his eyes and asked what my name was. Then he'd burst out laughing, GOT YA BABY. Andy, the definition of friend.

Patrick Rick Geurin, 91 and John Gold 89. My US and UK mentors respectfully and buddies of the heart. I dearly miss them

Jackie Collins, Errol Brown, Leslie Bricusse, Jay Handleman, Chris and Mickey Most, Philip Kingsley and Jan Gold. The world was better for them being in it. They make heaven a better place.

Victoria Goldman, writer/editor, for her comments.
(https://vgoldmanbooks.com)
Debbie Burke – for help on the very first draft, way back when.
(Queen Esther Publishing LLC)

JJ TINKER, for building my office/shed where I spent the time writing this book.

©Starman WGAW * the script used to make the movie Starman was not written by me.

Glynis Barber Brandon for everything. For putting up with me and loving me for over thirty-five years and not suing me over this book.

& My son Alex.

More About The Author

Michael is known in the theatre world for originating the role of Jerry Springer in the Royal National Theatre production of *Jerry Springer - The Opera*, transferring to The Cambridge Theatre, West End. He was nominated for an Olivier Award for best actor in a musical.

Other theatre credits include: His theatre debut in the New York Broadway Production of *Does a Tiger Wear a Necktie?* with Al Pacino at the Belasco Theatre and Lady and the Clarinet with Stockard Channing at the Long Wharf Theatre.

Other London West End productions include *Singin' in the Rain* at Chichester and the Palace Theatre London and *Wet Weather Cover* at Kings Head and then at The Arts Theatre.

Other London Productions, *Other People's Money, On the Waterfront, Off the Kings Road* with Jeff Bridges, *The Long Road South* for which he was nominated for an Offie, Arthur Miller's *A View from the Bridge* and *White Christmas* at the Dominion.

His TV credits include four seasons playing Elliot Salad in 'Episodes' with Matt LeBlanc, The Tracey Ullman Show, Dynasty, Mr. Selfridge, Galivant, The Katherine Tate series,

The Bill, The Knock, Lynda LaPlante's Trial and Retribution, Miss Marple, Dinotopia, Ally McBeal, The Practice, New Tricks, Death in Paradise, , Hustle and Dr Who -the Finale' with David Tennant. Danny Boyle's series, Trust with Hillary Swank. James Dean and dozens of other tv films.

Michael is best known for his portrayal of Dempsey in the iconic 80's TV cop series 'Dempsey and Makepeace'

Film Credits include Captain America- The First Avenger, The Times of Our Lives with Joan Collins, Me and Orson Wells with Zak Efron, HBO's The Contaminated Man, George Cukor's last film 'Rich and Famous' with Candice Bergman and Jaqueline Bisset, Change of Seasons with Anthony Hopkins and Shirley MacLaine, Lovers and other Strangers with Bea Arthur, Diane Keaton and Deja' Vu with Vanessa Redgrave, and Anna Massey. FM, and Renegades.

Michael was the North American voice of Thomas the Tank Engine for eight years and has recorded audio books for Michael Connelly, David Baldacci, Martin Cruz Smith and his late friend, Jackie Collins.

Michael was born in Brooklyn, New York. April 20, 1945 UK/US citizenship